A PORTABLE GOD

A PORTABLE GOD

The Origin of Judaism and Christianity

RISA LEVITT KOHN
AND
REBECCA MOORE

ROWMAN & LITTLEFIELD PUBLISHERS, INC.
Lanham • Boulder • New York • Toronto • Plymouth, UK

ROWMAN & LITTLEFIELD PUBLISHERS, INC.

Published in the United States of America
by Rowman & Littlefield Publishers, Inc.
A wholly owned subsidary of The Rowman & Littlefield Publishing Group, Inc.
4501 Forbes Boulevard, Suite 200, Lanham, Maryland 20706
www.rowmanlittlefield.com

Estover Road
Plymouth PL6 7PY
United Kingdom

British Library Cataloguing in Publication Information Available

Library of Congress Cataloging-in-Publication Data:
Kohn, Risa Levitt.
  A portable God : the origin of Judaism and Christianity / Risa Levitt Kohn and
Rebecca Moore.
      p. cm.
  Includes index.
  ISBN-13: 978-0-7425-4464-2 (hardback : alk. paper)
  ISBN-10: 0-7425-4464-8 (hardback : alk. paper)
  ISBN-13: 978-0-7425-4465-9 (pbk. : alk. paper)
  ISBN-10: 0-7425-4465-6 (pbk. : alk. paper)
  1. Judaism—Origin. 2. Christianity—Origin. 3. Judaism—Relations—Christianity.
4. Christianity and other religions—Judaism. I. Moore, Rebecca, 1951– II. Title.
  BM602.K64 2007
  296.09'01—dc22   2007015184

Printed in the United States of America

∞™ The paper used in this publication meets the minimum requirements of American
National Standard for Information Sciences—Permanence of Paper for Printed Library
Materials, ANSI/NISO Z39.48-1992.

CONTENTS

Preface   vii

Acknowledgments   ix

Introduction   xi

CHAPTER 1
Biblical Studies Is Not Bible Study . . . and Vice Versa   1

CHAPTER 2
Israelite Religion and Its Legacy   21

CHAPTER 3
Hellenism and Apocalypticism: Globalization and Millennialism in a
Different Era   45

CHAPTER 4
Sects and the City   73

CHAPTER 5
Communicating with God outside the Temple Walls   95

CHAPTER 6
Where Is God? Divine Presence in the Absence of the Temple   119

CHAPTER 7

"By What Authority Do You Say This?" Interpretation, Authority, and the Claim to Israel   139

CHAPTER 8

The Question of the Messiah   165

Glossary   177

Index   195

Preface

W̲E BEGAN CONSIDERING THE IDEA of writing this book in 2000 when, as relatively new faculty members at San Diego State University, we were awarded a grant to team-teach a course on Jewish and Christian origins. It became evident that there was no single volume available that dealt adequately with both the Jewish and Christian content and provided sufficient emphasis on the ancient Israelite influence on the period of origins, especially in the first century C.E.

As we gave lectures and heard each other's lectures, it became clear that much could be gained by engaging all three traditions—ancient Israel, early Judaism, and early Christianity—in dialogue with one another. Indeed, the sacred vocabulary of ancient Israel appears in a variety of first-century Judaic groups, although usually in a reinterpreted format.

Attempting to identify and place the points of contact between early Jewish and Christian traditions took the two of us on a fascinating and compelling journey. In conjunction with the historical and religious aspects of our academic research went the engagement of a Jewish professor and biblical scholar and a Christian professor and scholar of Christian traditions in their own dialogue.

Our ongoing exchange of ideas has resulted in this book. It is not the case, as may be expected in a coauthored volume, that we divided the writing and worked on sections independently. Each chapter in this book is truly the product of our joint thinking and scholarship, the product of numerous discussions held in classrooms, adult education settings, faculty offices, and our local coffeehouse.

A Portable God: The Origin of Judaism and Christianity demonstrates that the God of early Judaism and Christianity is not confined to the Jerusalem temple or to any fixed location. God, for several Judaic groups in the first century, exists, or can be found, in a number of places: in Torah, in Jesus, in the community, in the home. Or, as the Chagall art on our cover implies, God moves out of heaven and into the community via the covenant (the text) and its interpreters.

We might call this book a *quest* for the origins of Judaism and Christianity, taking off from Albert Schweitzer's notable book, *The Quest of the Historical Jesus*. We believe this research and writing process, however, has made it clear that this book opens the door to the *question* of origins and allows us to explore fundamental issues regarding the formation of Christianity and Judaism.

This book considers the nascent traditions that eventually solidify and become Judaism and Christianity. We argue that these two faiths share their origins in the precepts and concepts of Israelite religion, although adherents make adaptations to fit the new historical realities in which they are living. In other words, Judaism does not precede Christianity: They both arise together. This is not an entirely new idea in contemporary Jewish and Christian studies. What *is* new is our concentration on the ways in which Israelite religion is transformed in the so-called Second Temple period. The areas upon which we focus are the "location" of God, the roles of sacrifice and the priesthood, and interpretive authority.

We are suggesting that, despite different practices and customs, the earliest Jews and Christians share common ideas and sources. They develop these sources—especially Israelite conceptions of the divine—in creative ways that advance their traditions into the faiths we eventually come to call Christianity and Judaism.

Our approach emphasizes the importance, strength, and longevity of Israelite religion and its practices. This religion serves as a sufficiently strong foundation for a number of variants—with spectacular differences in some areas—to be able to take root and evolve in different directions. Judaism and Christianity are two primary manifestations of these variants, but other strands also coexist in the first century C.E., and we examine some of these as well. In this regard, we hope that the title *A Portable God* will serve as shorthand for a number of ideas that join forces: a set of beliefs that invoke God, the presence of God, and the intentions and requirements of God as understood by the earliest Jews and Christians.

Acknowledgments

W E OWE A DEBT OF GRATITUDE to a number of people who helped us through the process of writing this book. While we cannot list everyone—and certainly not all of the scholars past and present whose creative thinking contributed to our conception of this volume—we want to note a few key people who assisted us greatly.

We first want to thank the retired chair of the Department of Religious Studies at San Diego State University, Dr. Linda Holler, for helping us get this project off the ground by encouraging collaboration on a number of projects. Linda guided us through the grant-writing process and was instrumental in getting us release time through the support of the Baron Fund for Ethics in Education to co-teach a class in Jewish and Christian origins in 2000. That same year, the SDSU Office of International Programs provided funding for travel to Israel to do on-site research. The SDSU College of Arts and Letters in conjunction with the Office of Faculty Affairs also awarded each of us sabbatical time to work on this project—although not in the same semesters! The institutional support we received from San Diego State University has been extremely helpful.

Other colleagues and associates at San Diego State University have also been supportive. These include Elaine Rother and Margie Hoagland, administrative coordinators for the Department of Religious Studies. We would like to recognize a number of students who assisted us in our work: Darren Iammarino helped to identify sources and create a bibliographic database, which Stephanie Padilla enlarged. Kyle Davidson noted words needed for the glossary. We are grateful for the insights of our students, both those mentioned here and those in our classes who challenged us to explain complex ideas in accessible ways. SDSU student Martin Schuler created all of the maps and illustrations in this book. We are greatly indebted to him for his remarkable talent and creativity.

We certainly appreciate the anonymous reviewers whose comments greatly contributed to the reconceptualization of key themes and ideas. We are grateful for the close reading they gave the manuscript and for their helpful insights and suggestions. We would also like to thank Dr. William H. C. Propp of the University of California, San Diego, for reading the manuscript carefully and for suggesting wording and language to clarify important concepts. Dr. Martin G. Abegg of Trinity Western University and the Rev. Lawrence Frizzell of Seton Hall also made helpful comments and suggestions. We want to thank Rabbi Scott Meltzer of Congregation Ohr Shalom as well. Rabbi Meltzer provided valuable insights into the arcana of rabbinic literature and theology. Clearly any errors or omissions are our responsibility alone.

We especially thank Brian Romer of Rowman & Littlefield for his remarkable patience throughout the long process of writing and rewriting. Despite delays, Brian stuck with us and with the project. We could not have completed the project without his tremendous fortitude. Sarah Stanton and Erin McGarvey were most able assistants as the book entered the production process.

Most importantly, we express our profound gratitude to our respective families for putting up with hours—and days—away from home and for tolerating our distraction when the writing grew intense. We look forward to being reunited with them in meaningful ways—such as going to the beach, taking long walks, and just hanging out in the backyard.

Introduction

> *The mere use of such terms as "Islam," "Buddhism" and so on,*
> *tends to make us think of a religion as a kind of block, an*
> *eternal object that is always the same—somehow outside of the*
> *historical process.*

CLIFFORD GEERTZ[1]

C HRISTIANS AND JEWS TEND TO BELIEVE that their faiths developed independently and apart from each other. Although they have many things in common—especially sacred texts and an ancient history—most Jews and Christians believe that their religions are distinct from, and perhaps even antagonistic toward, the other.

Many Christians, for example, usually tell their story in the following way: The Israelites described in the Old Testament are a faithless, "stiff-necked" people who always seem to disobey God. They ignore their own prophets time and again and face war and destruction as a result. But God promises to raise up a messiah, an anointed figure, who will usher in a new era and who will write the laws of the Old Testament upon the hearts of all people, not just Jews. That messiah is Jesus Christ, who preaches a gospel of love, not law, and extends God's grace from Jews to Gentiles, that is, non-Jews. Jesus is in constant conflict with Jewish religious authorities over issues of belief and practice. These religious leaders prompt the Romans to execute Jesus, but this is part of God's plan, since Jesus' death serves as a redemptive sacrifice for all who believe in him. While New Testament scholars do not tell the story this way, this is the narrative that Christian theologians have used for centuries. Contemporary Christians who have

Jewish friends also reject this narrative, but many, if not most, Christians still subscribe to this account.

Paul the apostle explains God's plan and the significance of Jesus further in letters he writes to the churches he establishes in the Mediterranean world. Paul argues that Judaism is a religion of "works righteousness," so the story goes, which means that we can earn our way into heaven. But Christianity is a religion of grace, not laws or rituals and requirements, and so all we need to do to be saved is to believe that Jesus died a sacrificial death to atone for our sins. Christians therefore reject Judaism because it conflicts with the teachings of Jesus and Paul. Moreover, Christianity surpasses Judaism because the "new law" of forgiveness and grace through Jesus replaces the "old law" of commandments and observances. Jews, both then and today, do not understand that the earthly messiah whose arrival they expect has been replaced and superseded by a heavenly messiah whose kingdom is not of this world. In the same way, Judaism has been replaced and superseded by Christianity.

Most Jews tell a different story of their origins and history, stretching from the present back to the biblical figures of Abraham and Moses. Abraham is the first to practice circumcision, which is the sign of his covenant—or pact—with God. God promises the land of Canaan to Abraham and his descendants. This agreement is extended to the entire people of Israel at Mount Sinai, where God enters into a special relationship with the Israelites, and they promise in return to be God's holy nation. At Mount Sinai, Moses receives written instructions, called Torah, and these comprise some, though not all, of the writings that exist in the Hebrew Bible. Many Jews today believe that Moses also receives a set of oral commandments, which are faithfully transmitted for centuries until they are begun to be written down in the third century of our era. These instructions—both written and oral—spell out the requirements of being members of the covenantal group with God.

The Bible tells how the Israelites conquer and inhabit their promised land, in which they anoint kings and build a temple to their god in Jerusalem. They communicate with this god through sacrifices performed by priests. Several serious political and religious disasters occur in this history, however, with the worst being the Babylonian destruction of the temple in Jerusalem in 587/586 B.C.E. The Babylonians deport Israelite leaders to Babylon, where they are forced to rethink their covenantal obligations to their god. Upon their return to the land of Israel, the Judahites (since they are from Judah) rebuild the temple and continue as before. But when the Romans destroy the second temple in 70 C.E., Jews realize that worship, study of Torah, and good deeds (*mitzvot*) can please God in the absence of temple sacrifices. Sages, who are forerunners to rabbis, explicate the commandments and interpret God's will. They set the stage for the dramatic transformation of Judaism in which Jews begin to believe that worship consists of the study of God's teachings as they exist in written and oral Torah.

Jews, for their part, tell the story of Christianity as one of misunderstanding and misrepresenting the Hebrew Bible, especially the books of the prophets, when Christians contend that Jesus is God's messiah. In claiming that Jesus negates the necessity of following God's covenant, Christians selectively appropriate various texts and traditions and ignore others. In addition, pagan elements enter Christian thought, such as the idea of a trinitarian god or a divine human being, which makes Christianity suspect to Jews for many centuries. Moreover, a long history of Christian anti-Judaism—which can be traced from the late Roman empire through the Middle Ages and into our own day with the Holocaust—seems to contradict any sense of kinship between Jews and Christians, despite the biblical stories they share. Jews today, then, are often wary and critical of Christian beliefs and assertions.

This book departs from the stories that assume the birth of Judaism and the birth of Christianity are two separate, unrelated events. Their origins cannot be seen as following a linear or chronological process that places the Israelites in the beginning, followed by the Jews, and finally the Christians. On the contrary, both Judaism and Christianity emerge from the same religious tradition—that of ancient Israel—at the same time. Both claim to be Israel. Indeed, both initially identify themselves as Israel, and not as Jews or Christians. Even today, Christians and Jews consider themselves the descendants of Israel. They do not mean exactly the same thing by the concept of "Israel," however, as we shall see.

This common tradition is written down in the Torah (or Law, as it is translated in Greek), the Prophets, and the Writings. First-century Judeans—and these include the followers of Jesus and Paul, Peter, and James—accept the authority of these sacred texts.[2] Through a careful reexamination of the material and textual evidence from the period of 200 B.C.E. to 200 C.E., this book demonstrates how various communities draw upon the same traditions and read the same texts, responding in remarkably similar ways. These communities all attempt to live as the descendants of Israel within a new historical context. Different interpretive communities rely upon the same God and share the same beliefs, yet they also transform these beliefs in self-conscious efforts to justify their claims to be the true "children of Israel." Upon the return from the Babylonian Exile, each of these groups sees itself as the bearer of Israelite tradition in a new age, as each struggles to comprehend the meaning of God, Torah, temple, and sacrifice under new and changing historical circumstances.

A significant change as a result of the experiences in Exile and upon return is the recovery of the idea that God's presence is "portable." God moves with the people, remains with the people, and is present to the people just as God appears to the Israelites in the story of the Exodus. Some exilic Prophets, such as Second Isaiah and Ezekiel, actually see the Exile and the return as a type of "second exodus" and God's redemption of the Israelites yet again. This time, some Judahites remain in Diaspora and need God there, while others return to the land but seem to struggle with the issue of God's presence there as well.

Jesus and his followers are all "products" of ancient Israelite society and its worldview. They believe that the Law and the Prophets convey the word of God, and they understand themselves and their place in the world in terms similar to those of their contemporaries, including Sadducees and Pharisees, the community responsible for the writing of the Dead Sea Scrolls, and diaspora Judeans (that is, Judeans living outside of Judea). Each of these groups believes it is living in accordance with the dictates of God in the situations in which it finds itself. Each is reinterpreting its history, practices, and sacred texts in light of its experiences of oppression under foreign domination.

An examination of the writings that depict what scholars today call "biblical Israel" reveals profound concerns about the relationship between God and Israel. The covenant—or contract—between the two parties establishes a range of obligations and privileges that require ongoing interpretation, even in the earliest times. The Torah and the Prophets provide a dramatic record of how the Israelites maintain the covenant and what happens when they break it. The Writings collect a variety of different genres, such as psalms, poetry, novellas, proverbs, aphorisms, liturgy, laments, histories, and apocalypses.

These writings serve as the raw materials that later readers use to understand themselves and their identity. The descendants of Israelites living in the Persian, Greek, Egyptian, Syrian, and Roman Empires—stretching across Egypt, Greece, Italy, Turkey, and beyond—and those living in what had once been the kingdoms of Israel and Judah, look at their texts and traditions with new eyes. Some of these groups look at their written heritage and see in it explanations of their experience and understanding of a charismatic prophet known as Jesus of Nazareth: Who was he? Why did he die? What should his followers emphasize? The early Jesus Movement provides many different answers to these questions, so there is no single Christianity, no normative belief system, for several centuries after Jesus' death. Even today we find great variety in the three large streams of Christianity—Catholic, Protestant, and Orthodox. Other Judaic groups[3] search the scriptures to answer similar questions: Who is the king of the Judeans? How should sacrifices be performed, especially in the absence of a temple? How can we live in holiness? How do we keep our covenant with God? Several groups answer these questions in a way that accommodates distance—physical and psychological—from the temple in Jerusalem. At the same time, they continue to value all of the ideas associated with the temple, such as priesthood, sacrifice, and holiness.

This book looks at how disparate interpretive strategies dictate different conclusions and yet address identical concerns. We begin by considering key elements of Israelite religion that carry through from the earliest times to the latest. We also examine the history of the Israelites and their dealings with foreign cultures and empires. We regard the ways the history of first-century "Judaism" and "Christianity" (and we will explain later on why we put "Judaism" and "Christianity" in quotation marks) has been told—a tale of competing sects and parties—and why we think there are better, more accurate and appropriate ways to view Judaic religions of that time. The destruction of the temple in Jerusalem in 70 C.E. has a profound effect on the array of interpretive communities we are studying, and we will see how they respond to the absence of the temple.

Several groups struggle with questions of how to maintain the covenant with God even before the destruction of the temple. They ask: Is God confined to the temple in Jerusalem or to any single fixed place? Can one worship the God of Israel outside of Israel? We find that a number of first-century groups—those living at Qumran, those living in Diaspora, the Jesus Movement, the Pharisees—are forced through circumstance, but also through choice, to move God beyond the traditional Israelite boundaries of the tabernacle, temple, and Jerusalem. In doing so, these groups must continuously confront the priestly issues of holiness, purity, and the distinction between sacred and profane. If God is present at all times and in all places, then how do the people of God maintain a state of worthiness for this presence? How do they ensure that their immediate surroundings also remain sanctified?

In rethinking what it means to be Israel, two main groups ultimately prevail: that which serves as the basis for rabbinic Judaism and that which serves as the basis for Christianity. Using similar texts and traditions, adherents of the two groups come up with creative, alternative, and different understandings of identical sources. This use of the same terminology—the very same words—to describe vastly different concepts accounts for the misunderstanding and hostility followers of these new religions experience, even as they are appealing to the same audience. The Christian reading of scripture reinvigorates the Israelite notion of divine kingship and widens the covenant to encompass the world, while the Jewish reading reinvigorates the Israelite notion of Torah and extends human responsibility to God and neighbor. These competing interpretations lead to clashes over authority and to questions about who has the right to interpret the scriptures of Israel. Both traditions, however, extend the presence of God into the life of the community. No longer mediated by priests in a fixed temple, God's presence is accessible to all, especially in the practice of eating a common meal.

When we approach understanding the origins of Christianity and Judaism in this way, we gain a greater appreciation of the commonalities between these two world religions. Far from being completely different, or even antithetical, they share the same texts and traditions, with the same theological foundations. But what they do is take these texts, traditions, and concepts and interpret them in extremely different ways.

By telling the common story, rather than diverging stories, of Jewish and Christian origins, we begin to see Jews and Christians as siblings, as Alan Segal calls them in his book *Rebecca's Children*, rather than as parent and child. This has the advantage of avoiding the problem of Christian supersessionism, that is, the idea that Christianity replaces, or supersedes, Judaism. Most importantly, this approach shows that the similarities between Judaism and Christianity far outweigh their differences.

Suggested Readings

Julie Galambush. *The Reluctant Parting: How the New Testament's Jewish Writers Created a Christian Book*. San Francisco: HarperSanFrancisco, 2005.

Michael Goldberg. *Jews and Christians, Getting Our Stories Straight: The Exodus and the Passion-Resurrection*. Nashville: Abingdon, 1985.

Martin S. Jaffee. *Early Judaism: Religious Worlds of the First Judaic Millennium*, 2d. ed. Bethesda, Md.: University Press of Maryland, 2006.

Amy-Jill Levine. *The Misunderstood Jew: The Church and the Scandal of the Jewish Jesus*. San Francisco: HarperSanFrancisco, 2006.

Jacob Neusner and Bruce Chilton. *Jewish and Christian Doctrines: The Classics Compared*. London and New York: Routledge, 2000.

George W. E. Nickelsburg. *Ancient Judaism and Christian Origins: Diversity, Continuity, and Transformation*. Minneapolis: Fortress Press, 2003.

Alan F. Segal. *Rebecca's Children: Judaism and Christianity in the Roman World*. Cambridge, Mass.: Harvard University Press, 1986.

Notes

1. "The Discussion," in *Religion and Progress in Modern Asia*, ed. Robert N. Bellah (New York: Free Press, 1965), 155.

2. Judeans refers to the people living in Judea, which is what Greeks and Romans call the land that is identified as Judah in earlier times. We explain the transition from Israelites to Judahites to Judeans to Jews in chapter 3.

3. We are using the word *Judaic* rather than *Jewish* to encompass a variety of groups that cannot quite be considered Jewish in the modern sense of the word. In other words, first-century Judaic groups may exhibit some, but not all, elements of contemporary Judaism.

Biblical Studies Is Not Bible Study . . . and Vice Versa

1

THERE IS A DIFFERENCE BETWEEN Bible study and biblical studies. While Jews call it "Torah study" and Christians call it "Bible study," both processes occur within a confessional setting, that is, a location in which a group of believers or members of a community read what they consider to be an inspired text. Jews and Christians study the Torah and the Bible as sources of moral guidance, inspiration, comfort, and even history, philosophy, and truth, though not necessarily in that order! They scrutinize scripture—that is, the sacred texts of Judaism and Christianity—because they believe that it reveals the nature and intent of the divine, of God.

Biblical scholars take a different approach because they are asking different questions of the same texts. Scholars studying the Bible investigate issues of authorship and dating; questions of textual authenticity; matters of history, sociology, culture, politics, and economics; and even the subjects of medicine, botany, and zoology. Rather than assume that the Bible reveals religious truth, scholars assume that the Bible reveals what an ancient group of people believed was religious truth.

Biblical studies and Bible study are, therefore, two radically different ways to read the same book. Both are legitimate methods; both have value; both are needed. But it should be clear that both tend to occur in different venues, with Bible and Torah study taking place primarily in church and synagogue, and biblical studies happening in schools and universities. This is not a hard and fast rule, however. It is clear that ordinary Christians and Jews are asking increasingly scholarly questions about their sacred texts and frequently take academic approaches in religious settings to help inform their reading. On the other hand, there are a number of scholars who defend a confessional approach to biblical studies. When we teach biblical studies in the classroom, we try to take what is called a "critical approach" to reading scripture. This does not mean that we criticize or disparage the text, but that we believe religious texts are open for questioning and investigation.

This chapter presents some of the presuppositions scholars bring to their study of the Bible. It is important to lay these assumptions out at the beginning for two reasons. First, we need to understand how contemporary biblical scholarship works in order to understand the arguments scholars are making. Second, this volume uses a number of terms and concepts from biblical studies, and a brief introduction to some vocabulary will help readers understand what follows.

The (Un)Common Era

You will note that the introduction indicates dates with the initials B.C.E. and C.E. These stand for "before the Common Era" and "Common Era" and correspond to B.C. and A.D., "Before Christ" and "Anno Domini," or "Year of the Lord." B.C. and A.D. come from an explicitly Christian orientation and view of history. Jews and Muslims have entirely different dating systems, which reflect their own sacred histories. Jews, working on a lunar-solar calendar, date their years reckoning back to the creation of the world, while Muslims, also working on a lunar calendar, begin with Mohammad's *hijra* to Medina (622 C.E.). But because Europe was Christian—in the sense that ruling elites belonged to churches—and because European values were spread throughout the world via exploration, missionization, and colonization, the Christian point of reference became used universally.

The fact is, however, biblical scholars come from a variety of religious traditions, as well as from no religious tradition at all. The designations B.C.E. and C.E. were adopted, therefore, in recognition of this. Although they follow the traditional Christian dating system, they do not have an overtly religious reference point. While some might call this being "politically correct," we prefer to think of it as being sensitive to the religious worldviews of others and as being inclusive of as many perspectives as possible. It is the "Common Era" because we share it in common with billions of people around the world.

There are a few additional time frames we should introduce. The first, called Exilic, refers to the time of the destruction of the first temple in Jerusalem and the exile of many of Judah's inhabitants to Babylon, from

587/586 B.C.E. to approximately 539 B.C.E., when Judahites are permitted to return to Judah under the Persian ruler Cyrus. Pre-Exilic denotes the period before this Exile, while post-Exilic designates the period afterward. Another important era is identified as Second Temple Judaism to signify both the religion—Judaism (which we discuss as a complicated category in chapter 3)—and the age in which the second temple in Jerusalem is in existence. This epoch runs from about the fourth century B.C.E. to 70 C.E., when the temple is destroyed by the Romans.

Torah

The Hebrew word *Torah* literally means "instruction." In the Hebrew Bible, this instruction comes from God and serves as both teaching and guidance for Israel. Israel's compliance with these instructions is part of its perceived covenantal relationship with God. The biblical Israelites would not have understood Torah in its modern sense, a specific canon of authoritative texts comprising the Pentateuch, or the first five books of Moses (Genesis/Bereshit, Exodus/Shemot, Leviticus/Vayikra, Numbers/Bemidbar, Deuteronomy/Devarim).

When Ezra, a priest and scribe, returns to Jerusalem from exile in Babylon he reportedly carries with him the "the Torah of Moses which YHWH God of Israel gave" (Ezra 7:6; see also Neh 8:1, 13:1).[1] This is also called "YHWH's Torah" (Ezra 7:10) and the "law of your God" (Ezra 7:14). This document is generally equated with the first five books of the Hebrew Bible as we have them today. In other words, Ezra returns to Judah with the full Torah, which he may in fact have compiled and edited. By the time the Jerusalem temple is rebuilt toward the end of the late sixth century B.C.E.—consecration occurs around 515 B.C.E.—there is already an authoritative body of texts that a variety of groups consult and interpret to determine their appropriate ethical, ritual, and theological behavior with the express purpose of maintaining their covenantal relationship with God. As a result, for the post-Exilic populations discussed in this book, Torah can mean either a specific set of precepts or the collection of authoritative texts we refer to as the Pentateuch or both.

Modern Judaism appropriates the term *Torah* and uses it in a variety of ways: to refer to the Pentateuch, to the Hebrew Bible as a whole, and to the entire body of Jewish law and teachings, including the Talmud and other rabbinic texts (see below). In other words, we must consider the context in which the word *Torah* appears in order to understand what is meant.

Hebrew Bible, Jewish Scripture, Tanakh, or Old Testament?

While Jews and Christians historically have taught that Moses transcribed the first five books of the Bible, scholars present an alternative theory: A body of literature describing the history of the Israelites is spoken, written, and collected over a period of centuries. Large chunks of it are put together sometime around the Babylonian Exile, according to most biblical scholars, although some parts of it are written long before. When Judahites living in Judah are deported to Babylon in 587/586 B.C.E., they bring with them memories, stories, and texts. In Babylon they piece together their traditions into a mostly coherent collection of writings that tells the history of their nation and its relationship with its god. Many scholars discuss these traditions in terms of hypothetical documents that reveal some component of Israel's history and belief system. These sources have been identified as: the Yahwist (J), the Elohist (E), the Priestly Source (P), and the Deuteronomist (D). We catch glimpses of these sources in two different names for God: YHWH in the Yahwist source J, and Elohim in the Elohist source E. The redactors—that is, the editors of these texts—blend these two names for the divine (which reflect different theologies and divinities) so that those living in exile know it is one and the same god. Although each strand of JEPD, and other sources, presents a specific platform or viewpoint, an editor, or editors, weaves the strands together into a coherent narrative to tell the story of Israel's origins and history.

These writings are initially called the Law and the Prophets, or the Torah (teachings or instructions) and the Nevi'im (prophets).[2] A third collection of texts is assembled and called the Writings, or Ketuvim, and this is where Jews get the acronym TaNaKh for their Bible: Torah, Nevi'im, and Ketuvim, or law, prophets, and writings. The Torah comes first in the arrangement of Tanakh because it is the key part of the Bible; the Prophets come next; and finally the Writings, which are important, but not as authoritative as either the Prophets or the Torah. Tanakh ends with 1 and 2 Chronicles, which are not considered to be as reliable as other, older books describing the same subjects: 1 and 2 Samuel and 1 and 2 Kings.

Christians know Tanakh as the Old Testament, or more literally, the Old Covenant, which describes the original covenant, or agreement, that God makes with the Israelites. Christians contrast this with a New Covenant as foretold in Jeremiah:

> Behold, the days are coming, says the Lord, when I will make a new covenant with the house of Israel and with the house of Judah . . . This is the covenant that I will make with the house of Israel after those days, says

the Lord: I will put my law in their minds, and write it on their hearts; and I will be their God, and they shall be my people. (Jer 31:31, 33)

The teachings of the New Covenant appear in the New Testament, a collection of texts that includes letters, sermons, revelations, and gospels describing Jesus and his followers.

A few of the books of the Christian Old Testament differ from Tanakh, at least for Catholic and Orthodox Christians. While Protestant Christians include the exact same books as Tanakh in their Old Testament (although in a different order), Catholic and Orthodox Christians include a number of texts that are written in Greek. These texts contain the books listed in the accompanying chart, including the books of the Maccabees, a version of Esther with Greek additions, the Wisdom of Solomon, and the book of Jesus ben Sira, also known as Sirach or Ecclesiasticus. Sometimes these Greek texts are called deuterocanonical, meaning "second canon," and that term suggests they are not as authoritative as the strictly canonical texts. They are also commonly called apocryphal. Deuterocanonical, however, is somewhat preferable because it is less pejorative and a bit more scholarly. The term *apocryphal* has the connotation of being far out or far-fetched. It is important to remember that so-called deuterocanonical texts are in fact canonical for Catholic and Orthodox Christians.

To avoid the problem of theological exclusion that comes from calling Jewish sacred texts an "old" testament, scholars have come up with a number of different synonyms. Hebrew Bible is one euphemism used. The problem with this is that parts of some biblical texts—for example, Ezra, Nehemiah, and Daniel—are written in Aramaic, a Semitic language very similar to Hebrew, rather than in Hebrew. Calling the body of texts Jewish scripture solves that problem but creates another, since Jews, Christians, and even Muslims share these writings or the stories contained in them: They do not solely belong to a single religious group. Calling the writings Tanakh makes them distinctly Jewish, in the same way that calling them the Old Testament makes them distinctly Christian.

Texts and Translations

What complicates matters is that no single volume—from Genesis (Bereshit) to 2 Chronicles for Jews or from Genesis to Revelation for Christians—exists in the period we cover in this book, namely 200 B.C.E. to 200 C.E. At that time, each book is contained on a scroll, on a collection of scrolls, or on papyrus in a little codex, so no Bible is available to

Table 1.1.

The Jewish Tanakh	The Protestant Old Testament	The Catholic/Orthodox Old Testament
Torah	Genesis (Gen)	Genesis
Genesis (Bereshit)	Exodus (Exod)	Exodus
Exodus (Shemot)	Leviticus (Lev)	Leviticus
Leviticus (Vayikra)	Numbers (Num)	Numbers
Numbers (Bemidbar)	Deuteronomy (Deut)	Deuteronomy
Deuteronomy (Devarim)	Joshua (Josh)	Joshua
	Judges (Judg)	Judges
Nevi'im	Ruth (Ruth)	Ruth
Joshua (Yehoshua)	1 Samuel (1 Sam)	1 Samuel
Judges (Shoftim)	2 Samuel (2 Sam)	2 Samuel
1 Samuel (1 Shmuel)	1 Kings (1 Kgs)	1 Kings
2 Samuel (2 Shmuel)	2 Kings (2 Kgs)	2 Kings
1 Kings (1 Melakhim)	1 Chronicles (1 Chr)	1 Chronicles
2 Kings (2 Melakhim)	2 Chronicles (2 Chr)	2 Chronicles
Isaiah (Yisheyah)	Ezra (Ezra)	Ezra
Jeremiah (Yermiyah)	Nehemiah (Neh)	Nehemiah
Ezekiel (Yechezqel)	Esther (Est)	Tobit
Hosea (Hoshea)	Job (Job)	Judith
Joel (Yoel)	Psalms (Ps)	Esther (includes Greek
Amos	Proverbs (Prov)	additions)
Obadiah (Ovadyah)	Ecclesiastes (Eccl)	1 Maccabees
Jonah (Yonah)	Song of Solomon (Song)	2 Maccabees
Micah (Mikhah)	Isaiah (Isa)	Job
Nahum	Jeremiah (Jer)	Psalms
Habakkuk (Chavaquq)	Lamentations (Lam)	Proverbs
Zephaniah (Tsephanyah)	Ezekiel (Ezek)	Ecclesiastes
Haggai	Daniel (Dan)	Song of Songs (Song of
Zechariah (Zekharyah)	Hosea (Hosea)	Solomon)
Malachi (Malakhi)	Joel (Joel)	Wisdom of Solomon
	Amos (Amos)	Sirach
Ketuvim	Obadiah (Obad)	Isaiah
Psalms (Tehilim)	Jonah (Jonah)	Jeremiah
Proverbs (Mishlei)	Micah (Micah)	Lamentations
Job (Iyov)	Nahum (Nahum)	Baruch
Song of Solomon (Shir Hashirim)	Habakkuk (Hab)	Ezekiel
Ruth	Zephaniah (Zeph)	Daniel
Lamentations (Eichah)	Haggai (Hag)	Hosea
Ecclesiastes (Qohelet)	Zechariah (Zech)	Joel
Esther	Malachi (Mal)	Amos
Daniel (Daniyel)		Obadiah
Ezra		Jonah
Nehemiah (Nechemiyah)		Micah
1 Chronicles (1 Divrey Yamim)		Nahum
2 Chronicles (2 Divrey Yamim)		Habakkuk
		Zephaniah
		Haggai
		Zechariah
		Malachi

individuals the way it is today. Moreover, there are a number of texts in circulation at the time that are authoritative to a particular group, but not to all groups, and are not canonical to any religious group today. (The canon of scripture is the official inventory of books that are considered to have significant religious authority. A canon is a rule, or a list.) The Dead Sea Scrolls, for instance, a body of literature found in the Judean Desert, include a number of writings unique to the group living at Qumran, near the Dead Sea—such as the *War Scroll* or the *Community Rule*—as well as books that make it into the canon—such as the book of Isaiah. The idea of canon takes centuries to develop, however, and it is somewhat anachronistic to use the term when discussing the sacred texts of this time.

In addition, until the end of the first century C.E. many different Judaic groups accept the Greek texts that later make up part of the Catholic and Orthodox Old Testament. The fact that many Jews live outside Judea and speak only Greek necessitates a translation of Hebrew scripture. This translation is called the Septuagint, a Greek version of all the books of Torah, Prophets, and Writings that is made in Alexandria, Egypt, on the orders of Ptolemy II (r. 285–246 B.C.E.). An interesting legend surrounds this translation. Seventy-two translators take seventy-two days to complete the translation. Miraculously, the story goes, each translation is identical with the other. Although the legend says seventy-two translators are involved, the Septuagint is indicated by the Roman numeral LXX, or seventy, and the name itself—Septuagint— reflects this.

Obviously the purpose of the legend is to lend credibility to the translation. But even if the translations were, amazingly, the same, key concepts are still translated from the Hebrew mind into Greek idiom. For example, the word *torah*, which means "instruction" or "teaching" in Hebrew, becomes *nomos*, or "law" in Greek. The Hebrew word *almah*, which means "young woman," becomes *parthenos*, which means "virgin." Later writers, such as Aquila, Symmachus, and Theodotion, who translate Judaic texts from Hebrew into Greek are somewhat more faithful to the literal sense of the Hebrew original. The authors of the New Testament, however, who are all writing in Greek, know scripture via the Septuagint. Indeed, the LXX may be the only scripture they know until the end of the first century C.E., with the notable exception of a large body of literature called Pseudepigrapha.

Authentic Fakes

There is a wealth of texts that do not make it into the Bible. Some of these come from the Judean Desert (see below). The Old Testament Apocrypha ("hidden works") are sometimes called intertestamental literature or Pseudepigrapha. Apocrypha here indicates texts that neither Jews nor Christians include in their canons; this differs from the deuterocanonical texts, which are recognized by some, but not all, Christians. Almost all Pseudepigrapha are apocryphal, but not all apocryphal literature is Pseudepigrapha. For example, there are many Christian legends—such as the story of Veronica, who wipes Christ's brow with her handkerchief during his passion, or the existence of another wife for Joseph—that make up the New Testament Apocrypha. But these are not Pseudepigrapha.

Pseudepigrapha literally means "with false subscriptions" and refers to a diverse set of writings composed between 250 B.C.E. and 200 C.E. Many pseudepigraphical texts—which are preserved in Greek, Coptic, Ethiopic, or other languages and now exist in English and other translations—may have originally been written in Hebrew. Pseudepigrapha are writings that appear to be by or about biblical figures—such as Abraham or Moses or Enoch—and provide "the further adventures of . . .," especially in the form of heavenly travels and angelic visions. They elaborate upon and expand stories and legends from the Hebrew Bible and convey important messages from God that seem relevant to the problems of the present. They also comprise wisdom and philosophical literature, that is, writings that consider the nature of knowledge and wisdom and what it means to understand the nature of reality. The Pseudepigrapha include prayers and psalms and make up a type of devotional literature as well.

The Hebrew Bible/Old Testament actually contains an example of Pseudepigrapha. The book of Daniel purports to have been written during the Babylonian Exile, under the rule of Nebuchadnezzar, but scholars agree that it was written around 168 B.C.E. during the time of the Maccabean Revolt (see chapter 3).

The title of this section comes from David Chidester's book *Authentic Fakes*[3] because it is an apt description of Pseudepigrapha. These texts are "fake" in the sense that Jews and Christians today do not accept them as either inspired scripture (with the exception of Daniel) or historical or truthful accounts of past events. Neither group accepts the authenticity of the *Life of Adam and Eve*, for instance. But they are authentic in the sense that they *are* meaningful, significant, and profoundly inspiring to their authors and their audiences. They retell a number of biblical stories—such as the chronicles of Job or of Enoch—for a new era, one during which people are undergoing oppression and are seeking help not just from God but also from God's own messengers, the angels.

The Dead Sea Scrolls

The discovery of the Dead Sea Scrolls in eleven caves near the site of Khirbet Qumran has revolutionized our knowledge about both Jewish and Christian origins and the process of biblical transmission. More than 900 fragments of Bible, apocrypha, Pseudepigrapha, and commentaries are included in the Dead Sea Scroll library.

Most interesting for our study is the group of texts commonly referred to as the "sectarian" or non-biblical scrolls, thought by many to be written by the members of the Qumran community. These documents contain a wealth of information about the group's beliefs, practices, daily life, and thoughts on their current era and on the end of days. The texts enable modern readers to learn more about this group than about any other community in the first centuries B.C.E. and C.E. While the determination of the specific authors of the non-biblical scrolls is beyond the scope of our investigation, we do view this material as representative of an interpretive community in the first centuries B.C.E and C.E. (to 68 C.E.). For the sake of clarity, we refer to this group as the Qumran community, recognizing that the relationship between the site of Qumran and the provenance of the scrolls is still debated in modern scholarship.

The translation and publication of these scrolls helps scholars understand the way in which the community's beliefs evolve over time. Some argue that members of the community may have at one time been associated with the Jerusalem priesthood and that over the course of decades they develop a community with unique views about itself as the legitimate inheritor of Israelite tradition. This evolution is reflected in community members' writings, especially among editions of the same text that appear to have been composed at different times. We cite selections from the scrolls listed in the chapters that follow.

Pesharim: A pesher, or commentary, constitutes one of the unique ways the community at Qumran interprets its "Bible." After each biblical verse copied on a scroll, the authors of the text provide their own commentary or interpretation of the verse's meaning. This analysis is more often than not related to their understanding of contemporary events. The community at Qumran believes that these sacred texts contain hidden messages and esoteric secrets concerning its future. Community members have faith that their specific brand of righteousness empowers them to reveal these secrets. (Pesharim is the plural of pesher.)

Community Rule (1QS): The *Community Rule*—also known as the *Manual of Discipline*—is a set of rules according to which the community members at Qumran conduct their lives. The document contains principles regarding religious practice, justice, and conduct of the members of the community. It describes the way in which one can become a member of the group and details daily life, work, prayer, study, and the steps taken to discipline those members who violate any of the stated rules.

Damascus Document (CD): Fragments of this text were found in caves 4, 5, and 6 at the Qumran site. Scrolls with nearly identical contents were discovered in 1896 by Solomon Schechter in the genizah (depository for old books and scrolls) of the Ezra Synagogue in Cairo. This text addresses a community that is reported to have fled from Judea to the "Land of Damascus." Scholars posit that "Damascus" in the text may refer to the Syrian city or may simply symbolize "exile" in general. The text urges the community to remain faithful to the covenant and then sets out a list of legal precepts, rituals, and rules for the community to observe.

War Scroll (1QM): This scroll describes the final apocalyptic war between the Sons of Light, presumably the members of the Qumran community, and the Sons of Darkness, called kittim, after which a new world order will reign. The text explains how people will be recruited for the battle and provides various details concerning battle strategy. It includes descriptions of soldiers' weapons and blessings to be recited during the various stages of the battle.

The New Testament

The Christian New Testament is made up of twenty-seven books, all written in Greek. The majority of these books consist of letters, most of which are written between 50 and 60 C.E. by a man named Paul to churches he had established. The letters of Paul are the oldest writings in the New Testament, with 1 Thessalonians being the oldest. Some New Testament scholars believe, however, that several letters attributed to Paul were actually written by some of the apostle's own followers. Because Paul is so highly regarded, his name is used to provide authority and weight to the theological opinions expressed in letters written under his name. These letters are called the deutero-Pauline, or "second Pauline," corpus and include the Pastoral Letters (1 and 2 Timothy, Titus), Ephesians, and possibly Colossians and 2 Thessalonians. While most Christians believe that Paul wrote these letters, there are enough differences in vocabulary, theology, and concepts to raise questions about actual Pauline authorship for many New Testament scholars. The issue of authorship becomes important in conflicts over authority and interpretation, especially when people use texts to wage theological battles.

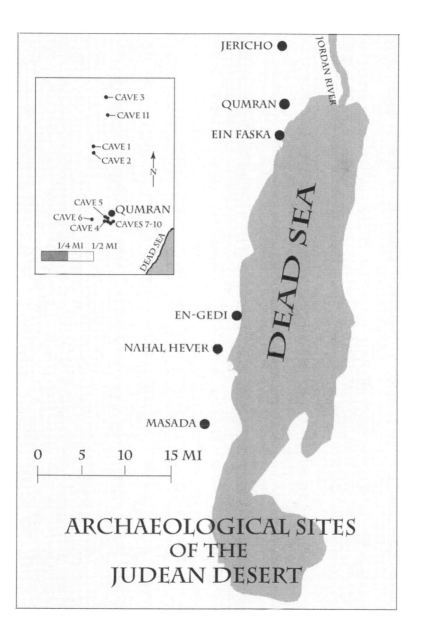

JERICHO ●

QUMRAN ●

EIN FASKA ●

JORDAN RIVER

DEAD SEA

EN-GEDI ●

NAHAL HEVER ●

MASADA ●

0   5   10   15 MI

● CAVE 3
● CAVE 11

● CAVE 1
CAVE 2

CAVE 5
CAVE 6 →
CAVE 4

QUMRAN
CAVES 7-10

N

1/4 MI   1/2 MI

DEAD SEA

ARCHAEOLOGICAL SITES
OF THE
JUDEAN DESERT

Although the New Testament begins with the four Gospels, or accounts of Jesus' life and teachings—Mark, Matthew, Luke, and John—these are among the latest, or youngest, texts in the New Testament. You may have observed that we have listed the Gospels in the order in which most scholars believe they were written. Mark seems to be the oldest gospel, probably written between 68 and 70 C.E. Matthew and Luke seem to have rewritten parts of Mark and incorporated them into their own subsequent accounts, written in the 80s, although some scholars date Luke into the early second century. The authors of Matthew and Luke seem to have had several other sources besides Mark, including a written collection of Jesus' sayings, which scholars call "Q" (which is short for Quelle, or "source," in German). Because Mark, Matthew, and Luke are quite similar in many respects (though different in others), scholars call them the Synoptic Gospels because they can be "seen together" (syn-optic). There are close parallels between these three gospels in what Jesus says and does that John's gospel does not reflect. Though the synoptic depictions of Jesus vary, they nevertheless show him as a human preacher and teacher who speaks in parables

Table 1.2.

New Testament	
Paul's Letters (in chronological order)	1 Thessalonians (ca. 50) 2 Thessalonians (Paul?) 1 & 2 Corinthians (ca. 54–55) Galatians (ca. 56) Romans (ca. 56–57) Colossians (Paul?) Philippians (ca. 61) Philemon (ca. 62)
Synoptic Gospels	Mark (ca. 66–70) Matthew (ca. 80–85) Luke and Acts (ca. 85–120)
General, or "Catholic," Epistles	James, 1 Peter (ca. 85–95) Jude, 2 Peter (ca. 130–150, though some date Jude to 50)
Johannine Literature	Gospel of John (ca. 90–95) Letters of John (three of them) (ca. 95–100) Revelation of John (ca. 95)
Deutero-Pauline	Hebrews, Ephesians (ca. 85–95) 1 & 2 Timothy and Titus (ca. 110–130)

and aphorisms, unlike the portrait of Jesus in the Gospel of John, which features a somewhat ethereal figure who comes down from heaven and gives long sermons and speeches. Scholars estimate that John was written at the end of the first century C.E.

There are a number of Christian texts that do not make it into the New Testament canon. These are the gospels and other sacred writings composed by Gnostic Christians in the first three centuries of the Common Era. Until the twentieth century, most of our knowledge about Gnostics and their beliefs came from early Christian heresiologists, or heresy-hunters, like Irenaeus of Lyons (ca. 115–202) and Epiphanius of Salamis (ca. 375). But in 1945, a cache of Christian codexes, or little leather-bound papyrus books, was found on the upper Nile in Egypt. These books provide elaborate mythologies; sayings of Jesus; appearances of Jesus to various disciples, such as Philip and Mary; and new revelations not contained in the canonical gospels. The Infancy Gospel of Thomas, for example, relates Jesus' actions as a little boy—a not very nice little boy with divine powers. The Gospel of Mary presents Mary as Jesus' favorite, who receives wisdom directly from the risen lord and communicates it to the other disciples. The Gospel of Thomas is a collection of sayings from Jesus, some of which appear in the canonical gospels and some of which do not, such as: "Blessed is the lion which becomes man when consumed by man; and cursed is the man whom the lion consumes, and the lion becomes man" (Tho 7); or, still more cryptically, "Become passers-by" (Tho 42). Although some early Christian communities use these texts, the majority rely on the gospels and letters that eventually become canonical

Most Christians today believe that the books of the New Testament are inspired by God and that they faithfully report the events and sayings in Jesus' life. New Testament scholars are a bit more skeptical about the historicity of the Bible. ("Historicity" refers to the historical reliability of an account.) Many would say that the Gospels are theological reflections, rather than accurate biographies, about the life and teachings of Jesus. They would add that using the New Testament as a historical source is tricky. Can we trust what it says about the Pharisees, or are the texts written at a time when there is conflict between different Judaic groups all claiming to be Israel? How do we account for the fact that the Synoptic Gospels have Jesus die on one day, while John's gospel has him die on a different day? Historical questions like these become important when we try to deduce the origins of what eventually become Judaism and Christianity. This minefield of conflicting claims and questions will become problematic when we try to understand various Judaic groups.

A final note on the New Testament: It does not exist in the first century. We do not have a fairly complete listing of New Testament texts until the late second century, and it is not until the fourth century that we have a preliminary canon identified in the letter of Athanasius, a bishop from Alexandria. We know that some early communities have only the letters of, or a letter from, Paul; some have a single gospel; some have texts that do not make it into the New Testament canon, such as the Gnostic gospels and apocalypses; some explicitly reject texts that are eventually canonized, such as the book of Revelation or the book of Hebrews. It is important to keep in mind, then, that the only scripture Jesus' followers know is Jewish scripture, at least initially. Oral traditions about Jesus, which transmit his sayings, teachings, and events about his life, circulate for decades. Even when they are committed to writing, people have only bits and pieces, not a complete library as we have today in the New Testament.

Rabbinic Literature

Another source we will be using to understand the origins of Judaism and Christianity is rabbinic literature, a broad catch-all term that describes a number of Jewish texts compiled after 200 C.E. Jewish tradition teaches that when God gives the Written Torah to Moses at Mount Sinai, there is a second body of material handed down to Moses orally at the same time. Jews believe that this Oral Torah was faithfully passed down by word of mouth to the leaders of each generation from the time of Moses up to the end of the second century. According to this tradition, God knows that the Written Torah will not suit the needs of the Jewish people after their wanderings in the desert and in changing historical situations. In this sense, the Oral Torah is understood to contain all of the information required for adapting the written text to future generations and situations. Scholars recognize that the idea of Oral Torah probably begins to develop after the Babylonian Exile as a secondary interpretive tradition that serves to keep the legal commandments outlined in the Torah relevant and observable in the face of changing times. It is clear that even within the Hebrew Bible itself, later texts often comment upon and interpret earlier traditions.

In response to the loss of political independence that begins with the Babylonian Exile and continues for more than 400 years into the Greco-Roman period, numerous interpretive traditions circulate and help define how Torah laws and rituals can continue to be observed. Moreover, in response to the rise of Christianity, respected and authoritative teachers begin to articulate their own theology and ideas about the God of Israel.

These teachers, called sages or rabbis, have followers who memorize and transmit their teachings about halakah, or observing the commandments, as well as their instruction regarding interpretation of Torah. Rabbinic sages are often noted for their ability to adapt and change Israelite tradition to meet both the internal and external challenges faced by the descendants of Israel in the time of Second Temple Judaism and later. It is this adaptation and change that serves as the Oral Torah of Jewish tradition.

The teachings of the sages that are compiled over a period of several hundred years are put together in one collection around 200 C.E. This text is called the Mishna, which means "repetition," suggesting the idea that the information had been learned and transmitted by repetition. The Mishna collects legal material and teachings and is divided into six major chapters, each of which is subdivided into tractates, or books. The chapters include:

Zeraim (Seeds), which deals with agriculture and tithing in the land of Israel;

Moed (Times), which deals with laws about observing Sabbath and festivals;

Nashim (Women), which deals with women, especially the regulations regarding betrothal, marriage, and divorce;

Nezikim (Damages), which deals with civil and criminal law;

Kodshim (Holiness), which deals with rules of sacrifices at the temple; and

Taharot (Purity), which deals with laws of purity and impurity.

These chapters are preceded by a short book called *Pirke Abot*, or *Sayings of the Fathers*, which gathers together ethical words of wisdom from sixty-five sages, whose decisions make up the rest of the Mishna. These sages, or rabbis, are known as the *Tannaim*, the Aramaic word for teachers. A compilation of supplementary rulings—known as the Tosefta—elaborating upon the same subjects, is put together around 300 C.E.

New situations arise in the period from the final editing of the Mishna until 400 to 500 C.E., which are not addressed in the Mishna. Many relevant teachings grow out of ongoing rabbinic discussions on Torah and Mishna. In response, a fresh generation of sages, called the Amoraim—Aramaic for explainers or interpreters—compile and edit a second collection of discussions known as the Gemara. The Gemara weaves together legal debate, folklore, history, biography, and personal stories of the sages. The Gemara contains both Jewish law (halakah) as well as narrative (aggadah). Two Gemaras develop somewhat simultaneously, one in the land of

Israel (ca. 425 C.E.) and one in Babylonia (ca. 500 C.E.). The combined Mishna and Gemara is called the Talmud. The Babylonian Talmud is considerably longer, at thirty-seven volumes, than the Jerusalem Talmud from the land of Israel.

For Jews today, Torah—as God's instruction—encompasses much more than the Bible. It includes the Mishna as well, and certainly the Talmud. Following the compilation of the Talmud, Talmudic authorities and teachers are looked to as the spiritual leaders of the Jewish people, because only those steeped in study of the tradition can master the large collection of legal precedents, ethical teaching, legends, and commentary.

The Mishna is the most important component of rabbinic literature for the purposes of this book, because it contains information about sages living in the first centuries, the period we are studying. Like the New Testa-

Table 1.3.   Jewish Scripture (Partial list, only up to sixth century C.E.)

Written Torah	
Tanakh	
Torah	Redacted ca. 5th century B.C.E.
Prophets *(Nevi'im)*	Redacted by ca. 2nd century B.C.E.
Writings *(Ketuvim)*	Redacted by ca. 1st century C.E.
Oral Torah	Also known as Rabbinic Literature
Mishna	Compiled ca. 200 C.E.
Pirke Abot	Compiled ca. 250 C.E.
Zeraim (Seeds)	
Moed (Times)	
Nashim (Women)	
Nezikim (Damages)	
Kodshim (Holiness)	
Taharot (Purity)	
Literature from the land of Israel	
Mekhilta of Rabbi Ishmael (commentary on Exodus)	Compiled 3rd to 4th century C.E.
Sifra (commentary on Leviticus)	Compiled 3rd to 4th century C.E.
Sifre (commentary on Numbers and Deuteronomy)	End of 4th century C.E.
Bereshit Rabba (commentary on Genesis)	Redacted by 5th century C.E.
Vayikra Rabba (commentary on Leviticus)	Redacted by 5th century C.E.
Tosefta	Compiled ca. 300 C.E.
Gemara	
Jerusalem Talmud	Compiled ca. 350 C.E.
Babylonian Talmud	Compiled ca. 500 C.E.
Talmud = Mishna + Gemara	

ment, though, the Mishna has a theological agenda. We cannot consider either text to provide "pure" history, though we can glean some historical information from both of them. In other words, the Mishna is just as problematic as the New Testament in terms of historicity.

The "Top Ten"

The Dead Sea Scrolls, the New Testament, and rabbinic literature are not written in a vacuum, but rather rely extensively on the Hebrew Bible. Each set of authors employs a variety of interpretive strategies in its respective reading of the Hebrew Bible, and each moves beyond biblical thought as it offers its own theological agenda. We can get glimpses of what each interpretive community finds important by examining the texts it uses the most. The Psalms, Isaiah, and Deuteronomy are the three most popular works among the Dead Sea Scrolls—at least in terms of the number of copies discovered—and are cited most frequently in the New Testament. In the Mishna, however, the most frequently cited texts are Exodus, Numbers, Deuteronomy, and Leviticus—all from the Torah. The Qumran and New Testament writers likely turn to Deuteronomy to discuss the theme of covenant because they each put forward their own covenant. They probably rely upon the book of Isaiah for support of their belief in imminent redemption and upon the Psalms in expectation of a messianic figure like David. The Mishna shows the interest of the Tannaim, the sages, in the works of the Pentateuch, especially the legal issues of Leviticus and Deuteronomy, although Isaiah and Psalms also occur in their "Top Ten."

Table 1.4.   The "Top Ten"*

	Qumran	No. of Copies	New Testament	No. of Citations	Mishna	No. of Citations
10.	Minor Prophets	8	Proverbs	4	Ezekiel	12
9.	Daniel	8	Jeremiah	5	Minor Prophets	14
8.	Leviticus	9	Daniel	7	Proverbs	16
7.	Exodus	14	Leviticus	17	Isaiah	26
6.	Jubilees	15	Minor Prophets	30	Genesis	35
5.	Enoch	20	Genesis	39	Psalms	41
4.	Genesis	20	Exodus	44	Exodus	133
3.	Isaiah	24	Deuteronomy	54	Numbers	133
2.	Deuteronomy	27	Isaiah	66	Deuteronomy	234
1.	Psalms	34	Psalms	79	Leviticus	349

*Thanks go to Peter Flint and Martin Abegg for providing the information for the "Top Ten."

Extra-biblical Sources

What is the evidence outside the New Testament for the existence of Jesus? Or outside the Talmud for the existence of rabbis Hillel or Shammai? If we pose these questions more broadly, we might ask: What is the historicity of the stories about Jesus? What is the historicity of stories about Hillel and Shammai? Can we take them as historical documents? The problem of historicity exists with a variety of sources. Most of our information about the Maccabean revolt of the second century B.C.E., for example, comes from texts written with a political and religious agenda. Most of our information about the sages who live contemporaneously with Jesus comes from theological writings. Of course, that is true of almost all the characters and events that appear in the Bible, with certain exceptions. Archaeologists have found material evidence that *refers to* King David, although that is not the same as saying that they have evidence for King David. They also have found inscriptions that describe the destruction of both the first and second Jerusalem temples.

Scholars look to extra-biblical sources to confirm or verify conclusions they draw from the Bible itself or from other religious texts, such as the Mishna. Extra-biblical simply means "outside the Bible." Just as navigators triangulate by using three points of reference to determine their location, scholars and researchers try to triangulate by using different points of reference to justify and support the conclusions they reach. Even pagan sources might serve as one of these points of reference, and indeed these do fill in some details about biblical narratives, both in the Hebrew Bible and the New Testament. These sources help researchers date biblical events.

In addition to pagan authors who recount first-century history, such as Tacitus, Suetonius, and Pliny the Younger, there are other Judaic writers who are about as reliable, or unreliable, as the New Testament and rabbinic literature. The historian Josephus, who fights with Vespasian against the Judeans in the First Jewish War (66–73 C.E.), writes far-reaching narratives that attempt to interpret biblical history and Judean culture for a pagan audience. Scholars rely extensively on Josephus for understanding the rule of the Hasmonean dynasty and for grasping the nature of Roman-Judean conflict, as well as for gaining insight into various Judaic philosophies. Philo is another extra-biblical source. Philo is an Alexandrian Judean who also lives in the first century. His writings focus on biblical interpretation and philosophy, but he does provide information about beliefs and customs of the Judeans. We will return to Josephus and Philo in chapter 3.

Biblical Scholarship

The ideas and vocabulary we discuss in this chapter are intended to introduce readers to the language of biblical scholarship. It is an alternate way of thinking about texts that many people hold sacred. It should be clear by now that things are more complicated than they may first appear, especially when we talk about texts and people from the first century. Readers will find that many of the conclusions we present are tentative and provisional, rather than hard and fast. That is because the history of late antiquity, and of Jewish and Christian origins, is undergoing intense revision and reevaluation. In short, it is being rewritten as we are reading and writing.

There is a lot to understand, and much to master, in the language and thought world of biblical studies that is foreign to our usual way of thinking about religion. We will continue to introduce new vocabulary as we proceed. And we will present our argument, which both confirms and challenges new and old theories of origins. To help readers navigate the unfamiliar terrain, we append a glossary at the end of the book and provide suggested readings at the end of each chapter.

Suggested Readings

Bart D. Ehrman. *Lost Christianity: The Battles for Scripture and the Faiths We Never Knew*. New York: Oxford University Press, 2003.

Richard Elliott Friedman. *Who Wrote the Bible?* New York: Summit Books, 1987.

Barry W. Holtz, ed. *Back to the Sources. Reading the Classic Jewish Texts*. New York: Simon and Schuster, 1984.

James L. Kugel. *The Bible as It Was*. Cambridge, Mass.: Belknap Press, 1997.

Burton L. Mack. *Who Wrote the New Testament? The Making of the Christian Myth*. San Francisco: HarperCollins, 1996.

Bruce M. Metzger. *The Canon of the New Testament: Its Origin, Development, and Significance*. Oxford, U.K.: Clarendon Press, 1987.

Bruce M. Metzger and Michael D. Coogan, eds. *The Oxford Companion to the Bible*. New York: Oxford University Press, 1993.

Jacob Neusner. *Rabbinic Literature: An Essential Guide*. Nashville: Abingdon, 2005.

Notes

1. Practicing Jews would not use the term *YHWH*, but instead would use a euphemism for the sacred tetragrammaton (or four letters) denoting the name of God. Scholars, however, use these four letters or may even transliterate them as Yahweh.

2. We are not following academic transliteration guidelines in this book, but rather are presenting to lay readers the way in which words sound and are pronounced today.

3. David Chidester, *Authentic Fakes: Religion and American Popular Culture* (Berkeley: University of California Press, 2005).

Israelite Religion and Its Legacy   2

I N RETELLING THEIR RESPECTIVE STORIES of origins, most Christians and Jews use a variety of terms—Israel, Jew, Christian—interchangeably. That is to say, Jews identify themselves at once as descendants of Israel and as Jewish, while Christians see themselves as Israel too. Our imprecise use of terminology and religious labels reinforces the lineal approach to understanding origins: Israel—Jew—Christian. These labels often tend to be tossed around without a very clear understanding of when it is historically or theologically appropriate to use one or the others. If we consider a modern analogy, identifying oneself or others as liberal or conservative can have very different meanings depending upon when, historically, the term is being used, and by whom.

Who then is the first Jew and the first Christian, and when is it appropriate to begin employing the terms "Jew" and "Judaism" or "Christian" and "Christianity?" Though the question seems simple enough, the response is rather complicated. Answering this and other queries takes us back to Israelite religion, the common ancestor, which is where we need to begin.

The People of the Hebrew Bible

When we ask a room full of students—either college-age or adult learners—who is the first Jew, typically two or three names predominate: Abraham, Moses, or even Adam. What qualifies these characters for the title role of "First Jew"? Most say their early appearance in the Hebrew Bible and their special relationship with God indicates their originary status. Abraham, they say, is the first to enter into a covenant with the God of

Israel. Moses is the first lawgiver. But are they Jewish? Most students are surprised to learn that none of these characters are called "Jews" in the Hebrew Bible. In fact, the word "Jew" scarcely appears in the Hebrew Bible, and when it does, it occurs in two post-Exilic books: Ezra and Nehemiah. Who, then, are the people of the Hebrew Bible/Old Testament?

In the text of the Bible, the term *Israel* first appears in Genesis in connection with Abraham's grandson Jacob. In Genesis 32, Jacob has an interesting encounter with an odd being. At the conclusion of this episode, Jacob's name is changed to Israel: literally, "the one who struggles or strives with God." From this point forward in the text, the members of Jacob's family are called the "sons of Israel." Literally then, the biblical Israelites are the children and grandchildren of Jacob. Therefore, Abraham is not, technically speaking, an Israelite, nor is he a Jew.

Israel also represents a national identity in the Bible. The book of Judges remarks that after the twelve tribes of Israel settle in Canaan, Israel has no king (Judg 17:6). Israel in this sense means a people and incorporates all twelve tribes into this unity. The elders of Israel beg the prophet Samuel for a king, and he anoints Saul, a Benjaminite, the first king of Israel (1 Sam 10:1). Under the reigns of Saul, David, and Solomon, the kingdom consists of the territory inhabited by the twelve tribes of Israel. When Solomon dies, the united kingdom splits into two. The northern kingdom keeps the name Israel and is composed of ten tribes, while the southern kingdom adopts the name Judah and consists of the tribes of Judah and Benjamin. Thus, Israel is now a geographic region.

The biblical text rarely differentiates between the various ways in which "Israel" is to be understood, and modern readers are often left to determine this on their own. English translations of the Bible do not distinguish among the familial term Israel—as in, literally, the sons of Jacob—Israel in the sense of a larger group of people or a nation, and Israel in the sense of a religion in which people worship a particular deity. The first chapter of Exodus, for example, seems to refer both to the literal "sons of Israel" and to the general descendants of Israel (Exod 1:1, 7). When we see the term "Israel" (all Israel, the house of Israel, the sons of Israel, the Israelites, etc.) in the Bible or in history books, we need to ask: Is Israel a family, a place, a nation, a people, a religious grouping, or even all five at once?

There is yet another Israel to be aware of. This is the modern nation of Israel, created in 1948. The citizens of this country are not called Israelites, but Israelis. If you go up to a group of Israelis on the street and ask to speak to an Israelite, they might wonder what century you are living in.

The People of the New Testament

When we ask a group of students a question about who the first Christian is, many say Jesus, although those raised in a Christian tradition might say Paul, or even name Jesus' disciple Peter. The early followers of Jesus, who understand themselves as "children of Israel" do not call themselves Christians. If Paul is the first Christian, he does not appear to know it, since he characterizes himself as a Hebrew, a Pharisee, and an Israelite (2 Cor 11:22, Phil 3:5). He also calls himself a Jew, or Judean (1 Cor 9:20), some terminology we discuss in chapter 3.

The disciples and members of the early church in Jerusalem consider themselves to be both Jews (or Judeans) and followers of The Way, or part of the church. "The Way" appears seven times in the book of Acts to indicate Christianity, a word which never appears in the New Testament, although the word "Christian" appears three times. In one instance, King Agrippa asks Paul, "Are you so quickly persuading me to become a Christian?" (Acts 26:28). In 1 Peter, the text says, "Yet if any of you suffers as a Christian, do not consider it a disgrace, but glorify God because you bear this name" (1 Pet 4:16).

Some extra-biblical sources from the second century do employ the name "Christian." Pliny the Younger describes practices of Christians in a letter to the Emperor Trajan. Tacitus notes that Nero blames Christians for the fires that engulfed Rome during his reign in the 60s C.E. Suetonius writes that "Chrestus" is executed as a rebel during the time of the Emperor Claudius. We also find the word "Christian" in some extra-biblical Christian sources from the end of the first century and the beginning of the second. A text called "Clement's First Letter" is one of the earliest Christian writings outside the New Testament (ca. 96 C.E.). In the letter to the Church of Corinth, Clement refers to "Christian faith," which he says confirms a number of ethical principles. Later on he chastises the Corinthian Church for being unworthy and unfaithful to its "Christian upbringing." In these instance, Clement is employing "Christian" as an adjective to describe a body of teaching, and even a way of life, rather than using it as a name for members of the church. Finally, the late second-century Christian apology *Epistle to Diognetus* describes Christians as a "new race," neither Judean nor Gentile.

We eventually see the word *Christian* used as a form of self-identification in the letters of Ignatius written at the beginning of the second century. Bishop of Antioch in Syria, Ignatius is known only from seven letters he wrote to various churches in Asia Minor as he marched as a prisoner to his martyrdom in Rome sometime during the reign of the Emperor Trajan (r. 98–117 C.E.). In his letter to the church at Magnesia, a town fifteen miles from Ephesus, Ignatius writes that, "We have not only to be called Christians, but to *be* Christians" (Magnesians 4). He reiterates the sentiment in his letter to the church at Rome: "It is not that I want merely to be called a Christian, but actually to *be* one. Yes, if I prove to be one, then I can have the name. Then, too, I shall be a convincing Christian only when the world sees me no more" (Rom 2–3). A few lines later he refers to "[t]he greatness of Christianity."

We can deduce several things from Ignatius' comments. First, Christian seems to be a label that outsiders use to characterize members of churches in various communities around the Mediterranean. We see this in King Agrippa's question to Paul: Are you trying to convince me to be a Christian? Second, it seems that those associated with the movement are beginning to use the term to identify themselves and to portray their movement as Christianity. We see this in Acts 11:26, where we learn that the disciples are called Christians in Antioch. Finally, the fact Ignatius uses Christian as a name in the same way that 1 Peter does might indicate that 1 Peter is written at a later time—a time in which followers of The Way are now calling themselves Christians.

Although we could call Ignatius the first Christian, since he views himself as one, perhaps a better candidate—and one Christians today would probably accept—is the first martyr, that is, the first person to be killed for professing Jesus. If we use this as our criterion, then Stephen, although he clearly believes himself to be Jewish, might be called the first Christian. Acts 7 describes his indictment of fellow Israelites, who he claims repeatedly persecute the prophets and turn away from God. But even if we call Stephen rather than Ignatius the first Christian, we need to remember that these are our own explanations, manufactured after the historical facts rather than generated at the time. The Christianity practiced by the early church resembles Christianity today, but is not identical; just as the Judaism of the first century also differs from that observed by modern Jews.

Understanding Israel and Judah

The division of Israel into two kingdoms in 922 B.C.E. leads to the birth of the biblical nation referred to as Judah—named after one of Jacob's sons—as noted above. Judah (*Yehuda* in Hebrew) occupies the central hill country between Jerusalem and Hebron. As a kingdom, Judah exists from ca. 922 B.C.E. to 587 B.C.E. To complicate matters, the people living in

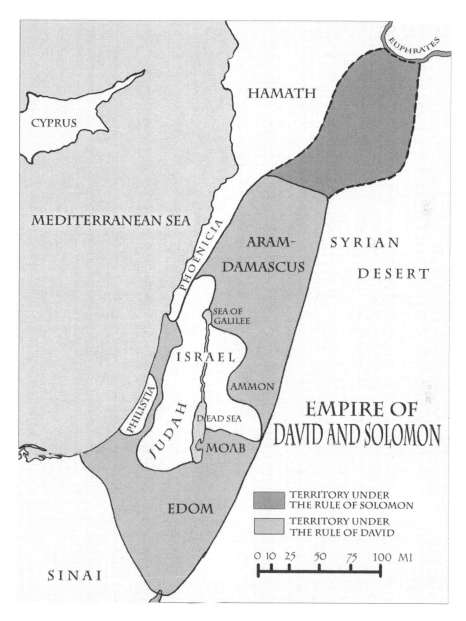

CYPRUS

HAMATH

MEDITERRANEAN SEA

PHOENICIA

ARAM-
DAMASCUS

SYRIAN

DESERT

SEA OF
GALILEE

ISRAEL

PHILISTIA

AMMON

JUDAH

DEAD SEA

MOAB

EMPIRE OF
DAVID AND SOLOMON

TERRITORY UNDER
THE RULE OF SOLOMON

TERRITORY UNDER
THE RULE OF DAVID

EDOM

0 10 25   50   75   100 MI

SINAI

EUPHRATES

Judah are also called, and refer to themselves, as Israel and the descendants of Israel, although they also retain their national identity as "children of Judah" or "men of Judah" (e.g., 2 Sam 1:18; 19:14, 16). They do this even after the geographic and political entity known as Israel no longer exists

(722 B.C.E.) as a result of the Assyrian invasion. Even after their own nation of Judah is destroyed by the Babylonians in 587/586 B.C.E., the Judahites call themselves Israel.

The inhabitants of Judah share the worship of the same god with their Israelite/northern kingdom counterparts and see themselves as Israel, the identity of a group of people who live in a covenantal relationship with their god. The Judahites, along with the Israelites (we are using the terms as geographical identifiers now), are not represented as Jews in the Hebrew Bible in the way we would understand Judaism today. What is perhaps most confusing is that in Hebrew the words *yehudi* and *yehudim* (Judahite, Judahites) can refer both to the inhabitants of the ancient land of Judah or to the early and modern practitioners of Judaism.

Throughout its history, the self-understanding of Israel and of Judah is neither monolithic nor static. Israel begins as a group of tribes connected by a common ancestor, but then grows into a nation ruled by kings. When Israel and Judah exist as two separate national entities, we know that the northern kingdom has its own sacred sites, which we see some of the prophets condemn (e.g., Amos 6:1, 7:9, 9:1). It is clear, then, that different historical realities over time result in a variety of ways that Israelites might perceive their place in the world and their relationship to their god. So too, a wealthy merchant in Jerusalem and a peasant living in the countryside in the ninth century B.C.E. may both worship the same god, although their individual beliefs, rituals, behaviors, and cultic sites need not be identical.

There is a tendency among most readers of the Bible to see the inhabitants of Israel and of Judah collectively as Jews, unconsciously linking these groups with modern Judaism. Although the worship of the god of Israel, in its various forms, has much in common with later Judaism—as well as with Christianity—it is not identical to either tradition, although this distinction is seldom made outside of scholarly circles.

A Word on the Hebrews

While in English the term *Hebrew* or *Hebrews* is often used synonymously with *Jew* or *Jews*, the Bible employs the term *ibrim* in several limited situations. Most notably, when non-Israelites come into contact with Israelites, or people from Israel, the non-Israelite identifies the Israelite as a Hebrew. This suggests there is a time when Israelites do not call themselves Israelites, or it may indicate the independence of biblical traditions that recount experiences in Egypt. We see Hebrew used in the Joseph narrative, for ex-

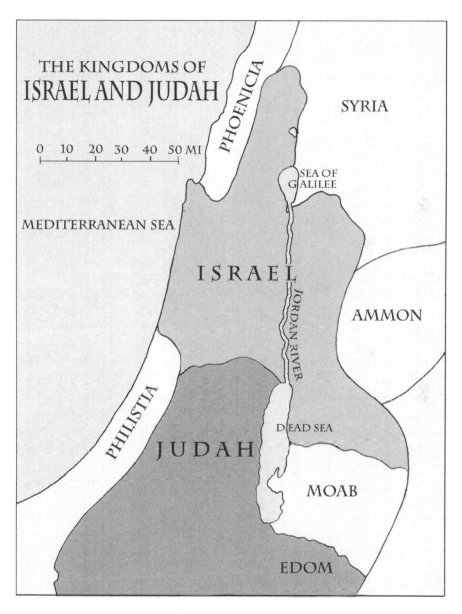

THE KINGDOMS OF
ISRAEL AND JUDAH

0 10 20 30 40 50 MI

MEDITERRANEAN SEA

PHOENICIA

SYRIA

SEA OF
GALILEE

ISRAEL

JORDAN RIVER

AMMON

PHILISTIA

JUDAH

DEAD SEA

MOAB

EDOM

ample, when Potiphar's wife identifies Joseph as a Hebrew (Gen 39:14). We also find references to Hebrews in Exodus, when Pharaoh's daughter calls the infant Moses "a Hebrew child" (Exod 2:6). The Philistines also use Hebrew in 1 Samuel 4. On occasion, an Israelite might use the word Hebrew when talking with a non-Hebrew (Gen 40:15, Exod 2:7). This reinforces the idea that Hebrew is a word used with outsiders instead of insiders. Most occurrences of Hebrew in reference to Israelites appear in the first five books of the Bible and in the books of Samuel and Kings.

What's in a Name?

We are introducing one additional term that is familiar in contemporary scholarship regarding Jewish and Christian origins, but is unfamiliar to most Christians and Jews. That is the word *Judaic*. Unlike the word *Jew*, Judaic neither designates nor implies the fully developed religion of Judaism. Scholars use it to describe the religions of Judea in the first centuries B.C.E. and C.E. While Jacob Neusner, the dean of Jewish studies in America, describes this period as one of "Judaisms" (see chapter 4), Judaism or Judaisms also signifies a more elaborate or coherent world religion than actually exists then. Others, such as Martin Jaffee, use "Judaic religion" to express the tentative, unfinished nature of all of the groups that claim to be Israel. This means that we can call the Jesus Movement and early Christianity a Judaic religion, just as we can call Pharisaical religion, the beliefs of those at Qumran, and the practices of those in the diaspora Judaic religions. Clearly this is a descriptive term scholars use, and not one that the groups themselves use: They all see themselves as Israel.

What should be clear from this brief introduction is that the words Israel, children of Israel, Israelite, Israeli, Judah, Judahite, Jew, Jewish, Judaic, and Judaism cannot be used interchangeably. We must always be aware of the particular historical circumstances in which each term is being used. We also need to be alert to the fact that translations often confuse matters further by introducing differences that may not exist in the original text. Yet translations also attempt to clarify how the same word means different things in diverse contexts.

If Israelites are not Jews, and Jews are not Israelites, what do we need to know about Israelite religion—the religion of the Bible—and what relevance does it have for the self-understanding of those who later claim the heritage of Israel as their own, that is, the Judaic religions? Because it is clear that various Judaic communities of the first centuries B.C.E. and C.E. view themselves as the inheritors of the traditions of Israel in terms of their authoritative texts, it is extremely important to understand how these groups interpret the various themes and concepts presented in the Hebrew Bible. The historicity of biblical texts is irrelevant in this regard: What is important is that people believe these writings are inspired by God and delivered to trustworthy people.

The various forms of material and archaeological remains that have been uncovered in what was the ancient land of Israel do not always support the narrative of Israel as it is portrayed in the pages of the Hebrew Bible. Archaeologists are often quick to point out a host of discrepancies between the Israel of the biblical text and the picture of Israel that emerges from the archaeological record. For example, statues of rotund females found in Israel suggest that the Israelites are not quite as monotheistic as their subsequent interpreters might like. As archaeology illustrates, there are a variety of ways in which an Israelite can worship YHWH, the god of Israel. Some of this worship is condoned by the biblical authors, while other practices are condemned; still more has probably been intentionally deleted. What we read in the Hebrew Bible with respect to Israelite belief does not necessarily represent what all Israelites believed or how all Israelites behaved. The Bible itself reveals conflicts over kingship, over the location of sacrifices, and over the importance of Jerusalem. Undoubtedly we are witnessing only a fraction of the actual discord that occurred.

In order for us to appreciate the various changes that take place in transforming ancient Israelite beliefs and practices into the various Judaic religions we examine in this book, we must obtain as clear an understanding as possible of what these beliefs and practices may have been from the texts of the Hebrew Bible. This is because various communities of interpretation take their cues from the Torah, the Prophets, and the Writings.

In formulating their individual conceptions of Israel, the Judaic communities of the first centuries B.C.E. to C.E. rely heavily on interpretation of their sacred texts. The first five books of the Bible seem to have been assembled into the cohesive unit known as the Torah in the Exile. When communities of displaced Judahites seek to define or even redefine their relationship with their god, they look to the Torah as the key instrument for this self-definition.

The Story of Israel

The story of the origins, birth, zenith, and decline of ancient Israel, from a group of wayward nomads to a nation wheeling and dealing with the superpowers of its time, is woven throughout the books that make up the Hebrew Bible. According to Susan Niditch, the story goes something like this:

> The world is created, ordered and peopled by God. Next emerge Israel's earliest ancestors from origins in the Fertile Crescent, migrating to a promised land upon orders from Yahweh, their God.

In Israel, Abraham and Sarah parent Isaac who marries his cousin Rebecca. Her son, Jacob, marries Rachel and Leah, his cousins, as generation follows generation. Pictured as sojourners or alien residents, the patriarchs and their families move their flocks, establish altars and sink wells. They are born, marry, vie for supremacy with one another, die, and bury their dead, laying a physical claim to the land . . .

The sons of Jacob father the tribes of Israel, whose number multiplies in accordance with God's covenantal promises of plenty. A fearful and tyrannical Pharaoh eventually enslaves and oppresses the Israelites, but they are liberated through God's miracle acts, plagues and an event at the Red Sea, and are led out of slavery by Moses and Aaron of the priestly tribe of Levi. The Israelites spend forty years in the wilderness, having experienced God's numinous power and receive his law, which they disobey frequently, setting a pattern of sin, punishment and forgiveness, which comes to characterize their relationship with the deity. Finally, they enter the promised land and attempt to settle it. At this time the people live politically and worship in decentralized fashion, without a capital, king or temple. Led by charismatic leaders called judges whose victories and defeats are often recounted in the bardic style of epic, the Israelites survive encounters with better-armed enemies in the land, Canaanites and Philistines and others who finally prove too strong for the fledgling Israelite state. The people demand a king and with great regret God acquiesces. Then come the monarchies: a united kingdom under Saul; then David, his usurper; the rule of David's son Solomon; and separate northern and southern kingdoms thereafter following a post-Solomonic schism. Many prophets arise declaring God's approval or disapproval of Israel's rulers and providing an ongoing evaluation of the people's faith. The court histories of the kings, especially David, are filled with intrigue, murder, adultery, incest, and rebellion, although David and his dynasty, which lasts for hundreds of years, are recalled idyllically, David himself becoming ancestor-hero of a hoped for messiah.

Finally, the kingdoms are conquered, the North by the superpower Assyria, the Southern Davidic kingdom by Babylonia, events regarded as punishment for Israel's sin. The temple has been destroyed and the elite of Jerusalem exiled in the so-called Babylonian exile, but they are permitted a safe return and some do return to rebuild the temple. New prophets arise such as Haggai and Zechariah declaring God's forgiveness and support for the restoration predicted by their predecessors, Jeremiah, Ezekiel and Deutero-Isaiah. With non-monarchic leaders such as Ezra and Nehemiah a small Judean polity reemerges under political control of Persia.[1]

Long passages detailing all kinds of legal precepts to be followed by this group of people are interspersed throughout this narrative. The laws are not handed down by a foreign despot, however, but are seen as the requirements of a contract between the people of Israel and their god. Failure to observe the various rituals and legal rulings contained within the covenant results in a failure to meet the terms of the agreement and often carries harsh consequences.

A number of themes recur throughout the narrative of the Israelites. The descendants of biblical Israel attempt to practice these elements in faithfulness to their understanding of the text. Although they inhabit a new world, distant from prophets and kings, the text remains true for them. Thus in order to understand how various interpretive communities work with the texts, we need to first look at the foundational concepts they use.

Historical Time Line from King David to Babylonian Exile

B.C.E. (all dates are approximate)	
1043 Saul becomes king	853 Ahaziah becomes king of Israel
1011 Saul and Jonathan slain; David becomes king of Judah	853 Jehoram becomes king of Judah
	852 Joram becomes king of Israel
1004 David becomes king over all Israel	852 Elisha begins to prophesy
	841 Jehu becomes king of Israel
971 Solomon ascends the throne	841 Ahaziah becomes king of Judah
966 Solomon begins to build the temple in Jerusalem	841 Athaliah seizes the throne of Judah
931 Rehoboam becomes king of Israel and Judah	835 Joash becomes king of Judah
931 Jeroboam rebels; sets up rival kingdom in the north	814 Jehoahaz becomes king of Israel
	798 Jehoash becomes king of Israel
913 Abijam becomes king of Judah	796 Amaziah becomes king of Judah
911 Asa becomes king of Judah	790 Uzziah becomes co-regent of Judah
910 Nadab becomes king of Israel	
909 Baasha becomes king of Israel	783 Shalmaneser IV becomes king of Assyria
890 Benhadad becomes king of Syria	
886 Elah becomes king of Israel; Zimri becomes king of Israel	782 Jeroboam II becomes king of Israel
885 Tibni becomes king of Israel	767 Uzziah becomes full king of Judah
883 Ashurbanipal II becomes king of Assyria	764 Amos begins to prophesy
	755 Hosea begins to prophesy
880 Omri becomes king of Israel	753 Zechariah becomes king of Israel
874 Ahab becomes king of Israel	752 Shallum becomes king of Israel
873 Jehoshaphat becomes king of Judah	752 Menahem becomes king of Israel
859 Shalmaneser III becomes king of Assyria	745 Tiglath-pileser III becomes king of Assyria
	742 Pekahiah becomes king of Israel
	740 Pekah becomes king of Israel

739	Uzziah dies; Isaiah begins to prophesy	686	Manasseh becomes king of Judah
739	Jotham becomes king of Judah	642	Amon becomes king of Judah
735	Ahaz becomes king of Judah	640	Josiah becomes king of Judah
732	Hoshea becomes king of Israel	612	Nineveh falls
727	Shalmaneser IV becomes king of Assyria	609	Jehoahaz becomes king of Judah
722	Sargon II becomes king of Assyria; Samaria falls	609	Jehoiakim becomes king of Judah
722	Israel (the Northern Kingdom) falls to Assyrian Army	605	Nebuchadnezzar becomes king of Babylon
722	Israelites deported to Assyria	605	The Babylonians invade Judah
715	Hezekiah becomes king of Judah	597	Jehoachin becomes king of Judah
705	Sennacherib becomes king of Assyria	597	Zedekiah becomes king of Judah
701	Judah invaded by the Assyrians	593	Ezekiel begins to prophesy
		587/586	The Babylonians destroy Jerusalem and the temple
		586	Judahites deported to Babylon

Key Concepts in Israelite Belief

God

In order to comprehend the way in which the Israelites envision their god, we must examine a number of texts. There is no biography of the god of Israel in the Hebrew Bible, no single place in the text where one can peruse a list of God's attributes and personality traits. There is no discussion regarding the birth of the god of Israel, and God's existence from the very outset of Genesis is entirely assumed. The authors of the Hebrew Bible do not feel compelled at any point in the text to prove, in a modern scientific sense, that their god exists. God begins history through actions and words in creation and remains throughout the force that directs and sustains all aspects of the universe and of human history.

The overarching image presented is of a single, all-powerful god. He is male, patriarchal, a ruler, a warrior, and a judge. He is not directly identified with any single force in nature. Though this solitary god is portrayed by the biblical authors as interacting on his own with the earliest of the patriarchs and matriarchs, most scholars recognize that this monotheistic view emerges somewhat slowly and does not always reflect the god of popular Israelite or Judahite belief. The god of Israel is referred to by a variety of divine titles: Elohim (God, a "plural of majesty with a singular meaning," according to *The Oxford Companion to the Bible*), El Elyon (God, the most high), El Qoneh (God, the creator), El Olam (God, the eternal), El Elohe Yisrael (God, the God of Israel), and El Shaddai (God of the steppe, or of the mountains).

We also find another title for God in the Hebrew Bible: YHWH, which sometimes appears as YHWH God of Hosts (YHWH Sabaoth).[2] After the Hebrew Bible is canonized, the custom develops not to pronounce this name out loud, so it is usually read, or pronounced, adonai, which means "Lord." Most translations write "LORD" in capital letters whenever the word YHWH appears in Hebrew. We frequently see both YHWH and Elohim joined together, as in Genesis 2:15: "The LORD God took the man and placed him in the garden of Eden." The name YHWH is as much a divine title as it is a representation of the Israelites' conception of divine nature and the relationship God has with the people. Most scholars see the name as a causative form of the verb "to be," meaning "he causes to be," or "he creates" (Exod 3:14).

This god combines a variety of often conflicting characteristics. He is a personal force in the lives of the Israelites, but also transcendent; he is angry and jealous, but is also merciful and compassionate. The centrality of YHWH worship in Israel is abundantly evident in the Bible and in Israelite material culture. Because the primary name used in the Hebrew Bible in connection with the God of Israel is YHWH, the religion of Israel is often called YHWHism by biblical scholars. Though there is a great deal of evidence that suggests that other gods are worshipped in Israel, there is little doubt that the worship of YHWH is primary throughout Israel's history.

Covenant

The relationship between YHWH and the people of Israel is described in the Hebrew Bible in terms of a covenant. A covenant is a contract between two parties in which both make promises under oath to perform or refrain from certain actions stipulated in advance. We see many instances of covenants executed between kings and their vassals throughout the ancient Near East, particularly when a king conquers and subjects a foreign people to his domination. The king agrees to protect his vassals, while they in turn pledge loyalty and taxes. Thus, the Israelites take the common legal language of their era to describe their relationship with their god.

According to biblical accounts, YHWH enters into these types of agreements with Noah, Abraham, Moses and all Israel, the priesthood, and with King David. The earliest covenant in Genesis occurs between God and Noah. At the conclusion of the flood, YHWH declares:

> "As for me, I am establishing my covenant with you and your descendants after you, and with every living creature that is with you, the birds, the domestic animals, and every animal of the earth with you, as many as came out of the ark. I establish my covenant with you, that never again shall all flesh be cut off by the waters of a flood, and never again shall there be a flood to destroy the earth." God said, "This is the sign of the covenant that I make between me and you and every living creature that is with you, for all future generations: I have set my bow in the clouds, and it shall be a sign of the covenant between me and the earth. When I bring clouds over the earth and the bow is seen in the clouds, I will remember my covenant that is between me and you and every living creature of all flesh; and the waters shall never again become a flood to destroy all flesh. When the bow is in the clouds, I will see it and remember the everlasting covenant between God and every living creature of all flesh that is on the earth." God said to Noah, "This is the sign of the covenant that I have established between me and all flesh that is on the earth" (Gen 9:9–17).

Later in Genesis, God makes a covenant with Abram, guaranteeing that Abram and his wife Sarah will be the ancestors of a multitude of nations and promising to give him and his descendants the land of Canaan (Gen 15:18–21). In Genesis 17, God changes Abram's name to Abraham, and specifies the terms of the covenant: Abraham must circumcise himself and all the males of his household. Circumcision serves as an essential component of what it means to be Israel, a visible marker of membership in the covenant with God. It becomes a contentious issue during the time of Hellenism in the second century B.C.E., when some wish to assimilate into Greek culture and attempt to remove the marks of circumcision, as well as in the first century C.E., when followers of Jesus must decide whether or not to require circumcision of Gentile members.

The covenant God makes with Moses and the Israelites at Mount Sinai (Exod 19–20) is central for Jews and Christians even today. At Mount Sinai (or Mount Horeb, according to the book of Deuteronomy), God gives the Israelites the Ten Commandments (Exod 20:1–17), which scholars call the Decalogue, or Ten Sayings. At the holy mountain God gives additional commandments for the Israelites to observe in order to create a holy people. "You shall be holy, for I the LORD your God am holy," God instructs Moses to tell the Israelite congregation (Lev 19:2).

By keeping the commandments to the best of their ability, the Israelites are fulfilling their contractual obligations to their god. They are differentiating themselves by their unique practices from the people occupying the land. More importantly, though, the commandments keep them mindful of God's goodness and graciousness. Obeying God's orders is not really an option, given the fact that the entire Israelite nation agrees to do exactly that in return for receiving God's favor.

With the Davidic covenant, God promises King David that a dynasty of kings will descend from his line. The prophet Nathan informs David that "Your house and your kingdom shall be made sure forever before me; your throne shall be established forever" (2 Sam 7:16–17). Although the line of David ends with the death of Zedekiah (587/586 B.C.E.), the legacy of the Davidic covenant assumes importance in the first century C.E. because it creates the expectation that an earthly king from David's progeny will eventually return to expel the Roman oppressors and ascend to a throne to rule a united Judah. This kingly figure—called "messiah," which literally means "anointed one"—will restore the independence of the Judeans and will bring about justice and righteousness on earth.

Each of the covenants we find in the Hebrew Bible has elements in common with the standard terminology of legal contracts found throughout the ancient Near East. But Israel is the only people we know of to date who envision their relationship with their god in terms of a legally binding contract that is dependent upon how faithfully the people live. The covenants recognize YHWH's role in guiding and protecting Israel and at the same time obligate the Israelites to maintain allegiance by adhering to a variety of stipulations that determine their social behavior among themselves and in relation to other social groups.

Tabernacle and Temple

In Exodus 25:8, God tells Moses to have the Israelites "make me a sanctuary that I may dwell among them." This sanctuary is called a tabernacle, which is a tent that, according to the biblical book of Exodus, Moses constructs while the Israelites are camped at Sinai. This tent houses their holiest religious object: the tablets of the Ten Commandments, the laws received by Moses at Mount Sinai. The tablets are kept in an ark—the ark of the covenant—a gold-plated wooden box kept in the holiest part of the tent, the "holy of holies." In the ancient Near East, covenants enacted between kings and vassals are kept in boxes—and they often serve as the footstool for the king, a physical and metaphorical reminder of the relationship between the two. As King David says, "I had planned to build a house of rest for the ark of the covenant of the Lord, for the footstool of our God" (1 Chr 28:2). It is no wonder, then, that the ark of the covenant has a special location in the tabernacle.

Because God commands the Israelites to construct the tabernacle while the people are encamped at Sinai immediately after the miraculous theophany (appearance of the divine) at the mountain, there are significant parallels between Sinai/Horeb as the meeting place between heaven and earth, and the tabernacle. It is almost as if the tent and ark are constructed in order to ensure that God, so clearly present at Sinai, would not be left there once the people continue toward Canaan. "The Tent is essentially a portable Sinai, wherever it stands bridging the gulf between heaven and earth"; its "function is to transport God's presence from Sinai to Canaan in a safe container."[3]

The rest of the book of Exodus is devoted to the assembly and function of this sanctuary. The text details the construction of the ark and of the tent in which it is housed. The ark and the tent often turn up together in the text and seem to be intimately connected. Both objects are directly associated with God's presence and both are seen as portable representations of this presence.

The tent is called both a dwelling place (*mishkan*) and a meeting tent (*ohel moed*), and appears in the Torah as the focal point of Israelite religious worship. It is the place where God speaks to Moses; it houses the ark of the covenant; and it is the only acceptable place to offer sacrifices, the primary mode of communion with the god of Israel. The glory of God (*kavod*) enters and resides in the tabernacle, and in that sense the tent seems to serve as a sign of God's presence in the camp. Consider the description of the function of the tent in Exodus 29:43–46:

> I will meet with the Israelites there and it shall be sanctified by my glory;
> I will consecrate the tent of meeting and the altar; Aaron also and his sons
> I will consecrate, to serve me as priests. I will dwell among the Israelites,
> and I will be their God. And they shall know that I am the Lord their God,
> who brought them out of the land of Egypt that I might dwell among
> them; I am the Lord their God.

The presence of God within the tabernacle demands constant covenant obedience within the Israelite camp. It becomes the task of the Israelites to keep their camp worthy of this presence on a variety of different levels. In addition, it is God's presence, or dwelling, within Israel that fulfills the promise he makes to the people in Exodus 29:45 that he "will be their God."

In the book of Deuteronomy we are told that the divine name dwells in God's sanctuary (12:5, 11; 14:23–24; 16:11). The resulting image, in the Torah, is that the mishkan is the dwelling place of God, the location of his glory and of his name on earth. William H. C. Propp's "nuclear power plant" analogy is instructive:

> Consider the Tabernacle as a *nuclear power plant*, channeling cosmic power from Heaven to Earth. It must be meticulously tended by specially trained personnel clad in protective garb, wearing special identity badges, who periodically deal with crises of contamination. The least breach of protocol can be disastrous, not just for the technicians but for the entire community. The most dangerous moment . . . is when it is switched on. In a split second, the shrine ceases to be a human artifact and becomes Heaven-on-Earth; the Impure and the Holy almost touch.[4]

The tabernacle, then, is not a communal place of worship, but rather a sacred site that must be protected from pollution and kept holy. It is not a gathering place for the community, like a synagogue or church, but rather is set apart from most people. In fact, the only ones who can actually enter the tent's precinct are the priests themselves.

Following the Israelite conquest described in the book of Joshua, the tabernacle is erected at Shiloh. It serves as the center for Israelite worship until King Solomon erects a permanent temple (1 Kgs 6–8 // 2 Chr 3–4), although sacrifices continue to occur in multiple places throughout Israel and Judah until King Josiah centralizes the temple cult in 622 B.C.E. The ark of the covenant is moved into Solomon's temple in a festival attended by priests, elders, and "all the congregation of Israel" (1 Kgs 8:4–5 // 2 Chr 5:5–6). After the priests place the ark in the inner sanctuary, they come out, and a cloud fills the holy place—the cloud is so dense that the priests cannot perform their duties, "for the glory of the LORD filled the house of the LORD" (1 Kgs 8:11). God's kavod pervades the temple, just as it does the tabernacle, but now the temple, a fixed location, serves as the

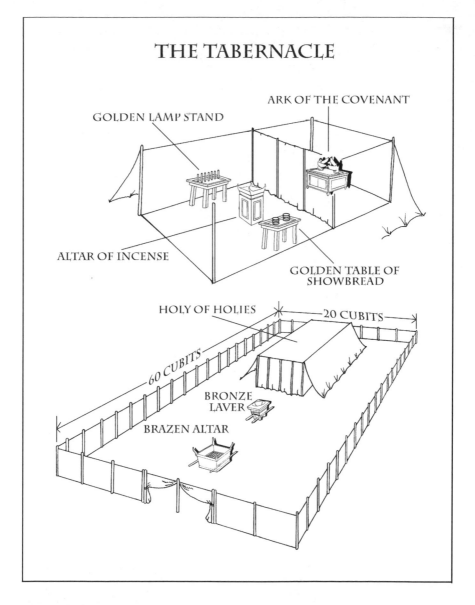

THE TABERNACLE

ARK OF THE COVENANT

GOLDEN LAMP STAND

ALTAR OF INCENSE

GOLDEN TABLE OF
SHOWBREAD

HOLY OF HOLIES

20 CUBITS

60 CUBITS

BRONZE
LAVER

BRAZEN ALTAR

meeting place between God and Israel. God's glory, now in residence at the temple in Jerusalem, remains there from the reign of Solomon until the temple's destruction by the Babylonians in 587/586 B.C.E. But ever afterward, God, or God's glory, extends beyond the priestly precincts, even though a second temple is constructed. This portable god serves to define a number of Judaic groups in the first centuries at the turn of the Common Era.

Sacrifice

The primary means of worshipping God in the ancient world requires offering animal and agricultural sacrifices. In English, the word "sacrifice" means to give up something—though frequently what is being given up is forfeited with the express purpose of achieving a specific goal or result. In baseball a "sacrifice fly" means that a runner gives up a base hit in order to let a teammate advance a base. Similarly, with the animal and agricultural sacrifices brought to the tabernacle or the temple, the worshipper gives up something of value—for example, the first lamb of the season or the first bushel of grain harvested—in the hope of gaining God's favor. Sacrifices may be offered to propitiate God, to wipe away uncleanness, to fulfill a vow or obligation, to indicate thanksgiving, or to make atonement for sin.

In Hebrew, the word for sacrifice, *korban*, has a deeper meaning. From the root *krb*, which means to bring close, the korban is intended to bring the worshipper closer to God. Thus, sacrifice is the primary way Israelites communicate with God: It is the way thanks are given, petitions made, and atonement sought. This would have been quite natural in the ancient Near East, where people communicate with each other by exchanging goods. Gift giving is formal and ritualized; the same holds true in the relationship between God and the Israelites.

The sacrificial ceremony as portrayed in the Torah is sacred and can only be performed by priests at the tabernacle or temple altar. In the Jerusalem temple, priests officiate at these offerings twice a day, with a large offering in the morning and a smaller one in the afternoon. Additional gifts are brought on the Sabbath and festivals, and people can also bring offerings for their own special occasions.

Additionally, the Torah presents a clearly articulated rationale for the practice of ritual sacrifice. If humans want to eat meat, they are required to recognize that they are taking a life. The slaughtering of an animal, therefore, is a sacred act and not, at least in theory, to be done on one's own and without special cause. Moreover, sacrifices are the primary way, if not the only way, people eat meat in the ancient world. This is particularly true of the Israelites, who require a religious professional to slaughter the animal—and make the sacrifice—in the proper way so that it is acceptable to God and to minimize human contact with blood, the life force directly associated with God. If humans want to eat meat, they have to recognize that they are taking a life and cannot regard the shedding of blood as an ordinary activity.

The image of a banquet is evoked when humans eat the food presented to God—except in the case of holocausts, which are whole burnt offerings.

In many ways, sacrifice serves as the way humans and the divine share a meal together. This shared meal is a form of communion. In Israelite religion, the priests mediate this communion, but later on, communion with God occurs in a number of different ways, both in the act of eating sacred meals and in other activities (see chapter 5).

Priesthood

The priesthood in Israelite religion is a hereditary position. Priests are not clergymen (or women!) as we have today, and the priesthood is not based on merit, calling, study, or ordination. Rather, priests are a limited group of men belonging to the family of Aaron, the brother of Moses. God appoints Aaron and his descendants to this job: "Aaron also and his sons I will consecrate, to serve me as priests" (Exod 29:44). In other words, Israelite priests are born into the profession.

In the text of the Torah, the *kohanim* (priests) are direct descendants of Aaron. The Levites, who serve as temple officials or functionaries, are members of the tribe of Levi and are also descended from Aaron. Some scholars even suggest that there may have been a "Mushite" priesthood descended from Moses that was often in conflict with the Aaronide priests. It is clear that the role of the priests and the Levites changes over the course of Israel's history and that there is often internal conflict regarding where the real power should lie.

Priests serve as ministers to God, presenting offerings on the altar and acting as intermediaries between the Israelites and their god. Offerings consist of meat, incense, grain, fruits, and oils. Coincidentally, these offerings help to support the priesthood. Although we may think of priests as performing animal sacrifices, it may be likelier that the Levites conduct the actual slaughtering, while the priests are the ones who place the gifts on the altar. Offering sacrifices is just one of several functions priests perform in Israelite society. They make oracular pronouncements and determine the will of God, often through consultation of the Urim and Thummim—which are possibly dice, pebbles, or sticks used when consulting the divine—and by casting lots (Deut 33:8–10. See also 1 Sam 23:6, 9–12; 30:7–8). The priests are entrusted with blessing the people (Num 6:22–27). They are also responsible for teaching the rituals, laws, and traditions of Israel to the Israelites (Lev 10:11; Deut 24:8, 33:10).

Many academics attribute the composition of large portions of the Torah to priestly groups. For example, the book of Leviticus is thought to represent the platform of the Jerusalem priesthood. Similarly, some see the book of Deuteronomy as the collected writings of another, perhaps even opposing, group of priests. That priests were engaged in the writing and editing of legal material is perhaps strengthened by the view that the sources that make up the Torah are probably compiled in the Exile by yet another priestly group.

In all of their activities, the priests mediate the covenantal relationship between God and the people of Israel by paradoxically serving as both a barrier and a bridge between the two. The average Israelite cannot enter their realm, but priests can move between the tabernacle/temple and the space outside. They serve as a sort of spiritual buffer in that they protect the people from the immediate power and presence of God.

The maintenance of God's holiness is ensured by having priests ritually purify themselves in a variety of ways before they offer an Israelite's sacrifices (Lev 21). It is the priests who determine what is clean and what is unclean and who separate the one from the other. Many things in everyday life cause impurity, especially blood—the life force—as well as other bodily fluids. Because priests move back and forth between the sacred and the profane in a unique manner, however, they must regain purity in order to serve God in a ritually holy state. The commandments in the so-called Holiness Code of Leviticus (Lev 19–25) pertain to priests and dictate how they should live in order to avoid defiling themselves and what they should do to regain purity once they have been defiled.

Kingship

While the idea of centralized leadership may seem natural today, it is unusual within the decentralized tribal societies of the ancient world. We may catch glimpses of tribal leadership in certain parts of the modern world, where groups joined by kinship, geography, and economics unite against other tribes, under the guidance of an elder (or what we may see these days, a warlord). Kings are required in highly organized, strongly centralized societies, predominantly urban, where a unifying force is required to maintain an army, to tax the populace for public works, and to defend the cities against invasion. It is unusual, then, that a rural group like the Israelites would desire a king. Still more unusual is the fact that the Israelites maintain a record of their life before the introduction of kingship.

Israelite society is initially tribal, and with tribal leadership the people do not find a human king necessary. Human intermediaries might determine God's will or follow God's guidance, but God is king of the Israelites during the period of the Judges (Josh and Judg). The Israelites eventually demand a human king, although the prophet Samuel warns them that the king will require thousands to plow his ground and reap his harvest, as well as women to cook and bake for him, and "will take the best of your fields and vineyards and olive orchards and give them to his courtiers" (1 Sam 8:14). The Israelites, according to the story, are nevertheless determined to have a king, so God sends them Saul, a mixed blessing. When we look at the biblical history of kingship, in fact, we can count the "good" kings on one hand: David, Solomon, Hezekiah, and Josiah. The rest seem to be corrupt, or corruptible, and even David and Solomon are far from perfect.

The Israelite king has a special title in Hebrew: *mashiach*, or messiah, which means anointed one. The inauguration of kingship is the anointing with oil by a priest. So any king is called a messiah, or anointed one. But other figures in Israelite religion are also anointed: namely, priests and prophets. The Torah describes the anointing of priests again and again (e.g., Exod 28:41; 29:7, 21), and prophets are anointed in Isaiah 61:1 and Ezekiel 28:14. In other words, we see at least three important figures in Israelite religion being anointed—prophet, priest, and king. Israelites generally understand messiah to refer to an earthly king. Moreover, "messiah" is a relatively unimportant term in Tanakh: "king" is much more central. But the concept of "messiah" assumes importance in the Pseudepigrapha of the first and second centuries B.C.E. and in the political and theological conflicts in the first and second centuries C.E., which we will address in later chapters.

Torah

Torah in Israelite religion does not have the same significance that it acquires after the Babylonian Exile. In pre-Exilic times it refers to God's instructions or teachings to the Israelites (e.g., Exod 16:4, 28), but it does not describe a written text, or texts. The Israelites, who have entered into a covenantal relationship with God, are to maintain the terms of the covenant. Following God's Torah, walking in the ways of the Lord, is part of the agreement.

Upon the return of the Judahites to Judah after the Exile, however, we learn of a written body of statutes and ordinances now called Torah. In the land of Yehud, as the Persians call it, Torah assumes enormous importance, since there is no longer any king or centralized Israelite government. Torah serves as a unifying feature, as well as a touchstone by which various communities understand and explain themselves to others. When different interpretations arise, Torah also becomes a divisive factor.

Conclusions: Or, Just the Beginning . . .

It is important to understand the significance of these concepts in Israelite religion because we will return to them again and again, just as the descendants of biblical Israel return to them. They are the defining characteristics of a people who saw themselves as chosen by their god and living in a covenantal, or contractual, relationship with that god. As times change, however, the interpretation of the covenant changes. This leads to great diversity among competing groups who all claim to be Israel, as we shall see.

Suggested Readings

Thomas Cahill. *The Gifts of the Jews: How a Tribe of Desert Nomads Changed the Way Everyone Thinks and Feels*. New York: Nan A. Talese, 1998.

William G. Dever. *What Did the Biblical Writers Know and When Did They Know It? What Archaeology Can Tell Us about the Reality of Ancient Israel*. Grand Rapids, Mich.: Eerdmans, 2001.

Barry M. Gittlen. *Sacred Time, Sacred Place: Archaeology and the Religion of Israel*. Winona Lake, Ind.: Eisenbrauns, 2000.

Paula M. McNutt. *Reconstructing the Society of Ancient Israel*. Louisville, Ky.: Westminster John Knox Press, 1999.

George E. Mendenhall and Gary A. Herion, eds. *Ancient Israel's Faith and History: An Introduction to the Bible in Context*. Louisville, Ky.: Westminster John Knox Press, 2001.

J. Maxwell Miller and John H. Hayes. *A History of Ancient Israel and Judah*. Philadelphia: Westminster Press, 1986.

Patrick D. Miller. *The Religion of Ancient Israel*. Louisville, Ky.: Westminster John Knox Press, 2000.

Nadav Naaman. *Ancient Israel and Its Neighbors: Interaction and Counteraction*. Winona Lake, Ind.: Eisenbrauns, 2005.

Richard D. Nelson. *Raising up a Faithful Priest: Community and Priesthood in Biblical Theology*. Louisville, Ky.: Westminster John Knox Press, 1993.

Susan Niditch. *Ancient Israelite Religion*. New York: Oxford University Press, 1997.

Notes

1. Summary quoted from Susan Niditch, *Ancient Israelite Religion* (New York: Oxford University Press, 1997), 7–8.

2. See chapter 1 for an explanation of the word *YHWH*.

3. William H. C. Propp, *Exodus 19–40: A New Translation with Introduction and Commentary* (New York: Anchor Bible, 2006), 688. For discussion of Sinai/Horeb as the locus of God's temple see D. N. Freedman, "Temple without Hands," in *Temples and High Places in Biblical Times*, ed. Avraham Biran (Jerusalem: Keter, 1981), 21–30.

4. Propp, *Exodus 19–40*, 690.

Hellenism and Apocalypticism: Globalization and Millennialism in a Different Era

❊

I MAGINE AN INVASION THAT WIPES OUT YOUR CITIES, annihilates your people, demolishes your holy sites, and destroys all that you cherish. Your god is supposed to protect you from such a disaster, but your god seems to have failed. Not only that, the holy place where god was believed to dwell in ultimate fullness and perfection is obliterated. And worst of all, you are exiled to a foreign nation, away from home, traditions, and God. All that remains is your memory of how things were, of how things are supposed to be.

This is an oversimplification of what it is like for the citizens of the kingdom of Judah in the sixth century B.C.E. when the Babylonians invade in 597 and when they destroy the temple in Jerusalem in 587/586 and deport the upper classes to the land east of the Euphrates River. Yet, historically speaking, we know that the Babylonians occupy Judah and the territories north and south of it and that they do deport the intelligentsia—the business and political classes—to Babylon, just as the Assyrians had done nearly two centuries earlier with the Israelites of the northern kingdom. Exile makes good strategic sense: If you cut off the head, the body cannot function.

This does not mean that the land left behind by the deportees is vacant. Far from it: People continue to worship the God of Israel and continue to practice sacrifices in Jerusalem, as well as in other places. It is ironic that when the deportees return they attempt to purify the priesthood by expelling foreign wives and their offspring. It is possible that these "foreigners" are actually the people who stay behind during the Exile. The rebuilding of the temple, however, renews concern for the purity of the priesthood. The centrality of the Jerusalem temple is restored, though not without some resistance, while the authority of the priests grows in importance from the Exile and beyond.

Although we catch glimpses of the pain of those in Exile—for example, Psalm 137 and the book of Lamentations—the experience of the deportees is not uniformly miserable. The period of formal exile is relatively short; that is, only a generation elapses before Persian armies conquer Babylon and not only allow but encourage the deportees to return home around 538 B.C.E. Many exiles remain in Babylon. In fact, so many stay that almost a thousand years later the premier schools of rabbinic Judaism are in Pumbedita and Sura in Babylon, that is, present-day Iraq.

The Persian period (539–323 B.C.E.) commences with the fall of the Babylonian Empire before the armies of the Achemenid dynasty, led by Cyrus the Great (ca. 590 or 576–529 B.C.E.). Cyrus is mentioned by name as a "messiah" in Isaiah (44:28, 45:1, and 45:13). The Persian king authorizes the return of the Judahites to the Persian province of Yehud (Judah) and the reconstruction of "the house of the Lord, the God of Israel—he is the God who is in Jerusalem" (Ezra 1:3). Completion of construction occurs in about 515, although Herod the Great (r. 37–4 B.C.E.) enlarges the complex considerably under Roman rule. With a new temple, the Judahites, especially the priestly and scribal classes, gain power, and Jerusalem regains the ascendancy over all other cities in Judah that it had before the Exile.

This is not the end of the story, of course, for the Persian Empire falls to the armies of Alexander the Great around 322 B.C.E. In fact, invasion after invasion sweeps through the tiny strip of land that serves as the bridge between Africa and Asia, between Egypt and Syria. The Ptolemaic dynasty of Egypt controls the territory of Israel and Judah for a century, from 301–201 B.C.E. Then the Seleucid dynasty of Syria controls it from 201–152, and the name Judea replaces Judah as the geographic designation. Finally, representatives of a priestly family claiming Israelite descent wrest control of the temple and the land from the Seleucids in a civil war fought between 168 and 153. This is the Maccabean, or Hasmonean, revolt, vividly described in the books of the Maccabees (see below). Even though the Seleucids continue to be a large presence in Judea, the Hasmoneans— the family name of the Maccabees—manage religious and political affairs in the land until the Roman conquest of 63 B.C.E.

As power changes hands many times between the sixth and the first centuries B.C.E., two major cultural shifts occur. Both profoundly shape the religion of Israel. First, Persian religion introduces a number of new ideas that lead to a dualistic theology that pits the forces of good against evil in a final battle waged on earth and in heaven. A large number of texts reflecting the influence of this theology emerge in the period 200 B.C.E. to 200 C.E., and because they reveal heavenly visions and dreams, they are called apocalypses (after the Greek word *apocalupsis*, which means "to disclose"). We see at least one apocalypse in Tanakh, that is, the book of Daniel, and another in the New Testament book of Revelation. We get the word *apocalyptic* from Revelation, which begins: "The apocalypse (revelation) of Jesus Christ, which God gave him to show his servants" (Rev 1:1). This apocalypse and many others help create the apocalypticism that shapes the outlook of many Judeans living in the shadow of imperial oppression.

The second major shift is the expansion of Greek culture throughout the Mediterranean. Called Hellenism after Hellas (Greece), it affects life and learning, both in Judea and in Diaspora. The Judahites, and then the Judeans, and finally all Judaic groups who consider themselves "Israel" adopt and adapt the language, literature, art, architecture, philosophy, and worldview of their surrounding culture. They become "Hellenized," in the same way that many in the world today have become "Americanized," by consciously or unconsciously taking on cultural values, assumptions, and even language from an alien world culture. The process of Hellenization is complex and takes centuries to occur, yet its impact is unmistakable.

In order to understand the profound impact these two cultural influences have upon the communities that see themselves as "Israel," we must

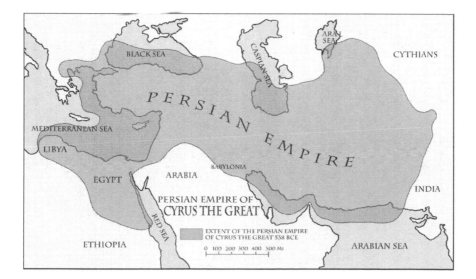

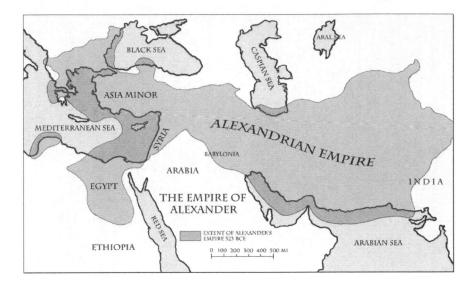

consider Hellenism and apocalypticism in some depth. In the past, some scholars wrote off these influences as not being "Jewish," or as somehow "defiling" Christianity. Historians today, however, realize how these forces inspired new literature, and even new religious movements, within the communities of Israel.

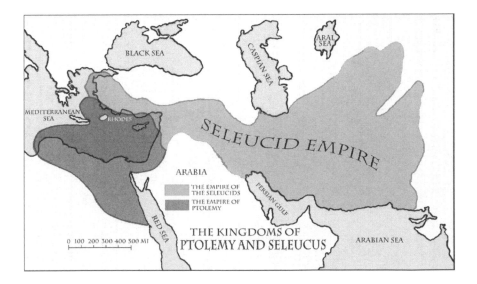

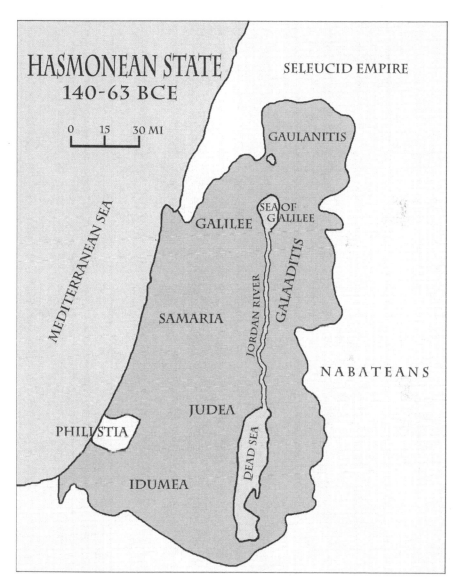

Hellenism: Globalization in a Different Era

When we consider globalization today, we might think of Iranian students wearing American-made blue jeans, South Asians answering our computer questions, or Americans driving Japanese-built cars. Viruses and diseases seem to travel the globe as easily as humans. We can watch CNN almost anywhere in the world, and we can feel the effects of global warming

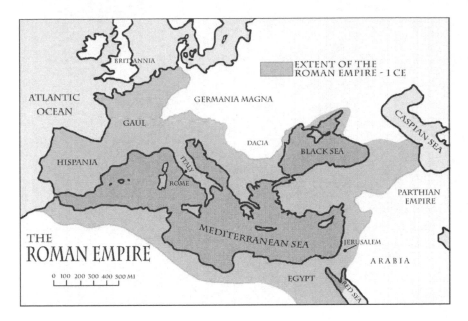

everywhere as well. It seems like our planet is getting smaller, especially when what people do in one country affects those in another. It is clear, however, that America dominates this global culture. We can find Mc-Donald's and Microsoft around the world, and knowing how to speak English is a survival skill in every country.

If we travel back to the turn of the era—from B.C.E. to C.E.—we find a strikingly similar time of globalization. Alexander the Great (356–323 B.C.E.) introduces Greek—that is, Hellenistic—mores to the nations he invades on his march to Asia, the Middle East, and North Africa. Although Alexander is a Macedonian, the culture he transmits is thoroughly Greek—in language, philosophy, religion, politics, and education. Hellenism is not limited to Alexander or Greece, however, since we find it long after Alexander's death in the Egyptian (Ptolemaic), Syrian (Seleucid), and Roman empires. It is a pervasive way of thinking and acting, and its influence suffuses the Mediterranean basin.

Our ideas about Hellenism are not static, and they change over the course of the twentieth century. They are first shaped by nineteenth-century German scholarship, in which Hellenism refers simply to the historical period between Alexander the Great and Roman Imperial rule. Eventually historians come to see Hellenism as the transformation of the ethnic-national culture of Greece into a universal culture and civilization that helps mold the ethos of the Roman Empire well into the Common Era. Martin Hengel argues that Hellenism has an omnipresent influence throughout the Mediterranean world and beyond. This includes the land of Judea. No area of life or thought is untouched, Hengel writes, from schools and education to language and literature. Even in Jewish literature—ranging from the book of Daniel in the Bible to the Copper Scroll found in the Judean Desert to Ben Sira in the Septuagint—one can find evidence of the influence of Hellenism.

Hellenism becomes the dominant paradigm by which various imperial forces judge a nation's traditions and customs. This paradigm is global and its practitioners adopt what they feel is a philosophy of universalism, that is, a belief that "one size fits all," culturally speaking. Hellenists generally accept polytheism, assuming a relatively tolerant perspective on one's belief system. At the same time, they strongly value piety, virtue, and rationalism. Above all, the Greek language is considered the idiom of learning and civilization.

Greek is the lingua franca of the ancient world—in the same way that French is in the nineteenth century, that English is today, and that Chinese or Arabic could be tomorrow. Not only do educated people speak Greek throughout the Hellenized world well into the fourth and fifth centuries—including what is western Europe today—but laborers who have to deal with employers also speak a kind of "street Greek," or *koine*, in much the same way that recent immigrants to the United States learn enough English to get by. Judeans in Diaspora certainly are fluent Greek speakers and, as we know from chapter 1, they get a Greek translation of Hebrew sacred texts during the third-century B.C.E. reign of the Egyptian king Ptolemy II. We can see clear influences of Hellenism in three members of Israel who are immersed in it: Philo of Alexandria (20 B.C.E–50 C.E.), Paul of Tarsus (d. ca. 65 C.E.), and Flavius Josephus (37–ca. 100 C.E.). Each of these figures, whom today we would call Jews, walks in two worlds: that of Hellenistic culture and that of the traditions and customs of Israel.

Philo lives in the Egyptian city of Alexandria, which is a completely Hellenized center of learning and commerce and home to a large number of diaspora Judeans. Philo knows Greek classical literature and philosophy, and he uses Greek allegorical methods to interpret scripture. Although he remains observant, worshipping the God of Israel, he uses allegory as a way to justify his customs. For example, he writes that the reason Jews should abstain from predatory animals is to avoid becoming predators themselves. Philo emphasizes the mystical, or contemplative, life and reads the story of Moses' ascent on Mount Sinai as an account of the mystical ascent of the soul to God, or the divine. He believes that the traditions of Israel pre-date those of the Greeks and argues that Moses is the teacher of Pythagoras. He is a good example of someone who uses Hellenistic culture to help people understand their own beliefs and traditions. Indeed he probably does not see a great divide between Greek and Judean culture.

Another Hellenized Judean is Paul, who grows up in Asia Minor, yet another member of the Diaspora. Paul writes in Greek and knows Greek rhetoric, logic, argumentation, and literary forms. Scholars today analyze his letters and their similarities to, and differences from, traditional Greek epistolary forms. Paul corresponds with Gentiles and Judeans who are also Hellenized and who probably understand the Hellenistic rhetorical devices Paul uses to compose his letters. When he becomes embroiled in a debate within the Jesus Movement, however, over what is required to be a follower—to keep the Torah commandments or not—he chooses the global culture of Hellenism over the ethnic culture of the Judeans.

A third Hellenized Judean is Josephus, whom we mentioned in chapter 1. Like Philo, Josephus interprets Jewish, or Judean, customs in Hellenized language and thought, but his audience appears to be non-Jews. He grows up in Judea, and during the First Jewish War he changes allegiances, first resisting Roman occupation and then serving as an advisor to Vespasian. Josephus lives out his days in Rome—again, in the Diaspora—and it is there that he composes several works that explain the history and customs of the Judeans. He first writes *The Jewish War*, followed by *Jewish Antiquities* and then his *Life*.

Hellenism is the background for understanding figures like Philo, Paul, and Josephus. It is also the setting for understanding various schools of thought that arise in Judea in the period 250 B.C.E. to 200 C.E. Just as the Greek philosophers have disciples who follow them around and take notes on their teachings, respected Judean teachers or sages also have disciples who learn their teachings. The disciples transmit the teachings of the sages orally until they commit them to writing at the close of the second century C.E.

Accommodation, Withdrawal, and Resistance

In the time of the second temple, we see three reactions to Hellenization: accommodation, withdrawal, and resistance. We have just described three important people who seem to accommodate Hellenistic thinking: Philo, Paul, and Josephus. Many other Judeans take on Hellenistic culture by accepting Greek language, literature, art, and architecture in the first centuries B.C.E. and C.E. We can see this in the thoroughly Hellenized architecture that exists in Judea, which includes synagogue design and decoration. We find elaborate mosaics that adorn synagogue floors and walls (though from a somewhat later era—third to sixth centuries C.E.) with depictions of human figures and even signs of the Zodiac! Even those who refuse to accommodate to global pressures are in some way touched by Hellenism, since their opposition triggers radical action in the form of withdrawal or resistance.

Those who withdraw include the community that leaves Jerusalem and establishes an outpost in the Judean desert at Qumran. Although Qumran is not as isolated as it is today, since the Dead Sea is larger then and serves as the site of several busy seaports, it is sufficiently far from Jerusalem for its founders to go in order to reject the Hellenized priests of the Seleucid and Hasmonean dynasties and establish a community with a purer priesthood—namely, their own. Some Judeans withdraw into apocalyptic dreams and revelations and produce fascinating literary works (see below). In the first and second centuries C.E., however, the apocalyptic imagination also fuels armed resistance to the Roman oppressors, whose Hellenized outlook ignores the sensibilities of Judean culture and custom.

Even though Judah/Judea falls under the domination of different empires, Hellenized culture remains throughout Greek, Egyptian, Syrian, and finally Roman rule. If we look at the "Scorecard for the Hellenistic Age" (see table 3.1), we see that the names of the high priests under Syrian, or Seleucid, rule are Greek—Jason, Menelaus, Alcimus—rather than Hebrew. When we get to the Hasmonean period (ca. 140–63 B.C.E.), we continue to see both rulers and priests named after Alexander. Although these signify accommodation to Hellenism, we see resistance as well. The Hasmoneans, for example, wage a culture war against a Hellenized priesthood. They resist assimilation and attack the Seleucids, but once they gain power, they become Hellenized themselves.

The Maccabean Revolt of 168–164 B.C.E., led by the Hasmonean family, occurs in the reign of the Seleucid king Antiochus IV (r. 175–164 B.C.E.). In collaboration with a corrupt priesthood, Antiochus tries to Hellenize the people of Judea. The books of the Maccabees, found in the Septuagint and the Catholic and Orthodox Old Testaments, describe the process of Hellenization in great detail, as well as Judean resistance to it:

> [The king] authorized them to observe the ordinances of the Gentiles. So they built a gymnasium in Jerusalem, according to Gentile custom, and removed the marks of circumcision, and abandoned the holy covenant. They joined with the Gentiles and sold themselves to do evil. (1 Macc 1:13–15)

Table 3.1.   Scorecard for the Hellenistic Age (332–63 B.C.E.)

333 B.C.E.	Alexander the Great defeats Persian King Darius III
	Greek/Macedonian control of Judea
ca. 305–198 B.C.E.	Ptolemaic control of Egypt and Judea
	Ptolemy I of Egypt takes Jerusalem
	Ptolemy II authorizes Greek translation of Torah
198–63 B.C.E.	Seleucid [Syrian] control/influence in Judea
	Antiochus III (223–187)
	Antiochus IV (175–164)
	Jason, High Priest (175–172)
	Menelaus, High Priest (172–162)
	Demetrius I (162–150)
	Alcimus, High Priest (162–159)
	Priesthood vacant for seven years* (159–152)
Maccabean Period	Jonathan "Maccabeus," High Priest/Commander of Army of Judea (152–143)
	Alexander Balas (152–146)
	Simon "Maccabeus," High Priest/Commander of Army of Judea (d. 134 B.C.E.)
ca. 140–63 B.C.E.	The Hasmonean State
	Simon, High Priest/Commander of Army of Judea (142–134)
	John Hyrcanus (Simon's son), High Priest/Commander of Army of Judea (134–104)
	Aristobulus (John's eldest son), High Priest who takes title of King (104–103)
	Alexander Jannaeus (brother of Aristobulus), High Priest/King (103–76)
	Salome Alexandra (wife of Aristobulus, then of Alexander), Queen (76–67)
	Hyrcanus II (son of Alexander Jannaeus), High Priest (76–67)
	Aristobulus II (son of Alexander Jannaeus), King and High Priest* (67–63)

*Historians are unsure whether the priesthood was vacant; no names for priests recorded.

And the king sent letters by messengers to Jerusalem and the cities of Judah; he directed them to follow customs strange to the land, to forbid burnt offerings and sacrifices and drink offerings in the sanctuary, to profane sabbaths and festivals, to defile the sanctuary and the priests, to build altars and sacred precincts and shrines for idols, to sacrifice swine and unclean animals, and to leave their sons uncircumcised. (1 Macc 1:44–48).

The construction of a gymnasium and the failure to circumcise sons or the removal of the marks of existing circumcision certainly sound like part of a program of forced Hellenization. In fact, the author of 2 Maccabees actually coins the term *Hellenization*:

[Antiochus] set aside the existing royal concessions to the Jews . . . and he destroyed the lawful ways of living and introduced new customs contrary to the law. He took delight in establishing a gymnasium right under the citadel, and he induced the noblest of the young men to wear the Greek hat. There was such an extreme of Hellenization and increase in the adoption of foreign ways because of the surpassing wickedness of Jason, who was ungodly and no true high priest, that the priests were no longer intent upon their service at the altar. (2 Macc 4:11–14)

The author goes on to say that the priests participate in the wrestling arena and watch the discus throwers, "disdaining the honors prized by their ancestors and putting the highest value upon Greek forms of prestige" (2 Macc 4:15).

The Maccabean revolt begins when the temple is profaned. The sanctuary is renamed the temple of Zeus. Prostitution is practiced there, improper animals are sacrificed, the books of the law are destroyed, and a

Table 3.2.   Scorecard for the Roman Period (63 B.C.E.–66 C.E.)

63 B.C.E.	Jerusalem falls to the Roman general Pompey
Herodian Period	Julius Caesar appoints Antipater (an Idumean) Governor of Judea
47 B.C.E.–6 C.E.	Hyrcanus II appointed High Priest
ca. 47 B.C.E.	Antipater appoints Phasael (his son) Governor of Jerusalem and entrusts Galilee to his second son Herod ("the Great")
40 B.C.E.	Herod named "King" by Roman Senate
37–4 B.C.E.	Herod the Great
	Ananel (not of Hasmonean line) appointed High Priest
35 B.C.E.	Aristobulus III (of Hasmonean line) appointed High Priest
31 B.C.E.–14 C.E.	Augustus Caesar (a.k.a. Octavian)
	Dissolves Roman Senate in 31 B.C.E.
4 B.C.E.–6 C.E.	Archelaus (son of Herod the Great) named "Ethnarch" by Augustus
	[Herod] Antipas (son of Herod the Great) named ruler of Galilee and Perea
	Philip (son of Herod the Great) given other territories
6–66 C.E.	Direct Roman rule of Judea; Capital city is Caesarea
6–41	Officials with title of "Prefect" put in charge
26–36	Pontius Pilate is Prefect
41–44	Herod Agrippa I rules as king (describes Pilate as "harsh, greedy, and cruel")
44–66	Officials with title of "Procurator" put in charge

"desolating sacrilege"—probably an idol of some sort—is erected. Mattathias, the patriarch of the Hasmonean family, kills a Judean offering an unfit sacrifice and also kills the king's officer who is enforcing the edict. Mattathias issues a call to arms, and his son Judas and nine others flee to the wilderness. There they regroup, take up arms, and win minor skirmishes against the Seleucid army. They take Jerusalem fairly easily and rule the city, and its temple, for the next hundred years, with Seleucid permission. We get the Jewish holiday of Hanukkah from the Maccabean rededication of the temple after it is profaned by Hellenized priests (1 Macc 4:36–59, 2 Macc 10:1–8).

Neither Judea nor Jerusalem is ever secure at this time, which is one reason the Romans are invited in: They unite with the Judeans against the Seleucids before taking Judea for Rome in 63 B.C.E.

Although the empire changes when the Roman general Gnaeus Pompeius Magnus—Pompey the Great—captures Jerusalem in 63 B.C.E., the culture of Hellenism remains pretty much the same: The rulers change, but the overall culture does not. The provinces on the eastern Mediterranean, and in the eastern Roman Empire in general, continue to speak Greek for many centuries. Although Herod Antipater and Herod the Great especially retain order in unruly Judea, things become chaotic under Herod the Great's sons, and so Rome governs Judea directly after 6 C.E., with prefects and procurators. Herod the Great emulates the great potentates of Hellenized civilization, and his expansion of the temple in Jerusalem is just one of many efforts he makes to show the rest of the world that Judea is not a rural outpost. Cultural accommodation continues to be the norm among the wealthy and the ruling classes under Roman rule.

At the same time, resistance to foreign domination—both political and cultural—begins among the dispossessed in the first century C.E. Judeans rebel in 66 C.E. and again in 132 C.E. The First Jewish War results in the destruction of the temple in Jerusalem in 70 C.E. but does not officially end until 73 C.E., when Roman troops take the Herodian fortress of Masada. The Second Jewish War, led by Simon bar Kosiba, results in the banishment of Judeans from Jerusalem and the promise by Emperor Hadrian to build a Roman city on the site.

Despite armed resistance on the part of the Judeans, the religion of Israel and its followers in Diaspora nevertheless remain generally well-accepted in the empire. Roman authorities respect and venerate the customs of Israel. The Judeans are exempt from certain civic rituals; they are allowed to raise money for the temple; and they can serve in the Roman Legion in their own cohort. It is a complex and confusing epoch, with both opposition to and acceptance of Hellenism, sometimes within a single individual. Although no group remains "pure" or untouched by the universal culture of Hellenism, a clear counterculture emerges to it, which offers a different set of values and customs.

A Counterculture

When we use the word *Judaism* today, a range of vivid and specific ideas and images comes to mind: synagogue, Torah, holy days, Shabbat, rabbis, Talmud, bar mitzvah, and so on. While many of these concepts pre-date the destruction of the temple, they assume new importance in the wake of its destruction. Rabbis take on a large role and develop a body of literature that serves as the foundation for what today we call rabbinic Judaism. Priests and temple sacrifices disappear, though not immediately. We argue that it is both anachronistic and inaccurate to speak of Judaism during the era of Hellenism, at least between 200 B.C.E. and 100 C.E. (and maybe even later). Nineteenth-century Christian theologians called the post-Exilic Israelite religion of this era "Late Judaism," which indicates their conviction that Judaism ended with the arrival of Christianity. Twentieth-century scholars define this religion as "Early Judaism" or "Middle Judaism," terms that recognize the fluid nature of a "religion" that has temples and priests—as in Israelite religion—but also has sages and synagogues—as in what becomes rabbinic Judaism. While these recent terms reflect the idea that Judaism is something new, they still follow the linear paradigm: Israel, Judaism, Christianity.

We are therefore going to use the original Greek word for Judaism—*Ioudaismos* (pronounced You-Die-ISS-Mos)—to break through our twenty-first-century thinking. Ioudaismos is a cultural entity of customs and practices that exists as an alternative to, and in competition with, Hellenism, or in Greek, *Hellenismos* (Hell-En-ISS-Mos). There is a growing body of scholarship that argues that Ioudaios (singular) and Ioudaioi (plural) should be translated as Judean and Judeans, rather than Jew and Jews. Christians concerned about New Testament anti-Judaism, for example, argue for this translation in the Gospel of John. We agree. Ioudaioi refers to an ethnic and geographical group, practicing certain religious customs, at least at this point in history (200 B.C.E. to 200 C.E.). This means that Ioudaismos (Judaism) refers to a cultural entity composed of Judeans, not to a religious entity as we would understand it today.[1]

The books of the Maccabees seem to use Ioudaioi as an ethnic or cultural identification that includes or encompasses religion, but is not religious as we understand the term today. Since the kingdom of Israel no longer exists after the Assyrian Exile, the writer of 1 Maccabees discusses Judeans, who continue to exist as a nation or ethnicity:

> When he had finished speaking these words, a *man of Judea* came forward (2:23).
> Judas, who is also called Maccabeus, and his brothers and the *people of the Judeans* have sent us to you (8:20).
> May all go well with the Romans and with the *nation of the Judeans* (8:30).
> And now I free you and exempt *all the Judeans* from payment of tribute and salt tax (10:29).
> In those days Jonathan assembled *the inhabitants of Judea* (11:20).

We might read these passages as being about Jews, and certainly English translators interpret Ioudaioi to mean Jews. But given the national and ethnic context of the conflict, Judeans seems more appropriate and in some places is grammatically preferable. This is one point that leads us to conclude that "Israel" refers to the beliefs and customs of Ioudaismos and that "Judean" refers to the nation, or culture, of Ioudaismos.

We also see Paul contrasting the cultures of Ioudaismos and Hellenismos. For example, he says, "Give no offense to Jews or to Greeks or to the Church of God" (1 Cor 10:32). The word *Ioudaioi* is normally translated as Jews, while *Hellenes* is translated as Greeks. Though we might think that "church of God" (10:32) refers to a religion, the Greek word *ekklesia* actually refers to a political body, namely the assembly. We find not two, but three competing worldviews then: Judean, Hellenistic, and the "church of God" (because we don't have the word "Christian" yet). This cultural distinction is perhaps clearer in 1 Corinthians 1:22–24, where Paul contrasts Judeans with Greeks (*Hellenes*) and with Gentiles (*ethnesines*):

> For *Ioudaioi* demand signs and *Hellenes* desire wisdom, but we proclaim Christ crucified, a stumbling block to *Ioudaioi* and foolishness to the *ethnesines* [nations], but to those who are called, both *Ioudaioi* and *Hellenes*, Christ the power of God and the wisdom of God.

Josephus offers additional support for our interpretation in his works, which introduce his people, the Ioudaioi, and their culture, Ioudaismos, to a Roman audience. The following examples show clearly why Judean(s) is a preferable translation to Jew(s):

Judea now became a province . . . Quirinius, a Roman senator of consular rank, was also sent by Caesar to be governor of Syria and assessor of property there and *in Judea* . . . While the *Judeans* reluctantly agreed to register their property, a certain Judas of Gamala claimed that this was tantamount to slavery, so he and a Pharisee named Saddok called for revolution, starting a fourth philosophy which led to ruin. Let me describe the various schools of thought among the *Judeans*. (*Ant.* 18.1; *War* 2.117)

And later on . . .

During the Roman procurator Coponius' administration in *Judea*, the priests, as was their custom, threw open the gates of the temple at midnight during Passover   Coponius returned to Rome . . . Tiberius, son of Caesar's wife Julia [Livia], who dispatched Valerius Gratus to succeed Rufus as procurator over the *Judeans* . . . Having stayed eleven years in *Judea*, Gratus retired to Rome and was succeeded by Pontius Pilate. (*Ant.* 18.29–36)[2]

In fact, *Jewish Antiquities* should probably be translated *Antiquities of the Judeans*, or even more literally, *Antiquities of the Judean Race*, since the Greek for "antiquities" (*archaiologia*) suggests a racial or ethnic history.

Once we start reading the word *Ioudaioi* as Judeans, rather than Jews, it becomes difficult to read texts any other way. For example, translating the inscription on Jesus' cross as "King of the Judeans," rather than "King of the Jews," reflects the reality of Jesus' execution as a political prisoner by crucifixion. Judea is a political entity that would require a king; Judaism, or Jews, however, would not. The Synoptics use the word for "Judean/Jew" infrequently, describing people instead by their affiliations or job descriptions: priests, Pharisees, scribes, Sadducees, Zealots, elders, and so on. It could be argued that in the Synoptics, the presumption is that everyone is either Judean or Roman, but that Judean/Jew is too large a category to be useful, so subdesignations are used instead. Clearly the distinction between Judeans and Samaritans, or Judeans and Galileans, is important at this time.

John's gospel, however, uses "Judeans/Jews" 73 times. Some scholars say that "Judean" is an appropriate translation in John's gospel, given the polemical period in which it was written. But we would ask the following question: Does the word *Ioudaioi* still refer to an ethno-geographical-cultural entity, or is it beginning to refer to a religious entity in John? Does salvation come from the Judeans, or from the Jews (John 4:22)? The animosity toward Judeans/Jews in John seems to point to religious differences rather than political or national conflict. This makes us think that "Jew" *might* be a preferable translation here. At any rate, we can see that at least up to the end of the first century, Ioudaioi seems to refer to the people who practice the customs of Ioudaismos, rather than the religion we know as Judaism today.

A final reason for thinking that "Judean" is a preferable translation to "Jew" is simply that the Hellenistic world has no concept of religion as we consider it today. On the contrary, religion is a cultural and ethnic commitment, a group of customs and observances. Although 1 Maccabees 1:43 is translated "Many even from Israel gladly adopted [Antiochus'] *religion*," the Greek word used is *latreia*, which actually means "service to the god(s)." A better translation is "Many from Israel [note Israel!] gladly took up serving Antiochus' god(s)." *Religion* is a Latin word, and it is a concept that comes into western culture relatively late. Daniel Boyarin argues that religion does not even begin to exist in the modern sense until the third or fourth centuries of the Common Era. At any rate, it certainly does not exist during the period of Hellenization.[3]

Instead, we see that it is the customs and beliefs of the Judeans that set them apart from the other nations of the Hellenized world. Ioudaismos is local, ethnic, and monotheistic. The Ioudaioi (Judeans) practice circumcision, keep certain food restrictions, and have their own philosophy written in sacred texts. Although the Ioudaioi welcome converts and encourage adoption of their customs, their traditions set them apart from the larger culture. Hellenismos, on the other hand, is global, universal, and polytheistic. Hellenists do not understand what they see as the religious "intolerance" of monotheism. They abhor any kind of genital mutilation and misconstrue unfamiliar dietary practices. For example, one observer writes that the Judeans abstain from eating pork because they worship the pig.

While Ioudaismos offers a clear contrast to Hellenismos, Judaism, the religion that begins to emerge in the first and second centuries C.E., absorbs elements of Hellenistic culture. We see this in the allegorical interpretation of scripture, in the philosophical schools of teachers and disciples, in art and architecture, and in literature and language. It is this cross-fertilization that eventually makes the practices of Judaism so attractive that some Gentiles become God-fearers and proselytes, willing to follow the ancient customs of the Judeans. For these reasons it is also what makes Christianity intelligible to the Greek-speaking world. It does not seem far-fetched to claim that Judaism, as well as Christianity, derives from a hybrid Hellenistic Ioudaismos or Judaic Hellenismos.

Israel and Ioudaismos

What do "Jews" call themselves, then, if not "Jews," when they refer to what we today would call their religion—remembering that this is a somewhat anachronistic category? We find some interesting things if we look at the language in 1 Maccabees. First, we note that *Israel* is the term used to denote the group of people who practice the customs of Ioudaismos:

> [Antiochus] went up against *Israel* and came to Jerusalem with a strong force (1:20).
>
> He suddenly fell upon [Jerusalem], dealt it a severe blow, and destroyed many people of *Israel* (1:30).
>
> [Jerusalem] became an ambush against the sanctuary, an evil adversary of *Israel* at all times (1:36).
>
> They kept using violence against *Israel* (1:58).
>
> But many in *Israel* stood firm and were resolved in their hearts not to eat unclean food. They chose to die rather than to be defiled by food or to profane the holy covenant; and they did die. Very great wrath came upon *Israel* (1:62–64).

Since we have just shown above that the writer of 1 Maccabees uses Judean to indicate a geo-political, ethnic, and cultural group, we have to ask what the use of Israel means in these examples. The kingdom of Israel no longer exists. The last citation seems to imply that Israel, not Judeans, is the collective identification for those who practice Ioudaismos; in this instance, the ones who observe certain dietary restrictions.

The members of the Qumran community view themselves as the remnant, or seed, of Israel, not as Jews or Judeans. They believe that they still live in the biblical age, which for them has not yet ended. The Damascus Document explains the birth of the community, saying that God "remembered the covenant with the forefathers [and] he saved a remnant for Israel and did not deliver them up to destruction" (CD 1.3–8).[4] It says again "And in all of them he raised up men of renown for himself, to leave a remnant for the land and in order to fill the face of the world with their offspring" (CD 2.11–12). The offspring, or seed of Israel (*zera yisrael*), will walk in the ways of righteousness and will not be cursed (CD 12.22).

It seems that the idea of zera yisrael, the seed of Israel, is shared by disparate communities of interpretation. In the Hebrew Bible and in rabbinic literature, however, it is interpreted literally rather than eschatologically.

Ezekiel says, "They shall not marry a widow or a divorced woman, but only a virgin of the stock [seed] of the house of Israel, or a widow who is the widow of a priest" (44:22). The Babylonian Talmud provides similar examples (*b. Kiddushin* 78a, *b. Gittin* 57b). The remnant of Israel (*sharit yisrael*) points to a small group in the eschatological future.

In the New Testament, Paul also refers to the remnant of Israel, using language in his letter to the Romans that echoes the Damascus Document:

> I ask, then, has God rejected his people? By no means! . . . So too at the present time there is a remnant, chosen by grace. But if it is by grace, it is no longer on the basis of works, otherwise grace would no longer be grace . . . For if their rejection is the reconciliation of the world, what will their acceptance be but life from the dead! If the part of the dough offered as first fruits is holy, then the whole batch is holy; and if the root is holy, then the branches are holy (Rom 11:1, 5–6, 15–16).

Paul also uses the word *Israel* differently than he does the word *Judean*, or *Jew*. In Romans, he contrasts Judeans and Gentiles (2:17; 3:9, 29; 9:24; 15:27) as two different ethnic groups. But when he focuses on the covenant community in his discussion in chapters 9 through 11, he calls the group Israel (9:4, 6, 27, 31; 10:19, 21; 11:1–2, 7, 11, 25–26). "Did Israel not understand?" he asks (10:19). "What Israel sought so earnestly it did not obtain, but the elect did" (11:7). "And so all Israel will be saved, as it is written" (11:26). In other words, Paul uses Israel to describe the people of God: "They are Israelites, and to them belong the adoption, the glory, the covenants, the giving of the law, the worship, and the promises" (9:4). (Note also that Paul employs four of the key concepts we identify in Israelite religion: God [the divine glory], covenant, Torah, and temple.

The deutero-Pauline text Ephesians reminds its audience that "you were at that time without Christ, being aliens from the commonwealth of Israel, and strangers to the covenants of promise, having no hope and without God in the world" (2:12). The commonwealth the author is discussing is not a geo-political reality, but rather the covenant community established at Mount Sinai. This is explained further in the next chapter: "The Gentiles have become fellow heirs, members of the same body, and sharers in the promise in Christ Jesus through the gospel" (3:6). The writer says that through Jesus, Gentiles have become part of the covenantal community of Israel.

Finally, the Gospels utilize Israel to depict the people who are in a covenantal relationship with the God of Israel. Jesus says "In no one in Israel have I found such faith" (Matt 8:10 // Luke 7:9), and he claims he "was sent only to the lost sheep of the house of Israel" (Matt 15:24). Matthew refers to the God of Israel, the twelve tribes of Israel, the people of Israel, and the King of Israel, while Luke tends to use Israel as a stand-alone word: "He has helped his servant Israel" (1:54); "The child grew and became strong in spirit, and he was in the wilderness until the day he appeared publicly to Israel" (1:80); "He was looking forward to the consolation of Israel" (2:25); "many in Israel" (2:34, 4:27); "many widows in Israel" (4:25); and so on. These are not geographic or political identifications, but rather cultural-religious classifications.

These examples from Josephus, 1 Maccabees, the Qumran community, Paul, and the Gospels highlight the difficulty in sorting out terms and terminology. Nevertheless, it appears that Israel, rather than Judea or Judean, specifies the group that maintains the covenant established at Mount Sinai. It is only when all but two competing claims to Israel have fallen, in the second century C.E., that Judeans become Jews and followers of Jesus, or followers of The Way, become Christians. Before this time, however, a variety of groups lay claim to the term *Israel*, seeing themselves as the inheritors of the traditions put forward in the Torah and the Prophets.

Israel is a significant identity given the conditions under which Judeans are living in the time of Hellenism. Repression and oppression make daily life difficult, to say the least, so nationalistic sentiment bubbles under the surface and breaks through at times, such as the rebellion led by the Maccabees. This period of persecution leads to the development of a body of literature that gives hope to those with nationalistic aspirations: God will redeem Israel, if not on earth, then in heaven. We thus see the rise of apocalypticism at this time.

Apocalypse Then

With the emphasis on "end-time thinking" among certain contemporary Christians, an apocalyptic climax to current affairs seems almost assumed by some. If people have not actually read any of the *Left Behind* series, which details the disasters following the "rapture" of Jesus' followers into heaven, they certainly have heard of the books. A number of national leaders appear to view the Middle East as the staging ground for the final battle of Armageddon, as described in the New Testament book of Revelation. Apocalypticism is not limited to Christianity, however. Muslim jihadists who fight holy wars and white supremacists and Neo-Nazis who anticipate RAHOWA (racial holy war) all share the apocalyptic worldview that the world is divided between good and evil and violent confrontation is inevitable.

A related term is *millennialism*, which initially described the belief in the *imminent* return of Jesus Christ amidst multiple world crises, followed by his thousand-year rule. The word *millennial* now describes a variety of religious groups—Christian and non-Christian alike—that live in the expectation of radical and enormous change on earth. Many New Age religious groups are millennialists, believing in a peaceful but sweeping transformation of the world and the cosmos. In the history of Christian thought, apocalyptic millennialism, which foresees violent change accompanying the return of Jesus, is relatively anomalous. While it is prevalent during the first centuries of the Common Era, once Christianity becomes established, millennialism and apocalypticism are too destabilizing, and potentially violent, for an institutionalized church to tolerate. There are moments of millennial fervor in Christian history, but these are the exceptions rather than the rule.

Regardless of its modern appearances and various manifestations, apocalypticism has its roots in the religion of Israel. In order to understand this heritage we must first go back to the time of the Exile and Israel's encounter with Persia.

Divine Justice According to Zoroaster

The god of Israelite religion is a providential god, responsible for everything that befalls Israel and Judah. This, at any rate, is the explanation the deported Judahites give while they are in exile in Babylon. They understand their misfortunes to be God's punishment for their own unfaithfulness. This is preferable to thinking that God has abandoned the people with whom the covenant had been made. God is just, however, and will never forsake the chosen people, according to the biblical text. Therefore, God is responsible and God is in charge. Even the book of Job, which blames Satan for Job's afflictions, depicts God as the one who allows Satan to act. Similarly, the wickedness of various kings draws down the wrath of God. God remains in control, no matter what.

Persian religion, under the influence of Zoroastrianism, has a different view of divine justice. Zoroaster, a Persian prophet who probably lived on the central Asian steppes in the second millennium B.C.E. (between 1400 and 1200 B.C.E.), teaches that there is one God, Ahura Mazda, who is wholly good and completely just. But there is also a competing evil spirit named Angra Mainyu, who is wholly evil and completely destructive.

These two beings wage cosmic war on a battleground that includes heaven and earth. Zoroaster prophesies that eventually Ahura Mazda will prevail over Angra Mainyu, but in the meantime, the evil spirit will corrupt and degrade the world that Ahura Mazda has created perfect and good. Because God can only be just, however, Zoroaster conceives of an afterlife in which people face an initial judgment three days after death. The good will ascend to heaven; the evil will be thrown into hell for punishment. After a time, there will then be a general resurrection and a final judgment, with the righteous being saved by God, but the wicked being utterly destroyed, including Angra Mainyu and his minions. The righteous will live forever with Ahura Mazda in an earth made new, and perfect, as it was originally intended.

Thus, Persian religion is dualistic, dividing the universe into two camps: one good and one evil. It sees the strife in the world as part of a cosmic battle between good and evil. Because the divine can only be just, however, the concept of resurrection—in other words, an afterlife—emerges to protect God's ultimate goodness. This reconciliation of the goodness of God with the evil that exists in the world is called theodicy: the vindication of God's justice in the face of radical suffering. The Persians preserve God's righteousness by eliminating God's responsibility for injustice. The Israelites preserve God's justice by interpreting suffering as God's judgment on their own faithlessness. The Israelites, then, believe that God acts in history, that is, in historical events, and that God's will can be known by interpreting those events correctly. The Persians, on the other hand, believe that while God acts in history, the real battle is heavenly, in one of seven realms created by Ahura Mazda. Only one of the realms is earth. The ultimate battle is otherworldly.

Israelite religion has almost always rejected the dualism we see in Persian religion. In the book of Job, for example, we see that Satan is not evil, but only doing his job, which is accusing God's favorites and testing them with God's approval. (That is the meaning of his name, the accuser, or adversary.) Moreover, Job never blames God for his woes. He merely observes: "Naked I came from my mother's womb, and naked shall I return there; the Lord gave, and the Lord has taken away; blessed be the name of the Lord" (Job 1:21). In the book of Zechariah, Satan appears as an accuser of Joshua, who is standing before the Lord. Although God rebukes Satan, again it appears that he is merely fulfilling his responsibilities (Zech 3:1–2). But in 1 Chronicles, a text written slightly later—that is, after the Exile and contact with the Persians—Satan has become evil, inciting David to take a census of Israel (1 Chr 21:1). As we move forward in history, we find

Satan assuming a more evil countenance. By the time we get to the New Testament, Satan has become a major figure who is opposed to the will of God.

Angels and Demons

When we think of the word *apocalypse*, rivers of blood, plagues of locusts, and worldwide disaster come to mind. These mental pictures reproduce some of the imagery contained in the book of Revelation, which is also known as the Apocalypse of John. There are many revelatory texts written between the return from the Exile and the destruction of the second temple. Scholars eventually identify apocalypses as a literary genre in which heavenly journeys, angelic visitations, and vivid dreams disclose unknown truths. While some revelations are bloody and violent, others unveil heavenly cities and perfect worlds.

Apocalypses express extreme pessimism about the present. It seems clear to their visionary creators that God must be directly involved, or must authorize a divine agent, if anything is going to change. At the same time, an underlying optimism about the future exists, since God is so powerful that whatever is occurring is happening according to plan. This kind of optimism asserts that it is the darkest hour just before dawn. Moreover, it is clear that the wicked will be punished and, further, will be absolutely destroyed. The good guys will win! The bad guys will suffer! The revelations in apocalypses explain past, present, and future events deterministically: All is foreordained. Only a few know the divine plan, however. Frequently these seers and prophets are figures from Israel's past, such as Enoch, Elijah, or Moses, speaking to the present condition in the Pseudepigrapha, as writers rework the traditions they receive from biblical Israel. These writers employ symbolism, myth, and code to retell the received traditions in a way that makes sense in the current age.

We catch glimpses of proto-Apocalyptic literature as early as the fifth and fourth centuries B.C.E. in Isaiah 24–27, in Third Isaiah 56–66, and in Ezekiel, especially 37–48. For example, we see both the punishment promised and the reward assured in Isaiah:

> For the Lord comes out from his place to punish the inhabitants of the earth for their iniquity; the earth will disclose the blood shed on it, and will no longer cover its slain. On that day the Lord with his cruel and great and strong sword will punish Leviathan the fleeing serpent, Leviathan the twisting serpent, and he will kill the dragon that is in the sea. (Isa 26:21–27:1)

Lift up your eyes and look around; they all gather together, they come to you; your sons shall come from far away, and your daughters shall be carried on their nurses' arms. Then you shall see and be radiant, your heart shall thrill and rejoice, because the abundance of the sea shall be brought to you, the wealth of the nations shall come to you. (Isa 60:4–5)

Jews and Christians are also familiar with the apocalyptic visions in Daniel 7–12, while Christians know of the apocalypticism present in 1 Thessalonians, 1 Corinthians, Romans, Mark 13, and Revelation. Indeed, the entire New Testament is suffused with apocalyptic expectation.

There is a wealth of texts that do not make it into the Bible, however. These stories are filled with angels and demons, battle scenes, and visions of the arrival of some sort of savior. The Pseudepigrapha contain elaborations and expansions of stories and legends from the Hebrew Bible. These include wisdom and philosophical literature, prayers and psalms, and a number of Hellenistic Judaic works. Angels and supernatural beings play large roles in these texts. The book of Jubilees, a rewriting of Torah, retells the story of creation, and adds the following:

For on the first day he created the heavens, which are above, and the earth, and the waters and all of the spirits which minister before him:
the angels of the presence,
and the angels of sanctification,
and the angels of the spirit of fire,
and the angels of the spirit of the winds,
and the angels of the spirit of the clouds and darkness and snow and hail and frost,
and the angels of resoundings and thunder and lightning,
and the angels of the spirits of cold and heat and winter and springtime and harvest and summer,
and all of the spirits of his creatures which are in heaven and on earth.
(Jub 2:2)

The angel Michael also plays a prominent part in a variety of different apocalyptic texts: canonical, apocryphal, and those from the Judean Desert. In the book of Daniel, for example, an angel appears to the prophet and tells him that Michael, "one of the chief princes," came to help him (the angel) in Persia and that "there is no one with me who contends against these princes except Michael, your prince" (Dan 10:21). Daniel concludes with the reassurance that "At that time Michael, the great prince, the protector of your people, shall arise" (12:1). Michael makes appearances in the

New Testament as well. The letter of Jude relates a story that claims that the archangel Michael rebuked the devil over the latter's attempt to interfere with the burial of Moses (1:9). Michael also appears in Revelation when war breaks out in heaven. He and his angels fight against "the dragon"—"that ancient serpent, who is called the Devil and Satan, the deceiver of the whole world"—which is defeated and thrown out of heaven (12:7–9). In the *Testament of Abraham*, a pseudepigraphical work dating to the late first century C.E., God assigns Michael the task of preparing Abraham for his death by first showing him a number of sights from a heavenly chariot. Thus, Michael is God's right-hand man, or angel, across various traditions in Israel.

The collection of the Dead Sea Scrolls—which includes items discovered around the Judean Desert—contains a number of pseudepigraphical works, including fifteen or sixteen copies of Jubilees, perhaps an indication of the community's own interest in apocalypticism. The community at Qumran also generates its own apocalyptic literature, and the *War Rule* (1QM) provides an extremely detailed battle plan for the final clash between God and Satan. The names of Michael and other angels—Gabriel, Sariel, Raphael—are written on the shields of towers (1QM 9.15–16), and God

> sends everlasting aid to the lot of his [co]venant by the power of the majestic angel for the sway of Michael in everlasting light, to illuminate with joy the covenant of Israel, peace and blessing to God's lot, to exalt the sway of Michael above all the gods, and the dominion of Israel over all flesh. (1QM 17.6–8)

The scroll makes it clear that it is only by the power of God's intervention that Israel is saved. "For the battle is yours! With the might of your hand their corpses have been torn to pieces with no-one to bury them . . . It is not our might nor the power of our own hands which performs these marvels, except by your great strength and by your mighty deeds" (1QM 11.1, 5).

We see then, that the dualistic vision of the cosmos introduced through Persian religion eventually pervades a wide variety of different types of groups all claiming to be Israel. The only remaining question is why.

A Time of Anguish

Apocalypses are created in times of intense oppression, when people are feeling that things are hopeless. The book of Daniel, which purports to be written during the Persian period but is actually composed during the repressive regime of the Seleucid dynasty, contains an apocalypse—or revelation—in the second half of the work:

> In the third year of the reign of King Belshazzar a vision appeared to me, Daniel, after the one that had appeared to me at first. In the vision I was looking and . . . I was by the River Ulai. I looked up and saw a ram standing beside the river. It had two horns. Both horns were long, but one was longer than the other, and the longer one came up second. (Dan 8:1–3)

Daniel learns that a wicked king will exalt himself above all else and will blaspheme the "God of gods" (11:36). When the archangel Michael arrives, however, "there shall be a time of anguish, such as has never occurred since nations first came into existence. But at that time your people shall be delivered, everyone who is found written in the book" (12:1). We can see that the apocalypse in Daniel describes current events in the Seleucid Empire in the future tense, but predicts a happy outcome. This prophecy written backward accurately describes the historical situation in symbolic language, although the apocalyptic outcome does not transpire exactly as foretold.

Initially, life under the Seleucid dynasty that is ruling Judea (198–63 B.C.E.) is not terrible. Antiochus III (r. Judea 198–187 B.C.E.) sets aside a fund to pay for animals and supplies needed at the temple and provides money for temple repairs. Judeans can live under their ancestral laws, and priests and scribes are exempt from paying taxes, as are the residents of Jerusalem. But all this changes as Syrian funds are depleted in wars with the Romans.

The situation changes dramatically under Antiochus IV (r. 175–164 B.C.E.). As noted above, a Hellenized ruler and a corrupt priesthood introduce new customs and require the abandonment of old traditions. The Judean high priest Onias is replaced by Jason, who bribes his way into the position. Jason is then outbid by Menelaus, who unfortunately falls into arrears in his payments to Antiochus IV. Meanwhile, the emperor wages war unsuccessfully against the Egyptians. On his return from his losses, he enters Jerusalem and desecrates the temple, stealing its gold and silver. Two years later, he returns to Jerusalem with a military force and attacks the city, tearing down its city walls and turning it into a military center under Seleucid control. That same year, 167 B.C.E., he begins imposing new, Hellenistic customs on the citizenry. The new edicts make it almost impossible to observe the customs of Ioudaismos. 2 Maccabees 7 describes the brutal torture of seven brothers and their mother for refusing to eat pork. "What do you intend to ask and learn from us," one of the brothers asks, "for we are ready to die rather than transgress the laws of our ancestors" (2 Macc 7:2). This drives the king into a rage, and he tortures each brother separately, which 2 Maccabees describes in great detail. But all of the brothers encourage the one being tortured to remain steadfast, and the mother is especially supportive, saying "The Lord God is watching over us and in truth has compassion on us, as Moses declared in his song that bore witness against the people to their faces, when he said, 'And he will have compassion on his servants'" (2 Macc 7:6). After all of the sons are killed, the mother dies, though it is not clear if she is abused or not. "Let this be enough, then, about the eating of sacrifices and the extreme tortures," the account concludes (2 Macc 7:42).

Even after the Maccabean Revolt and the accession of the Hasmonean family to the priesthood and leadership of Judea, the Seleucids maintain control of the territory. Moreover, the Hasmoneans are almost as Hellenized as the Seleucids, and their priests are not much better than their predecessors. There are repeated slaughters of Judeans by one party or another throughout this period. In addition, Judea continues to be a battleground between Syria and Egypt, and then between Rome and Syria. Ironically, the Judeans enter into an alliance with Rome against Syria. The Roman general Pompey is happy to oblige and in 63 B.C.E. marches into Jerusalem.

Life under Roman rule is no improvement, with the possible exception of the rule of Herod the Great (r. 37–4 B.C.E.) who, though Hellenized, extends the Jerusalem temple and attempts to demonstrate his legitimate claim to rule by supporting the customs of Ioudaismos. But when the Romans assume direct control of Judea in 6 C.E., they fail to take into account the cultural sensibilities of the people who live there. The temple treasury is constantly raided. Pontius Pilate, for example, uses temple funds to build an aqueduct. The Emperor Caligula (r. 37–41 C.E.) orders a statue of himself erected in the Jerusalem temple and dispatches a large number of troops to enforce the edict, although the local governor does not want the statue there. Violence against the Romans breaks out time and again, and it is brutally crushed, until the first revolt occurs in 66 C.E., when Judean rebel forces take Jerusalem and massacre Roman soldiers. The war lasts until 73 C.E., although Jerusalem is retaken in 70 C.E. by General Titus, and the temple is destroyed the same year.

A second revolt breaks out in 132 C.E., when Emperor Hadrian (r. 117–138) issues a ban on circumcision. He also plans to build a new city on the ruins of Jerusalem, which will contain a temple to Jupiter Capitolinus. The leader of the revolt, Simon bar Kosiba (also known as Simon bar

Kokhba) leads a guerilla war against the Romans, which is successful for three years. He takes Jerusalem early in the revolt, and some evidence suggests that his group starts to rebuild a temple and to institute (or continue) sacrifices. Rabbi Akiba (50–135 C.E.), who is martyred during the revolt, believes that bar Kosiba is the messiah and calls him Simon bar Kokhba (son of a star) after a messianic passage in Numbers: "A star shall come forth out of Jacob, and a scepter shall rise out of Israel" (Num 24:17). Bar Kokhba, who has taken the title "Prince of Israel," is killed in 135, and the revolt is crushed. Jerusalem becomes Aelia Capitolina, and Jews are barred from entering the city.

This summary shows the conditions of almost constant warfare or imperial domination under which the residents of Judea live from 200 B.C.E. into the second century C.E. Judea is an occupied nation, controlled by Hellenized rulers who care little about the local customs. Nationalistic resistance surges repeatedly against the outsiders, as rebels attempt to reinstate the traditions that have been observed at least since the return from Exile, if not before. It is no wonder, then, that a body of literature arises that looks to God and the angels for salvation. Battles on earth make changes only temporarily. What is needed is a radical transformation of the present evil age into an age in which God will rule, guiding the hand of the anointed ones: the king, the priest, and the prophet. That age seems extremely distant, and yet very close.

It is easy to imagine the hope that apocalyptic literature must have inspired. Despite political oppression and religious repression, people could believe that God will prevail; thus they gain the courage to resist or the prudence to withdraw. They are not alone, but are fighting in a cosmic battle—not just an earthly war—that engages all the forces of evil, not just those of a specific nation or empire. No wonder they are defeated again and again: The enemy is enormous. Only God can triumph in this cause.

This, then, is the situation in which the different communities of interpretation we discuss in the next chapter are working. They face cultural competition and the denigration or eradication of their traditions and beliefs. They face physical suppression: imprisonment, torture, and death. They face war, both against external forces and against internal traitors. In response, they choose to accommodate themselves to some elements, to resist, or to withdraw completely. Yet throughout it all, the people Israel have their sacred texts and their God, which sustain them. Although scripture remains their rock and their anchor, the situation changes, and as a result, so does interpretation as well as the very texts themselves.

Suggestions for Further Reading

Daniel Boyarin. *Border Lines: The Partition of Judaeo-Christianity.* Philadelphia: University of Pennsylvania Press, 2004.

John P. Brown. *Ancient Israel and Ancient Greece: Religion, Politics, and Culture.* Minneapolis: Fortress Press, 2003.

James H. Charlesworth, ed. *The Old Testament Pseudepigrapha,* 2 vols. New York: Anchor Bible, 1983.

Shaye J. D. Cohen. *The Beginnings of Jewishness: Boundaries, Varieties, Uncertainties.* Berkeley: University of California Press, 1999.

Louis Feldman. *Judaism and Hellenism Reconsidered.* Leiden and Boston: Brill, 2006.

Martin Hengel and Christoph Markschies. *The "Hellenization" of Judaea in the First Century after Christ.* London and Philadelphia: SCM Press and Trinity Press International, 1989.

Florentino García Martínez and Eibert J. C. Tigchelaar, eds. *The Dead Sea Scrolls Study Edition,* 2 vols. Grand Rapids, Mich.: Eerdmans, 1997–1998.

Jeffrey Siker. *Disinheriting the Jews: Abraham in Early Christian Controversy.* Louisville, Ky.: Westminster John Knox, 1991.

Shemaryahu Talmon, ed. *Jewish Civilization in the Hellenistic-Roman Period.* Philadelphia: Trinity Press International, 1991.

———. "Waiting for the Messiah: The Spiritual Universe of the Qumran Covenanters." In J. Neusner, W. S. Green, E. Frerichs, eds. *Judaisms and Their Messiahs at the Turn of the Christian Era.* Cambridge: Cambridge University Press, 1987.

James C. VanderKam. *An Introduction to Early Judaism.* Grand Rapids, Mich.: Eerdmans Publishing, 2001.

Margaret H. Williams. *The Jews among the Greeks and Romans: A Diasporan Sourcebook.* Baltimore: The Johns Hopkins University Press, 1998.

Martin O. Wise, Martin G. Abegg, and Edward M. Cook. *The Dead Sea Scrolls: A New Translation,* rev. and adapted. San Francisco: HarperSanFrancisco, 2005.

Notes

1. Shaye Cohen insists that Ioudaios acquires a religious meaning in the Maccabean period and should be translated as "Jew." Shaye J. D. Cohen, *The Beginnings of Jewishness: Boundaries, Varieties, Uncertainties* (Berkeley: University of California Press, 1999). We disagree, for reasons we present in the following discussion.

2. These two quotations by Josephus come from Paul L. Maier, trans., *Josephus: Essential Writings* (Grand Rapids, Mich.: Kregel, 1988), 260. All other citations to Josephus come from the Loeb Library, H. S. J. Thackeray, trans., *Josephus* (Cambridge, Mass.: Harvard University Press, 1976).

3. Daniel Boyarin, *Border Lines: The Partition of Judaeo-Christianity* (Philadelphia: University of Pennsylvania Press, 2004).

4. All citations from the Dead Sea Scrolls come from Florentino García Martínez and Eibert J. C. Tigchelaar, eds., *The Dead Sea Scrolls Study Edition,* 2 vols. (Grand Rapids, Mich.: Eerdmans, 1997–1998).

Sects and the City 4

P ICK UP MOST TRADITIONAL DISCUSSIONS of the Second Temple period and you are likely to come across a chapter called "The Diverse
World of First-Century Judaisms," or "Palestinian Judaism in the
Time of Jesus," or "Sectarianism in the Second Commonwealth." The prevailing image is that of a world populated by competing theologies and
feuding parties. The Sadducees, we are told, control the temple and the
priesthood. The Pharisees, led by lay leaders, represent the "common people." The Essenes are eccentric renegades who live in relative seclusion, dis-
tancing themselves philosophically and geographically from the other
groups. The Zealots are wild-eyed bomb-throwers, ready to install the first
messiah who comes along. One gets the impression that if we could walk
down the streets of first-century Jerusalem, we might easily identify and
differentiate card-carrying Pharisees from Sadducees or spot visible distinctions between Essenes and Zealots.

Even though we find these neat and tidy labels a convenient way to describe what seems to be going on in first-century Judea, we also know they
are historically anachronistic. In other words, the people of the period do
not necessarily identify themselves using these terms. The situation may be
better understood as one in which a variety of closely related groups view
themselves as maintaining and protecting the tradition of biblical Israel.
Each sees itself as descendants of Israel.

These successors of ancient Israel use the Torah, the Prophets, and
some Writings, such as the Psalms, as their guide to understanding what it
means to be Israel. In order for these texts to remain meaningful, communities read them in light of their current experiences and, by doing so, interpret or reinterpret these writings anew. This process is further complicated

when a number of different communities share the same texts but have different experiences and different interpretive views. Each community interprets scripture uniquely. The text does not change, but the opinions as to what a specific law or ritual may mean and how it should be followed are varied. This variation manifests itself in a number of theological worldviews and behaviors. Within a single entity identifying itself as "Israel," we find a number of interpretive communities, each attempting to uphold traditions it perceives as the embodiment of historical Israel and doing so in the face of changing historical circumstances. None of these communities necessarily has the intention of differentiating itself from the others; each strives to live in accordance with the Torah. Although their interpretations diverge, we cannot assume that these differences are evidence of deliberate forms of self-definition.

Yet the way scholars usually describe what is going on at this time is not by an examination of how Torah is interpreted, but rather by delineating the so-called sects of the Second Temple period. Each group—Sadducees, Pharisees, Essenes, Zealots, Samaritans, Boethusians, and the Jesus Movement—is compartmentalized into a theological cubbyhole. Their beliefs and practices are compared and contrasted, but there is little understanding of how, in essence, they all share the same identity, namely Israel.

We offer the concepts of Torah, priesthood, and temple—which all groups accept as central to their life and practice—as an alternative paradigm for understanding Judaic religion in the period of origins. When we look at the Qumran community, the Pharisees, and the Jesus Movement, for example, we find competing communities of Torah interpretation. These groups redefine, or rework, the concept of the priesthood in ways that provide each a sense of group identity on the one hand, but which do not necessarily make them sectarians on the other.

So Many Sects . . .

The traditional sectarian picture is drawn from a number of texts written in the first through sixth centuries C.E. These include the writings of Josephus, the New Testament, and rabbinic literature.

Josephus, a Jewish military and diplomatic leader, provides the earliest account of the so-called Judean groups, which he calls "philosophies." Writing in Greek for a Roman audience, Josephus is both interpreter and apologist for the customs of the Judeans. In his accounts of the history of the Judeans—*Jewish Antiquities* and *The Jewish [Judean] War*—Josephus describes four philosophies of the Judeans. These four groups have dominated almost all evaluations of first-century Judaic religion since the Enlightenment.

"Let me describe the various schools of thought among the Judeans" (*Ant.* 18.11; *War* 2.117). Josephus goes on to discuss the Pharisees, the Sadducees, the Essenes, and, probably, the Zealots. He says that the Pharisees:

> simplify their standard of living, making no concession to luxury. They follow the guidance of that which their doctrine has selected and transmitted as good, attaching the chief importance to the observance of those commandments which it has seen fit to dictate to them . . . Because of these views they are, as a matter of fact, extremely influential among the townsfolk, and all prayers and sacred rites of divine worship are performed according to their exposition. (*Ant.* 18.12–15)

He also notes that the Pharisees believe that souls survive death and are rewarded or punished based on moral conduct.

The Sadducees, in contrast, "hold that the soul perishes along with the body" (*Ant.* 18.16). In addition, the Sadducees "own no observance of any sort apart from the [written] laws" (*Ant.* 18.16). Josephus is rather critical of the Sadducees, saying they are somewhat argumentative and disputatious, although they are also "men of the highest standing" (*Ant.* 18.17). Elsewhere he notes that the Sadducees have the confidence of the wealthy alone and no following among the populace (*Ant.* 13.297). As a result, they must submit to the teachings of the Pharisees, "since otherwise the masses would not tolerate them" (*Ant.* 18.17). According to Josephus, the key theological conflict between the Pharisees and Sadducees is that the Pharisees:

> had passed on to the people certain regulations handed down by former generations and not recorded in the Laws of Moses, for which reason they are rejected by the Sadducean group, who hold that only those regulations should be considered valid which were written down (in Scripture), and that those which had been handed down by former generations need not be observed. (*Ant.* 13.297)

The third "philosophy" Josephus describes is that of the Essenes, who like the Pharisees believe in the immortality of the soul. Because they use a different purification ritual, they are barred from the temple sanctuary. They hold property in common, says Josephus, and live by themselves, without wives or slaves, establishing communities in cities and towns throughout the country. The absence of wives indicates that Josephus assumes the group is all-male. He discusses their form of community organization, their charitable endeavors, and—with particular emphasis—their piety, noting that "they are stricter than all Jews [Judeans] in abstaining from work on the seventh day," not even defecating on the Sabbath (*War* 2.148).

Josephus does not mention Zealots by name when he describes the fourth philosophy, but scholars assume that this is the group he means. The Zealots agree with the opinions of Pharisees, "except that they have a passion for liberty that is almost unconquerable, since they are convinced that God alone is their leader and master" (*Ant.* 18.23). Scholars have identified this group as a revolutionary body that emerged shortly before the First Jewish War. Paula Fredriksen calls this group the "Insurrectionists," Judeans who "focused on liberating Jerusalem and cleansing the temple."

Josephus discusses the Samaritans, but does not consider them a philosophy, or for that matter, Judeans. They interfere with the construction of the second temple, they marry foreign wives, and they persuade the Persians to let them build their own temple on the tallest mountain near Samaria, Mount Gerizim. He contrasts their ethnicity, as well as their behavior, with that of the Judeans. The New Testament also indicates dislike for Samaritans, suggesting general animosity toward them by Judeans.

There are several additional groups to consider that are not usually included in traditional lists of first-century "sectarian Judaism." These include God-fearers, proselytes, and a new category recognized by some modern scholars: Enochic Judaism. God-fearers are Gentiles who participate in the life of the Judean community, principally in the Diaspora. They observe the commandments, attend synagogue services, and can be considered converts to the Judean way of life. Proselytes are essentially God-fearers who have taken the radical step of being circumcised. In a Hellenistic society, which abhors what it considers to be genital mutilation, this is a dramatic act of faith. As such, some would argue that it is legitimate to say that God-fearers and proselytes become part of Israel in the period between 100 B.C.E. and 100 C.E. Similarly, a number of God-fearers become followers of Jesus in the first and second centuries C.E. The book of Acts mentions visitors from Rome, "both Judeans and proselytes" (2:10). While it is not quite accurate to call God-fearers and proselytes members of a sect, they nevertheless make up a unique and distinct group of people who claim the heritage of Israel.

Gabriele Boccaccini believes he and others have identified yet another sectarian group during the period of what he calls "middle Judaism," that is, from 300 B.C.E. to 200 C.E. "Enochic Judaism," as it is called, comprises a group or movement that takes the pseudepigraphical book of 1 Enoch as its central text. The theme running through 1 Enoch is that evil exists prior to human will and has subsequently contaminated human nature. Enochic Judaism also relies on other texts, such as Jubilees, *Testaments of the Twelve Patriarchs*, and 2 Enoch—books in which the biblical character of Enoch makes either a brief appearance or no appearance at all. What is significant about 1 Enoch in particular, and Enochic Judaism in general, is its emphasis on the "Elect One" and the "Son of Man." A heavenly redeemer plays an important role in many of the texts used by Enochic Judaism. Most of the evidence for this recently identified group comes from texts referring to Enoch or reflecting an apocalyptic view, rather than secondary reports of their activities or beliefs. Fragments from Enochic texts were found at Qumran—and texts from Qumran cite these sources—suggesting to Boccaccini that the group living on the shores of the Dead Sea was formed by Enochic Jews rather than Essenes.

New Testament Sectarians

The New Testament notes Sadducees, Pharisees, Zealots, and Samaritans, and also mentions scribes and elders, but it does not say anything about Essenes by name. We need to specify which New Testament writings we mean when we talk about the various groups that exist in the first century. For example, Paul's letters refer to Pharisees, but do not mention Sadducees, Samaritans, or Zealots. This probably reflects the fact that Paul is a Judean in Diaspora and thus has limited contact with Sadducees and Samaritans. They may not be germane to his arguments. Furthermore, his audience consists of non-Judeans, whose interest in "Jewish philosophies" would be limited at best. Finally, Paul's letters are written before the Zealots even exist, at least according to current analyses of Judean conflict with Roman authority.

The four Gospels—Mark, Matthew, Luke, and John—provide the most detail in the New Testament about first-century Judean groups. Yet the groups they highlight, and those they neglect, are intriguing. For example, one of Jesus' disciples, Simon, is identified as a Zealot (Mark 3:18 // Matt 10:4 // Luke 6:15). This is the only reference to the Zealots contained in the Gospels, although during Jesus' trial there is a reference to an insurrection (Mark 15:7 // Luke 23:25). The Sadducees also play a minor role, appearing only once in Mark and Luke, and not at all in John. Mark tells a story about them in regard to their lack of belief in the resurrection and their question to Jesus about a woman who dies with seven husbands (Mark 12:18 // Matt 22:23 // Luke 20:27). The inclusion of Sadducees in this pericope might have come from Josephus' discussion of Sadducean beliefs about the afterlife, since they merely serve as a framing device for

Jesus' observations about resurrection. In other words, the Sadducees, like the Zealots, play a small role in the Gospels. Scholars explain this by stating that the Sadducees vanish with the destruction of the temple in 70 C.E., and the Gospels—written at the end of the first century C.E.—reflect this loss. If the Gospels are historical, however, this may reveal the relative insignificance of the Sadducees in the first century.

The Gospels refer to the Pharisees (eighty-eight times) more than any other group—with the exception of priests (ninety-three times)—and they depict Jesus both in conflict and in conversation with them. The Pharisees seem to be concerned with following written Torah and the "traditions of the elders." They ask Jesus why his disciples violate the Sabbath by plucking some grain to eat and why they fail to wash their hands before eating. They get upset when Jesus heals a man on the Sabbath. The disciples ask Jesus why the Pharisees fast, but they do not. The Pharisees also practice tithing and are committed to supporting the temple. In fact, priests and Pharisees are mentioned together seven times, which is seven times more than priests and Sadducees.

Another group the Gospels mention is the Samaritans. This is an unpopular group among the Judeans, as we know from Josephus, and even Jesus and his disciples disdain them. For example, Jesus tells his disciples not to go to any towns with Samaritans in them (Matt 10:5). But Jesus also tells the parable of the kindly Samaritan who takes care of a mugging victim (Luke 10:29–37), and in John's gospel, Jesus' first non-Judean believer is a Samaritan woman of ill repute who persuades her Samaritan community that Jesus is a prophet (John 4).

Rabbinic Literature on the Sectarians

A final source to consider when attempting to identify different Judaic groups in the first century is rabbinic literature. Like the New Testament, rabbinic texts such as the Mishna (200 C.E.) and the Talmuds (fifth and sixth centuries) are compiled from oral traditions handed down over time. The rabbinic material contains stories about sages from the first century, such as Hillel and Shammai, and also cites legal decisions attributed to these teachers. As with the writings of Josephus and the New Testament, stories of first-century rabbinic sages and the "laws" ascribed to them are used in rabbinic writings to put forward a specific religious point of view not necessarily in accord with historical reality.

There are several passages where these writings may directly allude to the Pharisees and Sadducees by name, but even here no specific theologies or interpretive strategies are outlined. In addition, there are some people who separate themselves from those they consider less observant, but we cannot call them Pharisees.

The Mishna puts perushim and saddukim together in one text where at least some scholars believe we are dealing with the Pharisees and the Sadducees.[1] *M. Yad* 4:6–8 cites several disputes between perushim and saddukim relating primarily to ritual purity—corpse uncleanness and water flowing from a burial ground—and to an issue of civil law (the responsibility one has when an injury is caused by one's cattle). In *m. Para* 3:7f., the perushim want greater purity of the priest for the rite of the red heifer than the official ritual requires, and thus are in conflict with the saddukim. In general, the Mishna discusses perushim more often than saddukim and frequently shows the superiority of the perushim position. In other words, the texts are polemical rather than historical in nature. With that said, however, the perushim appear infrequently in the Mishna, while the saddukim are even less visible.

Second Temple "Judaisms"?

Based on the sources outlined above and others, scholars usually tell the story of Second Temple "Judaisms"—a phrase coined by Jacob Neusner to indicate the lack of any single normative Judaism at the time—as one of competing "sects" operating within an oppressive environment dominated by Hellenistic culture. The Sadducees are the upper class of society, linked directly with the priesthood and the office of high priest at the temple in Jerusalem. The Pharisees represent the "masses" and the "middle class" and are the "democratizers" of practice who apply traditionally priestly rites to non-priests. The Essenes are a radical monastic group that breaks from the establishment entirely and lives in total seclusion, practicing its own idiosyncratic form of Judaism. Most of the other groups—such as Judeans in Diaspora, Samaritans, and Egyptians—are neglected as relatively minor players in the story. The overarching view that one receives from this analysis is a society that is highly segmented and one that—with the exception of the Sadducees—is reacting to the corruption and Hellenization of the priesthood.

What this account fails to consider is the importance of the Torah as a unifying cultural symbol of profound social and political significance. In effect, the Torah is all that tangibly remains of Israel after the Exile of 587/586 B.C.E. It is during the early Exile that the text is edited, redacted, promulgated, and read in a variety of public settings. Even after the temple is rebuilt, the text remains the guide for how to live as Israel, both inside and outside of Judea.

Because the Torah serves as the springboard from which all daily life and practice is determined, all of the "sects" in question accept several basic principles vis-à-vis temple and priesthood. First, that God appointed a hereditary priesthood to act as the conduit for communicating his will by interpreting his law and by serving in the temple. Second, priests, through the practice of sacrifice, mediate that communication with God. Third, that the Sabbath and festivals mark significant experiences in the community's relationship with God; they are set apart as times when special behavior is required. In addition, the Torah concept of God's dwelling among the Israelites requires that the environment be in constant worthiness of this holy presence. As a result, purity is a concern as Israel strives to continue in its effort to live as a holy people (Lev 19:1–2).

The Torah is the primary—and at times, the only—remaining identity marker for the Israelites and the nation of Israel after the Exile. It is the text that provides a history of the nation and the people. As a result, the principles listed above—priesthood, sacrifice, temple, festivals, and Sabbath— take on paramount importance in the lives of different communities. Though the Torah discusses each of these issues in some detail, it provides few specifics with respect to behavior. It sets out the fundamental principles, but implementation is left to interpretation.

For example, the commandments to observe and keep the Sabbath holy (Exod 20:8 and Deut 5:12–15) do not explain what constitutes observance, how the day should be kept holy, and what activities should be and could not be performed. Exodus 16 hints at correct practice, however, when it describes the experience of the Israelites in the wilderness. God provides manna for them on six days, but on the seventh, Moses commands them to rest. "The LORD has given you the sabbath, therefore on the sixth day he gives you food for two days; each of you stay where you are; do not leave your place on the seventh day" (Exod 16:29). Pre-Exilic biblical texts say little with respect to Sabbath adherence, though Jeremiah prohibits carrying burdens outside of one's house (17:21–24). After the Exile, however, there is great discussion and debate about proper observance. Nehemiah forbids buying and selling on the Sabbath (13:15–22), and 1 Maccabees discusses whether or not the army should fight on the Sabbath (2:29–41). Josephus also raises the question of fighting on the Sabbath (*War* 1.145–7). Post-Exilic communities know from their "Bible" that the Sabbath is important and to be set apart from other days. They feel bound to continue this practice but in doing so are forced to speculate as to what the original precept requires of them.

Many scholars conjecture a shift from priestly to lay authority between Ezra in the mid-fifth century B.C.E. and the Maccabean Revolt of 167 B.C.E. They say that a popular and influential group of non-priestly teachers interpret Torah. In doing so, this group moves away from the past emphasis on priestly religion and leads to a "democratization" of Judaism. This lay opposition to an unpopular priesthood is often correlated by contrasting an autonomous synagogue and the hierarchical temple.

Second Temple sources provide little evidence to substantiate this vision. There is no textual support from this period to document a major transfer of power and authority from priestly to lay hands. To the extent that any change takes place, it occurs between competing priestly groups or between increasingly specialized subgroups. We are calling these subgroups—previously identified as sects—communities of interpretation.

What appears to have existed in the period of the so-called Second Temple "Judaisms" is a central priesthood, located in the temple, which interacts with and responds to the various explanations of Torah that these different interpretive communities present. We are arguing against the traditional understanding of a move in authority from the priesthood (Sadducees) to the laity (Pharisees) and to the ascetics (Essenes). It appears instead as though all three of these groups—and others as well—not only are composed of priests, at least in part, but also couch their philosophies in priestly vocabulary and matrices. Indeed, some of them see themselves as operating within the priesthood as outlined in Torah and in continuity with the priesthood as depicted in the redacted Torah. As Steven Fraade says:

> Those Second Temple groups that questioned or rejected the legitimacy or fitness of the Jerusalem Temple and its priesthood affirmed no less the principle that the descendants of Aaron and Levi were the authoritative purveyors of Israel's scriptures, their interpretation, and legal implementation. These groups to the extent that they distanced themselves from the Jerusalem Temple and its Priesthood, developed their own (from their perspective, more legitimate) priestly vision and praxis, including alternative or supplemental scriptures authenticated by their own priestly scribes and interpreters.[2]

In painting the political and theological picture of Second Temple "Judaisms," traditional scholarship emphasizes the sects themselves, highlighting their similarities and especially differences. A better starting point for understanding the variety of Judaic groups is to focus on the temple and the priesthood. This allows us to see a number of competing interpretive communities as claimants to the same heritage and at the same time to follow their shifting allegiances and alliances. This strengthens our perception that many groups remain within the boundaries of what they believe is Israel.

Torah, Temple, and Priesthood

The primary roles of the priests in pre-Exilic times are to communicate the will of God to the people and to impart the laws and associated rituals to the people. They also perform sacrifices and maintain the shrine in the tabernacle and the temple. These activities are echoed in the verb *yarah* (instruct/instruction).

While the everyday task of officiating at sacrifices is temporarily suspended during the Exile, there is little evidence to suggest that the priesthood continues as an empty vessel, defined solely through inherited identity. On the contrary, it is clear that at least some priests direct their energies towards the compilation of, interpretation of, and teaching of various texts. The prophet Ezekiel—probably a priest in Exile—and Ezra—a priest who brings the "Torah of Moses" back to Jerusalem—suggest that some priests are quite active in Babylon. In fact, there is a large group of scholars who attribute the composition of the Priestly Source (P) as a whole to the period of the Exile.

Moreover, there is evidence that the priesthood persists back home. Priests continue to conduct sacrifices at the ruins of the Jerusalem temple, as well as throughout the land. Samaritans later develop their own temple and cult, possibly during the reign of Alexander the Great, if not before. Recent archaeological evidence, which identifies the outlines of a sanctuary substantially different from that of Jerusalem atop Mount Gerizim, actually pushes the date of construction into the Persian period.

In addition, priests and temples claiming ties to Israelite religion also exist in the Diaspora, most notably in Egypt. The evidence from Elephantine, for example, indicates a sacrificial system that exists until the destruction of the Egyptian temple by the Persians in 410 B.C.E. Since Elephantine Judeans write to the high priest in Jerusalem, this implies that they do not oppose the temple at Jerusalem. A second temple built in Leontopolis in Lower Egypt, however, apparently is constructed in explicit competition with the Jerusalem temple. Confusing documentary evidence comes from Josephus, and while there is debate over this temple's origins, there is agreement that the temple is erected sometime between 163 and 145 B.C.E. as part of political conflict between the Ptolemaic and Seleucid empires.

The text of Torah gives legitimacy to the priesthood by God's appointment of Aaron and his descendants and by virtue of the ability of the priests to correctly divine God's wishes. The lack of political independence after the Exile heightens the importance of the temple and its managers. This in turn increases the significance of Torah as the cultural symbol of Israel. In short, the Torah, a priestly literary construct, reinforces the priesthood and the priesthood reinforces the Torah. In the absence of a king or an army or control over the land, the Judahites/Judeans find that the Torah serves as the ideological basis for national survival and identity. The Torah is a constitution, a history, and a source of authority. And those who interpret Torah have tremendous power derived from this interpretive authority.

The history of the priesthood from the return from Exile in the late sixth century B.C.E. through the end of the first century C.E. is fraught with conflict over maintenance of the temple apparatus and control of Torah interpretation. The books of the Maccabees detail some of this discord; Josephus relates conflicts; the New Testament reports other disagreements. 1 Maccabees, for instance, describes the violent opposition to a Hellenized and corrupt priesthood mounted by traditionalist Judeans. The Maccabean Revolt of 167–164 B.C.E. results in a change of administration in the priesthood. Josephus recounts these events, as well as the slaughter of various parties who fall out of favor with ruling authorities and priests. Jesus is said to have faced priests at his trial, while his followers encounter the anger of priests in the New Testament book of Acts. In other words, textual evidence from three fairly different types of sources documents the ongoing importance of the priesthood.

Even before the Exile it is clear that the priest serves as the interpreter of Torah as God's will and instruction. For example, Leviticus 10:11 shows God commanding Aaron to "teach the people of Israel all the statutes that the Lord has spoken to them through Moses." Deuteronomy gives the "Levitical priests" extensive power to judge cases of homicide, assault, and legal rights, saying that the Israelites should do what the priests say, "Carry out exactly the decision that they announce to you from the place that the LORD will choose, diligently observing everything they instruct you" (17:10). In fact, the person who does not obey the priest shall die (Deut 17:12). The Levites (or more precisely, Levi, ancestor of all priests and Levites) are supposed to "teach Jacob your ordinances and Israel your law," in addition to burning incense and making whole burnt offerings to the Lord (Deut 33:10).

After the Exile, we find allusions to the interpretive function of priests in Josephus, Philo, and, much later, the Mishna. Josephus says that it is the priests, and especially the chief priest, who are entrusted with the administration of Israel's divinely ordained constitution, not just in the area of worship, but also equally in matters of law and the training of the entire community. Philo similarly understands the priests, seeing their consecration to God's service as providing both a bridge and a buffer between the divine and human realms. In the Mishna, priests are the ones who bestow blessings over the congregation in the synagogue and who are given the honor of the first *aliyah* to the Torah.[3] (Being called up to bless the Torah before it is read is called aliyah, which means to ascend. It remains a great honor in synagogue services today.)

Although there is plenty of evidence to suggest the presence of conflicting ideas about who should run the temple and how it should be done, there is little evidence to suggest that any Second Temple Judaic groups would deny that the descendants of Aaron and Levi are the legitimate teachers and implementers of Torah in Israel. (We discuss the distinction between priests and Levites below.) To the extent that they distance themselves geographically or theologically from the temple, these groups cultivate their own priestly visions and programs.

The fact that diverse groups—all claiming to be Israel—appropriate the language, and even the functions, of the priesthood indicates the significance of priests, and the idea of priesthood, in the Second Temple period. Three examples show how different interpretive communities adopt and adapt these concepts, and how they all claim Torah, temple, and priesthood.

Qumran

The continued importance and prominence of the priesthood outside the realm of the Jerusalem temple is clearly evident in the Dead Sea Scrolls. Priesthood at Qumran is a matter of descent. It is not understood metaphorically, but in the very concrete sense of belonging to the "seed of Aaron." The sectarian writings found at Qumran outline a community clearly organized with Zadokite priests at the center. (Zadokite priests are the descendants of Zadok, one of David's two priests, and the priest who anoints Solomon at David's request. After the Exile, the Zadokites control the temple priesthood. Some scholars claim that the Qumran community is founded by disaffected Zadokite priests who leave Jerusalem during the Hasmonean period. They argue that the word "Sadducee" comes from "Zadokite.") The Levites appear in the scrolls in a manner similar to their depiction in the Torah: They serve as judges, officers, and leaders of the congregation; they act as servants of the priests. They are the mediators in a community composed of both priests and lay people. Similarly, the traditional Israelite distinction between priests, Levites, and laity is mentioned throughout the scrolls.

At the same time, it is clear that the Qumran community has at least temporarily removed itself from the temple and cult in Jerusalem. As a consequence, the "priests" at Qumran do not function as priests in quite the same way as their contemporaries at the temple do. Most significantly, they do not officiate at or make sacrificial offerings, and, as a result, they do not receive their share from such offerings. They do, however, preside over their meals, blessing the bread and wine and observing a ritual that may parallel, or replicate, the sacrificial system in Jerusalem, though there is no use of wine in the temple and very little of bread. "And when they prepare the table to dine or the new wine for drinking, the priest shall stretch out his hand as the first to bless the first fruits of the bread and the new wine" (1QS 6.4–5). Even in their visions of the end of days, the priests stand apart from the rest of the community as holding a special role.

The priests at Qumran also assume, or rather resume, several important functions attributed to the Israelite priesthood. According to several texts, they are involved in the judicial process and make oracular pronouncements by casting lots in connection with priestly verdicts:

> Only the sons of Aaron will have authority in the matter of judgment and of goods, and their word will settle the lot of all provision for the men of the Community and the goods of the men of holiness who walk in perfection. (1QS 9.7–8)

The priests also teach, providing instruction in the laws of Torah (Deut 33:8–10). A number of scrolls mention a Righteous Teacher (or Teacher of Righteousness) who guides the community with inspired interpretations of Torah. Similarly, the Zadokites at Qumran are assigned to:

> swear with a binding oath to revert to the Law of Moses, according to all that he commanded, with whole heart and whole soul, in compliance with all that has been revealed of it to the sons of Zadok, the priests who keep the covenant and interpret his will. (1QS 5.8–9)

The priests interpret Torah and gather the community together in order to remind them of the requirements of the covenant:

> When they come, [the priests] shall assemble all those who come, including children and women, and they shall read into [their] ea[rs] [a]ll the

precepts of the covenant, and shall instruct them in all their regulations, so that they do not stray in [the]ir e[rrors]. (1Q28a 1.4–5)

Finally, the priests at Qumran invoke the blessings of God upon the faithful, just as temple priests in Jerusalem do. The *Community Rule* states: "And the priests will bless all the men of God's lot . . . And the Levites shall curse all the men of the lot of Belial" (1QS 2.1–2, 4–5).

In sum, though not engaged in a sacrificial cult, the priests at Qumran continue to function as a clearly identifiable group with tasks specific to their hereditary positions. They are set apart from the rest of the community at Qumran in terms of the authority they wield and the tasks they perform. At the same time, as we will see below, their oft-noted obsession with purity and other priestly concerns is not unique to their community. Certainly it is not markedly different from the concerns shared with priests at the temple in Jerusalem, though specific practices are distinct. Moreover, they share with Pharisees and those in the Jesus Movement a concern about certain priestly duties.

The Pharisees

Notwithstanding the many difficulties we encounter in reconstructing their history and beliefs, the Pharisees appear at first glance to break away from the priestly model. They are most often described as the middle class, lay intelligentsia in opposition to the priests in Jerusalem. But there are Pharisaic priests. It is even possible that Pharisaic control of the priesthood during the Hasmonean period forces a group of Sadducean priests to withdraw from Jerusalem and found the community at Qumran. The Pharisees actually influence and control the priesthood in key moments prior to the end of the first century C.E.

Josephus describes a few of these moments. For example, the Pharisees are extremely popular with the Hasmonean John Hyrcanus (r. 134–104 B.C.E.), enjoying feasts and festivals with him. When he asks them if they notice him doing anything wrong, all the Pharisees praise him but one, who asks Hyrcanus to give up the high priesthood and simply be the political leader of the nation (*Ant.* 13.288–298). This comment so enrages Hyrcanus that he joins the party of the Sadducean group, according to Josephus. Yet Alexander Janneus, grandson of John Hyrcanus, reputedly begs his wife Alexandra from his deathbed to:

> yield a certain amount of power to the Pharisees, for if they praised her in return for this sign of regard, they would dispose the nation favorably to-

ward her. These men, he assured her, had so much influence with their fellow-Jews that they could injure those whom they hated and help those to whom they were friendly. (*Ant.* 13.400–401)

Alexandra becomes queen (r. 76–67 B.C.E.) and follows Alexander's advice, permitting the Pharisees to do whatever they like and commanding the Judeans to obey them. "And so," Josephus concludes, "while she had the title of sovereign, the Pharisees had the power" (*Ant.* 13.409). They exercise that power by freeing prisoners, recalling exiles, and even urging the queen to take revenge for the deaths of Judeans killed by her husband. "In a word, [they] in no way differed from absolute rulers."

The Gospels also link Pharisees with the Jerusalem power structure, frequently showing the Pharisees and priests, or high priests, in close association. John's gospel connects the Pharisees and chief priests several times:

The chief priests and Pharisees sent temple police to arrest him (7:32).

The chief priests and the Pharisees called a meeting of the council, and said, "What are we to do? This man is performing many signs" (11:47).

Now the chief priests and the Pharisees had given orders that anyone who knew where Jesus was should let them know so that they might arrest him (11:57).

So Judas brought a detachment of soldiers together with police from the chief priests and the Pharisees, and they came there with lanterns and torches and weapons (18:3).

While New Testament scholars frequently dismiss the historicity of the Gospels, in light of Josephus' earlier comments it seems fair to assume that the Pharisees are a powerful group, closely aligned with the priesthood, if not always the priests themselves.

Rabbinic literature may allude to the Pharisees in a number of places, though as we have said, these references are as problematic as are New Testament citations. The Mishna includes what seems to be a category of Pharisaic law, which comprises legal sayings attributed either to Pharisaic masters before 70 C.E. or to the houses of Shammai and Hillel. Beyond, there seems to be little that conclusively indicates Pharisaic theology or history.

Although extant Second Temple sources for the Pharisees are all biased and difficult to reconcile with one another, it is nevertheless evident that the Pharisees share a number of priestly concerns with the community at

Qumran. Both groups stress the importance of purity. The Gospels show Pharisaical concern with hand washing (e.g., Mark 7:1–13); Qumran literature describes purification baths, or *mikvaot*, required before eating. The Gospels show the Pharisees as strict observers of the Sabbath (e.g., Matt 12:1–14); Qumran literature indicates similar strictness in the desert community. The Gospels emphasize the Pharisees' practice of tithing for the temple; the Qumran community has set up an alternate temple (see next chapter). The fact that both groups are concerned with the issues of purity and ritual—on top of Sabbath observance and washing, there are tithes and diet—also likens them to the priests of the temple and the pre-Exilic priesthood. Their interests fall entirely in line with priestly concerns in general.

What differentiates the Pharisees from the temple priests on the one hand and the priests at Qumran on the other is that they extend priestly practices beyond the boundaries of the temple without entirely removing themselves from either the temple or the community. While it is true that some Essene communities live within and among cities and their inhabitants, they live communally in a way that differs markedly from that of the Pharisees. The Pharisees achieve a middle ground by legitimizing their practices and beliefs as coming from an authoritative body of teaching that exists in addition to the Written Torah—namely the "traditions of the elders." In place of an ancient genealogical claim to priesthood, the Pharisees hearken to an equally ancient tradition that, in their minds, is just as authoritative, binding, and old, but is not directly tied to the "seed of Aaron." The rabbis eventually trace these traditions back to Moses, but that does not occur until the mid–third century C.E.

The Pharisaic broadening of purity requirements beyond the temple, alongside their allegiance to extra-Torah tradition, has earned them the reputation among some scholars today as championing the extension of holiness to "all Jews equally."[4] In other words, the Pharisaic program is viewed as an effort to proffer the priesthood to everyone.[5] There is, however, no evidence that this is their intent, or that it even occurs:

> Rather it makes more sense to assume that the Pharisees, like the Qumran sectaries, undertook these supererogatory purity practices in order to distinguish themselves from, and to elevate themselves above, the rest of Israel, and to define for themselves a status approaching, but not equaling, that of priests.[6]

The Pharisees cannot break away from the priesthood because they are committed to Torah. However, by behaving more piously than the temple priesthood—in their opinion—and by justifying this behavior as belonging to an ancient tradition, they create for themselves, deliberately or not, a liminal position between the temple and Qumran; that is, between two other competing groups of priests. Though scholars have viewed the Pharisees as the lay leaders of Second Temple Judaism and as departing from the confines of established Israelite priestly religion, this is a gross exaggeration of what appears to have been the case. They cannot be a part of Israel without accepting the precepts of the Torah, and that includes the priesthood.

What the Pharisees do is move the priesthood outside the temple. In the process they expand the divine presence beyond the confines of the temple as well. By incorporating the "traditions of the elders" into their own lives, they extend the temple and enlarge the space in which God is found. Because God is now accessible in a number of places, not just a fixed location, people must be ready, and in a state of purity, for the encounter with God. The Pharisees facilitate this state of readiness by stressing a holiness accessible to all, not just temple priests.

The Jesus Movement

Although Christian theologians writing in the second and third centuries downplay the significance of the Levitical priesthood—focusing instead on the mysterious Gentile priest-king Melchizedek (Gen 14:18–20, Ps 110:4, Heb 7)—it is clear that the concepts of priesthood, temple, and Torah remain important for those in the early Jesus Movement. We see New Testament writers transforming these concepts in two main ways: by identifying Jesus as priest and temple and by identifying believers as priests and temple. In both instances, the traditional priesthood is reinterpreted in favor of a new and "improved" priesthood.

Paul redefines the temple as the community of believers who individually are the temple of God. His only explicit mention of the priesthood occurs in his final letter, which he concludes by saying that he is a minister of Christ Jesus to the Gentiles "in the priestly service of the gospel of God, so that the offering of the Gentiles may be acceptable, sanctified by the Holy Spirit" (Rom 15:16). Paul ties together the idea of priesthood and sacrifice with the notion of Gentile inclusion into the Jesus Movement. For him, what is important is the temple that exists in the hearts of believers. "Do you not know that you are God's temple and that God's spirit dwells in you?" he asks. "If anyone destroys God's temple, God will destroy that person. For God's temple is holy, and you are that temple" (1

Cor 3:16–17). Paul makes similar comments elsewhere in 1 Corinthians as well as in 2 Corinthians. For him, the temple exists in the heart.

It seems a short step to go from understanding the believers as God's temple to seeing the community of God's people as the priests of the temple, as later New Testament literature does. Exodus 19:6 provides the point of departure in Torah for this interpretation by New Testament writers: "You shall be for me a priestly kingdom and a holy nation." 1 Peter, probably written at the end of the first century to a community undergoing persecution by the Romans, reminds the group that they are "a chosen race, a royal priesthood, a holy nation, God's own people" (1 Pet 2:9). Revelation—probably written around the same time during the same persecution—also describes a "kingdom [of] priests serving his God and Father" (Rev 1:6); and later on, "You have made them to be a kingdom and priests serving our God, and they will reign on earth" (5:10). Near the conclusion of the apocalypse the author declares: "Blessed and holy are those who share in the first resurrection . . . They will be priests of God and of Christ, and they will reign with him a thousand years" (20:6).

In the Johannine literature, which is composed after 70 C.E., Jesus is identified as the temple of God, or the place where God "dwells." The author of John's gospel sees Jesus' body as the locus for the "dwelling" (or tabernacle) of the Logos (John 1:14),[7] but also as the temple itself (John 2:19–22). In his apocalyptic vision, another John—John of Patmos—says, "I saw no temple in the city, for its temple is the Lord God the Almighty and the Lamb" (Rev 21:22).[8] Revelation 21 alludes to John 1:14, when it says, "See, the home of God is among mortals. He will dwell with them as their God; they will be his peoples, and God himself will be with them" (Rev 21:3). These references all indicate that God's temple exists either in Jesus, or in the crucified lord of Christians, or that God is actually the temple. In any event, it is no longer a building. We discuss the distinction between temple and tabernacle in John's gospel in more detail in chapter 6.

If the Gospel of John and Revelation see Jesus as the temple and tabernacle, the book of Hebrews—probably written between 60 and 100 C.E.—views Jesus as the high priest. The author of Hebrews assumes the centrality of priesthood and temple but reinterprets them. The temple is subsumed by the tabernacle (Heb 9). Indeed, there is no temple at all, but rather the tent/tabernacle of meeting as described in the Torah (Exod 25:10–40, 26:1–37; Lev 24:1–4, etc.). Jesus appears as the "high priest of the good things that have come, then through the greater and perfect tent (not made with hands, that is, not of this creation)" (9:11). This perfect tent is the body of Jesus. We cannot assume that the author of Hebrews knows the Gospel of John, or vice versa, so the fact that both texts use the language of tent, tabernacle, and temple seems significant. The author of Hebrews asks if the sprinkling of bull's blood sanctifies the impure, "how much more will the blood of Christ, who through the eternal Spirit offered himself without blemish to God, purify our conscience from dead works to worship the living God?" (9:14). So Jesus becomes the priest, the temple, and the sacrifice.

These New Testament writings indicate a development in the thought of the early church. On the one hand, the priesthood and the temple are transferred to Jesus, who becomes the new central "institution" in the minds of his followers. On the other, the priesthood and the temple are transferred to the church, an institution that is growing in importance in the face of the delay of Jesus' return. Paul argues that believers, including Gentiles, are the temple of God in order to exhort Gentiles to be holy and to reject their former paganism. The authors of 1 Peter and Revelation go further, using the language of Exodus to apply it to all followers: All are holy, because they are a kingdom of priests.

Competing Communities of Priests

This brief survey illustrates how the priesthood, clearly defined in the Torah, is contested in the first centuries B.C.E. and C.E. Determining who has legitimate claims to the priesthood, however it is defined, reveals the much larger issue of which group or groups can claim the Israelite inheritance in terms of theological identity and interpretive authority. The image of the priesthood, so clearly established and central to the pre-Exilic Israelite cult, is still viewed as the central institution in the post-Exilic communities. But priestly behavior and interests now serve as platforms for competing ideas about leadership, authority, and maintenance of authentic Israelite tradition.

The concept of priesthood, along with that of temple and Torah, is a useful way to understand various Judaic groups that exist roughly between 200 B.C.E. and 200 C.E. and indeed is preferable to thinking along sectarian lines. Lawrence Schiffman criticizes the identification of various "Judaisms" of this period, saying that view "ignores the vast body of commonality which united them around adherence to the law of the Torah . . . [W]hat brought them together as a nation, civilization, and religion far outweighed the differences, which tended to be exaggerated in the sources."[9] The sources that discuss the various groups—from Josephus and the New Testament to the Qumran literature and rabbinic writings—are all polemical texts, written with theological or tendentious purposes in mind. In other words, they are not historical as we think of history today. Yet they provide glimpses of the thoughts and concerns of people two thousand years ago.

What is truly remarkable is how all of these texts indicate the centrality of priesthood, Torah, and temple to self-identity and self-understanding across time, space, and social location. As the descendants of Israel, claiming to be the rightful heirs to the covenantal tradition, the Qumran community, the Pharisees, the Jesus Movement, and others employ the same strategy, namely, to claim selected markers of Israel for themselves and not for others. While some reject cultural markers that serve a covenantal purpose, such as circumcision or dietary restrictions, all include Torah, an enlarged temple, and a newly defined priesthood. The reinterpretation of Torah and the reinvention of temple and priesthood all point to the recovery of the portable God of ancient Israelite religion. This becomes more apparent when we examine how God moves from the temple into the text.

Suggestions for Further Reading

Gabriele Boccaccini, ed. *Enoch and Qumran Origins: New Light on a Forgotten Connection*. Grand Rapids, Mich.: Eerdmans, 2003.

James H. Charlesworth. *The Pesharim and Qumran History: Chaos or Consensus?* Grand Rapids, Mich.: Eerdmans, 2002.

John J. Collins and Robert Kugler, eds. *Religion in the Dead Sea Scrolls*. Grand Rapids, Mich.: Eerdmans, 2000.

Steven Fraade. *From Tradition to Commentary: Torah and Its Interpretation in the Midrash Sifre to Deuteronomy*. Albany: State University of New York, 1991.

Paula Fredriksen. *From Jesus to Christ*, 2d ed. New Haven and London: Yale University Press, 2000.

Maxine Grossman. "Priesthood as Authority: Interpretive Competition in First-Century Judaism and Christianity." In *The Dead Sea Scrolls as Background to Postbiblical Judaism and Early Christianity*, ed. James Davila. Leiden and Boston: Brill, 2000.

Martin S. Jaffee. *Early Judaism: Religious Worlds of the First Judaic Millennium*, 2d. ed. Bethesda: University Press of Maryland, 2006.

F. G. Martinez. "Priestly Functions in a Community without Temple." In *Gemeinde Ohne Temple/Community without Temple*, ed. Beate Ego, Armin Lange, and Peter Pilhofer, with Kathrin Ehlers. Tübingen: Mohr Siebeck, 1999.

Carol A. Newsom. *The Self as Symbolic Space: Constructing Identity and Community at Qumran*. Leiden: Brill, 2004.

George W. E. Nickelsburg. *Ancient Judaism and Christian Origins: Diversity, Continuity, and Transformation*. Minneapolis: Fortress Press, 2003.

E. P. Sanders. *Jewish Law from Jesus to the Mishnah*. London: SCM Press, 1990.

Lawrence H. Schiffman. *From Text to Tradition: A History of Second Temple and Rabbinic Judaism*. Hoboken, N.J.: Ktav, 1991.

____. *Reclaiming the Dead Sea Scrolls: The History of Judaism, the Background of Christianity, the Lost Library of Qumran*. Philadelphia: Jewish Publication Society, 1994.

Notes

1. Several scholars posit that the occurrence of these two groups together in a given text suggests reference to Pharisees and Sadducees. See for example, E. Rivkin, *A Hidden Revolution* (Nashville: Abingdon, 1978), 125ff. and J. Lightstone, "Sadducees Versus Pharisees: The Tannaitic Sources," in J. Neusner ed., *Christianity, Judaism and Other Greco-Roman Cults: Studies for Morton Smith* (Leiden: Brill, 1975).

2. Steven Fraade, "Priests, Scribes and Sages in Second Temple Times," unpublished paper. See also Fraade, *From Tradition to Commentary: Torah and Its Interpretation in the Midrash Sifre to Deuteronomy* (Albany, N.Y.: State University of New York, 1991), 72–73. The authors would especially like to thank Dr. Fraade for sharing his work with us.

3. See *m. Ber* 5:4; *m. Meg* 4:5, 6, 7; *m. Sota* 7:6; *m. Tamid* 7:2; *m. Git* 5:8. Fraade, "Priests, Scribes and Sages in Second Temple Times."

4. Jacob Neusner, "Judaism in a Time of Crises," *Judaism* 21, no. 3 (1972): 322.

5. Oscar Skarsaune, *In the Shadow of the Temple: Jewish Influences on Early Christianity* (Downer's Grove, Ill.: Intervarsity, 2002), 120.

6. Fraade, "Priests, Scribes, and Sages." See also E. P. Sanders, "Did the Pharisees Eat Ordinary Food in Purity?" in *Jewish Law from Jesus to the Mishnah* (London: SCM Press, 1990), 244–45; and Daniel Schwartz, "Kingdom of Priests: A Pharisaic Slogan?" in *Studies in the Jewish Background of Christianity* (Tübingen: J.C.B. Mohr, 1992), 57–80.

7. Logos in Greek means "word," but it also means reason, rationality, and wisdom.

8. The Lamb in Revelation refers to the crucified Jesus in his form as the risen Christ.

9. Lawrence Schiffman, *From Text to Tradition: A History of Second Temple and Rabbinic Judaism* (Hoboken, N.J.: Ktav, 1991), 98.

Communicating with God
outside the Temple Walls

5

I N THE LAST CHAPTER WE DESCRIBED how various groups claiming the inheritance of Israel all value the priesthood, although in different ways. The Pharisees seek to achieve the purity of priests and thus extend the precincts of purity beyond the temple walls. Those at Qumran relocate the priesthood to the members of their community. The Jesus Movement and its later interpreters, such as Paul, see the community itself as a temple and understand the Exodus commandment to be a "kingdom of priests" as applying to themselves and the church.

Let us recall the tasks of priests in the post-Exilic period. A major responsibility of the priesthood is to perform sacrifices. If we remember that the meaning of the Hebrew word *krb*, "closeness" is embedded in the term for sacrifice—*korban*—then we can better understand the role of priests. They exist to help the people achieve or preserve closeness to God. They mediate this relationship in a variety of ways. Although one of the chief means is sacrifice, the purpose remains the relationship between the community and its deity. In addition to performing sacrifices, the priesthood is involved in interpreting Torah, teaching, overseeing prayer and rituals, providing blessings, and, in general, maintaining communication with God.

Once the priesthood moves beyond the bounds of the temple—as we have demonstrated to be the case, at least among some Judaic groups—it should come as no surprise to discover that the tasks of the priests move along with them. Sacrifice and the reading and interpretation of Torah occur outside the temple in divergent ways. The Torah travels into a variety of locations, which include the *proseuche*, or houses of prayer, described by Philo and others; the synagogue; and the home. Sacrifice also moves outside of the temple and in doing so is redefined in several different ways. If we think of sacrifice as a way to ensure closeness with God and to uphold the presence of God to the community and to the individual, we can observe examples of closeness and presence in the communal acts of eating and praying together.

Reading Torah, praying, and eating together not only draw the people closer to God, they draw the people closer to each other. These practices serve as identity markers and boundaries between the clean and the unclean, the holy and the impure, just as temple priests once delineated these boundaries. At the same time, new practices both divide and unite various interpretive communities. And throughout, we see God becoming more and more portable, dwelling in a number of new localities.

The Movement of Torah and the Presence of God

If current and prevailing biblical scholarship with respect to the compilation of the Torah is accepted, the Exile leads to the dispersion of numerous and varied traditions and laws pertaining to Israelite belief and practice. What emerges during the early restoration, most would say with Ezra, is a unified, albeit composite, constitution of Israelite history and ritual, namely, the Torah. In fact, if we return to our list of key concepts from chapter 2, the covenant as teaching and instruction—that is, as Torah—comes out of Exile as the most intact remnant of Israelite religion (ironically, it goes into Exile fragmentary but emerges whole). This is perhaps due to its inherent portability: Unlike the temple, the Torah can be moved. It continuously reveals the will of God and keeps the community bound to its god.

It does not appear that the public reading of Torah is connected in any way to the temple. This is not to say that it does not occur at the temple, but rather that it may have been ancillary to the sacrificial service. The earliest evidence we have for some sort of public reading of Torah appears in Nehemiah 8, where all the people gather in the square before the water gate and Ezra brings the law before the assembly so that they can hear it "with understanding." Ezra stands on a wooden pulpit made for this exact purpose. He opens the book and blesses God, and all the people lift up their hands and bow to the ground in worship. The Levites help the people interpret the law: They "give it sense." Nehemiah 13:1 again shows Levites reading from the "book of Moses" to the people. We see in Nehemiah many elements of contemporary Jewish worship: procession, adoration of the Torah, blessings, reading of the Torah, and explication of what the reading means.

Public reading of the Torah is something that can be done in Diaspora as well as back in Judea. It is an act that requires no specialized personnel, no specific location, and no regulated or fixed time of day, though doing so on the Sabbath and festivals would seem rather logical. Reading, listening to, and expounding Torah emerges from the Exilic period as a key mode of self-identity helping to connect scattered communities with their Israelite past. Torah thus moves beyond the priesthood after the Babylonian destruction of the first temple and exists outside the temple certainly before the Roman destruction of the second. It is surely no coincidence that the era that witnesses the movement of the priesthood beyond the confines of the temple also sees the transfer of scripture to a variety of locations as well.

The ceremony described in Nehemiah 8 and a commandment found in Deuteronomy 31:10–13 are the only passages in the Hebrew Bible that speak of public reading of Torah. A variety of Second Temple sources, however, illustrates the existence of the practice in the first centuries B.C.E and C.E.

The community at Qumran gathers together for communal Torah reading regularly. The *Community Rule* (1QS 6.7–8) states: "And the Many shall be on watch together for a third of each night of the year in order to read the book, explain the regulation, and bless together." This group reading is part of the Qumran community's daily routine. Similarly, the Zadokite fragments reinforce this scenario: "[And anyone who is not quick to under]stand, and anyone w[ho speaks weakly or staccato], [with]out separating his words to make [his voice] heard, [such men should not read in the book of] [the Torah], so that he will not lead to error in a capital matter" (4Q266 frag. 5.2). From this injunction it appears that the reader of the Torah must do so in a manner that guarantees that community members can hear and understand what the reader is saying.

Josephus also speaks of public Torah reading when he says that, "[Moses] appointed the Law to be the most excellent and necessary form of instruction . . . so that every week men should desert their other occupations and listen to the law to obtain a thorough and accurate knowledge of it" (*Apion* 2.175). Similarly in *Antiquities* 16.43 he reports, "We give every seventh day over to the study of our customs and our law for we think it necessary to occupy ourselves with [them] . . . to avoid committing sins." Josephus is thus used to hearing the Torah read on a weekly basis, probably for the purposes of study and discussion.

Neither the community depicted in the book of Nehemiah, nor that of Qumran, nor Josephus situate the Torah reading in a particular place. It is something that can and does occur anywhere. In Philo, though, we find Torah reading as something that takes place in what he calls the proseuche, literally, the "house of prayer": "[Augustus] knew therefore that they have houses of prayer and meet together in them, particularly on the sacred sabbaths when they receive as a body a training in their ancestral philosophy" (*Embassy to Gaius* 156). But in *On Dreams* 2.127, he uses the word "synagogue" to describe the place of assembly. "And you will sit in your *synagogoi* and assemble your regular assembly, and read in security your holy books expounding any obscure point and in leisurely comfort discussing at length your ancestral philosophy."

Public Torah reading is also mentioned in the New Testament. "And on the sabbath day they went into the synagogue and sat down. After the reading of the law and the prophets, the officials of the synagogue sent them a message, saying, 'Brothers, if you have any word of exhortation for the people, give it'" (Acts 13:14–15). In the Gospel of Luke (4:16–21), Jesus reads from Isaiah in the synagogue in Nazareth and then proceeds to interpret the reading. Both of these passages mention the reading of the *haftarah*, that is, the Prophets as accompanying a Torah reading. Both 2 Maccabees (2:13, 15:9) and Ben Sira (Prologue) mention the Prophets alongside the Torah as an authoritative and sacred body of texts.

Rabbinic texts are the only sources that connect Torah reading with the temple, specifically on the Day of Atonement, when the high priest reads from the Torah as part of temple liturgy (*m. Yoma* 7:1 and *Sotah* 7:7). In this latter passage, the rabbis talk about the high priest being given the Torah and reading portions of Leviticus to those present in the congregation. Though the rabbis describe this ritual in some detail, it is not clear from any of our other sources whether public reading of the Torah is part of a liturgy. Significantly, at Qumran and in the early rabbinic sources, the priest is the first to begin reading the Torah. Scholars do not know if public Torah reading and communal prayer were originally associated with one another.

Public Torah reading, therefore, is something that must have begun after the Exile and certainly before the destruction of the second temple. Though sometimes located in a house of prayer or synagogue, it is certainly not confined to these locations.

What is the purpose of this practice? It seems logical enough to assume that Judaic communities in Diaspora and back in Judea would want to consult the Torah for information on how to continue living in accordance with the laws of their covenant and as Israel. For these communities, hearing Torah read and expounded also functions as communion. It reinforces a community's distinctiveness as Israel, and it serves as an important identity marker—both for self-understanding and to distinguish the group and its history from others. Later, as we shall see, the rabbis connect the reading of Torah with the presence of God.

God in the Home and in the Marketplace

In addition to the movement of Torah into public spaces, specific Torah verses move beyond priestly purview and into the home. In Deuteronomy 6:8–9, the Israelites are instructed to bind the words of God to their hands, forehead, and the doorposts of their homes. The text itself does not clearly specify which words, but literary and archaeological evidence illustrates that a variety of Judaic groups follow this commandment rather literally. *Mezuzot*, or doorpost amulets, are mentioned in a number of sources. The *Letter of Aristeas*, a Hellenistic pseudepigraphical work that describes and defends the translation of the Septuagint, states:

> For he has marked out every time and place that we may continually remember the God who rules and preserves [us]. For in the matter of meats and drinks he bids us first of all offer part as a sacrifice and then forthwith enjoy our meal. Moreover, upon our garments he has given us a symbol of remembrance, and in like manner he has ordered us to put the divine oracles upon our gates and doors as a remembrance of him. (158–59)

Josephus implies that the employment of mezuzot was an old and well-established custom (*Ant.* 4.213). "They shall inscribe also on their doors," he says, "the greatest of the benefits which they have received from God." Philo mentions mezuzot, as does Proverbs 1–9, which seems to suggest *tefillin*,[1] or mezuzot, if interpretation is correct (3:1–3, 21–23; 6:20–22). The earliest mezuzah texts are found at Qumran (cave 8) and contain the Ten Commandments and passages from Deuteronomy (6:6–9 and 11:13–21). Each of these texts speaks of Israel's obedience to God and similarly requires the placement of these words on the doorposts. Additional evidence comes from the Aramaic Targumim. Onkelos, Jonathan Ben Uziel, and the Targum Yerushalmi (all three edited in the second century C.E., but likely composed much earlier) all translate the original commandment in Deuteronomy 6:9, "you shall write," as "you shall write and you shall affix."[2] Each of these sources attests to early traditions of affixing biblical texts to one's doorpost.[3]

Martin S. Jaffee writes that the placement of mezuzot on the passage between the home and the outside world changes the character of Judaic domestic space:

> The words of the Torah presided over a point of passage between two very different sorts of space. Beyond the door of the home lay "the world" at large, shared alike by Jew and non-Jew. It was a place of commonness, disorder and impurity. But the domestic space, even though it served the commonest of needs, could be evocative of the heavenly world from which the Torah originally came.[4]

The presence of Torah texts at the entrance of a house could transform the space into a place worthy of God's presence. As such, communication with God becomes possible in the home, just as it is in other places where the Torah is present. So too, the presence of a mezuzah on a home identifies the inhabitants as belonging to Israel.

A final identity marker that also keeps God in mind is the wearing of *tzitzit*, or fringes on the prayer shawls of Jewish men. A custom of the Israelites, it comes from the book of Numbers in the Torah, which reads:

> The Lord said to Moses: "Speak to the Israelites, and tell them to make fringes on the corners of their garments throughout their generations and to put a blue cord on the fringe at each corner. You have the fringe so that, when you see it, you will remember all the commandments of the Lord and do them, and not follow the lust of your own heart and your own eyes. So you shall remember and do all my commandments, and you shall be holy to your God." (Num 15:37–40)

Amy-Jill Levine compares tzitzit to contemporary WWJD bracelets, which remind their Christian wearers to be mindful of what Jesus would do. She also points out that the Gospels indicate that Jesus wears tzitzit: A hemorrhaging woman touches his fringes (Mark 5:27); those in the countryside touch the fringe of his cloak (Mark 6:56); and he criticizes the long fringes and tefillin of the Pharisees, suggesting that his own are short (Matt 23:5). Levine uses a modern idiom when she says Jesus wears Torah on his sleeve by wearing tzitzit.[5]

While tefillin and mezuzot are confined to private spaces, tzitzit are a public identity marker. All three, however, provide people with ways to be mindful of the commandments and service to God, not just in the temple or, possibly, in the synagogue, but in the home and the village square.

God at the Table

The presence of God can be experienced at the table as well, according to the understanding of several communities. What people eat, or do not eat, identifies one as a member of Israel, or not, and a number of Hebrew and Greek biblical texts illustrate the significance of food in creating communal identity. As early as Genesis 9, when God blesses Noah after the Flood, he also commands Noah not to consume "flesh with its life, that is, its blood" (9:4). The laws in the book of Leviticus go further, by specifying a range of animals that cannot be eaten, from camels and rock badgers to rabbits and pigs (Lev 11:3–23; see also Deut 14). The bread prepared for Passover cannot have leaven in it, while the bread for Shavuot must have leaven in it (Lev 23:4–6, 15–17).

In the Greek Old Testament, the Septuagint, we witness the deaths of seven brothers and their mother at the hands of the Seleucids: They refuse to eat pork (2 Maccabees 7). Eating together is also a rather divisive issue in the early church, when "circumcised believers" sit down to share a meal with "uncircumcised men." What can they eat? Peter explains that he eats with the uncircumcised after he has a dream and hears the spirit tell him "not to make a distinction between them and us" (Acts 11:1–18). And even though Paul reports that the Jerusalem church does not require the "uncircumcised" to be observant (Gal 2:7–10), the book of Acts tells the story differently, with James, the brother of Jesus, saying that, "I have reached the decision that we should not trouble those Gentiles who are turning to God, but we should write to them to abstain only from things polluted by idols and from fornication and from whatever has been strangled and from blood" (Acts 15:19–20). In other words, Gentiles can remain uncircumcised, but they must not eat any pagan sacrifices, and they must observe kosher food requirements and not eat anything with blood in it.

Not eating is an important identity marker as well. The Bible and other texts describe fasting, and this too sets the people of Israel apart. Third Isaiah criticizes the fasting of the Judahites, who apparently wonder why God is not noticing their fasts. He explains, "Look, you serve your own interest on your fast day, and oppress all your workers. Look, you fast only to quarrel and to fight and to strike with a wicked fist. Such fasting as you do today will not make your voice heard on high" (Isa 58:3–5). Isaiah then says that the fast that God wants is to loosen the bonds of injustice and to let the oppressed go free.

Fasting is also an issue in the New Testament, with perhaps the most famous fast that of Jesus, who spends forty days in the wilderness (Matt 4:2).

The Gospels mention the fasting of the Pharisees and John the Baptist several times (Matt 9:14, 11:18 // Luke 5:33, 7:33). Fasting also seems to be a practice of the early church, according to the book of Acts, with fasting and praying or fasting and worshipping the Lord noted (Acts 13:2–3, 14:23). An interesting post-biblical text, the *Didache*, compares the fasting of the "hypocrites" with that of the believers: "And do not keep your fasts with the hypocrites. For they fast on Monday and Thursday; but you should fast on Wednesday and Friday." The *Didache* is a type of instruction manual providing guidelines for rituals and practices for the early Christian community. Historians date the text to between 100 and 120 C.E., although the material it contains may be much older. Its comparison between "hypocrites" and "believers" indicates growing tension between followers of Jesus and others who are observing fasts.

In a culture of economic scarcity, it is no wonder that food is a consuming interest. Feasting and fasting assume supreme importance because people survive on very little food. The Bible is replete with references to food in abundance and to meager rations. The fact that biblical Israelites eat differently from their neighbors serves to set them apart. This diet is noticed by outsiders, who comment upon it and even attempt to force Judeans to eat food proscribed to them by God, as we see in the Maccabees. Plutarch (ca. 46–ca. 120 C.E.) observes the Judean abstention from pork and presents a dialogue in which one of the participants surmises that it "is that the beast enjoys a certain respect among that folk . . . I think the Jews would kill pigs if they hated them" (*Moralia* 8).

If food is an identity marker, how and when it is eaten is also part of this identity formation. The practice of eating meals together, saying special words, and giving the food sacred significance is a natural outgrowth of the concern about food. The boundary-setting nature of communal meals may at first glance seem to be an oxymoron: How can eating together set a boundary? But the limits occur in who is *not* sitting at the table. The limits define the group by indicating who is in and who is out. This might seem a bit foreign in our minds today, where in contemporary Judaism a Sabbath meal is shared in the home every Friday night, Saturday noon, and Saturday afternoon, and where in modern Christianity participants are welcome to the communion table.

When we look at the history of communal meals, we can see that they do indeed begin as a way to reinforce the beliefs and commitments of those gathered together. The Christian communion begins as a real dinner, with people sitting down and sharing bread. Do they gather in sadness, remembering their teacher Jesus? Or do they sit down together in joyful expectation of his imminent return? Or do they simply eat together as a way to preserve their identity as a group? When is the Sabbath meal instituted in Judaism? Does it exist in the first century C.E.? Or does it emerge much later, a response to the Christian appropriation of sacrificial language? These are questions on which scholars disagree, and to which current communities of interpretation—namely practicing Jews and Christians—would provide different answers.

Table Fellowship

Table fellowship does not begin with Israelites or first-century Judaic groups. In the wider Hellenistic world, the symposium brings people together for dinner and discussion. There is ample evidence—we have only to look at Plato—for the practice of "eating with a purpose" in Greek and Roman society, although there is plenty of evidence of debauched dinner parties as well. Civic associations' gathering for ritual meals is an important activity in the Greco-Roman world. Some texts indicate a definite hierarchy in the seating arrangement, with one's superiors sitting above and one's inferiors sitting below. We see a similar hierarchical arrangement at Qumran, and a recognition—and rejection—of the hierarchical seating arrangement in the Gospels, when Jesus admonishes his followers not to take the place of honor (Luke 14:7–14). There are also special rules of etiquette to be observed regarding eating, drinking, comportment, and even attire. What seems very clear is that the formal meal always involves friendship and hospitality, even if one's family members are absent from the table, as women and children are frequently excluded from symposia gatherings.

The communal meal among Judaic groups, however, has what today we would call a religious as well as social or cultural purpose. We can begin to get some understanding of its significance, and of the importance of eating together, by first examining the group at Qumran. If we study the text of the *Community Rule,* we find a number of descriptions of a special, sacral meal that seems to be different from ordinary times of eating. Some have speculated that this meal replicates the way priests at the Jerusalem temple eat the "bread of the Presence," that is, the special bread offered to God (Lev 6:16). Purification requirements are also specified for this meal, and instructions state how purification should be undertaken, what prayers should be given, and how people should be seated. Even a type of order of service is evident (1QS 6.4–5, 2.19–22, 6.13–23; blessings: 1QS 6.4–5, 1QSa 2.11–22). For example, the *Rule* advises, "And when they prepare the table to dine or the new wine for drinking, the priest shall stretch out his hand as the first to bless the first fruits of the bread and the new wine" (1QS 6.4–6). The bread is blessed first, then the wine. This is an important distinction, as we shall see.

If we take Josephus' description of the Essene meal to be the practice of those living at Qumran (a very big "if," given scholarly consensus about what was happening at Qumran), we find the same order of service. Individuals purify themselves, they seat themselves in silence, and "the baker serves the loaves in order, and the cook sets before each one plate with a single course." A priest gives a blessing before they eat, and then gives another prayer at the end (*War* 2:5, 8).

Philo observes a similar practice in *The Contemplative Life*, in which he discusses the Therapeutae, a group that at first glance appears similar to the Essenes. He says that on the seventh day all the members of the group come together, looking on it as a day "sacred and festal in the highest degree." They take a complete rest, and "they eat nothing costly, only common bread with salt for a relish flavoured further by the daintier hyssop, and their drink is spring water." On other occasions, when they actually eat meat, they pray that the entertainment may be acceptable to God. Women take part in the feast, "most of them aged virgins, who have kept their chastity not under compulsion, like some of the Greek priestesses, but of their own free will in their ardent yearning for wisdom." After the feast, the group celebrates all night, singing hymns to God, dancing and praying.[6]

Taken together, these practices all combine ritual, prayer, and communion with the God of Israel. The involvement of priests and the special role they appear to have in the recitation of blessings is significant. We note in chapter 4 that the one significant difference between the priesthood as it appears to have functioned at the Jerusalem temple and the priesthood at Qumran is that the Qumran priests do not officiate at or make sacrificial offerings. As a result, they do not receive their share of offerings as their counterparts at the temple do. After all, an important component of Israelite and Judaic sacrifice is the consumption of specific portions of the offerings by the priests and the people making the offering. There is, then, even in the Torah, an important connection between sacrifice (God's consumption of food) and eating (human consumption). The Torah precepts concerning food—restricting one's consumption to only those foods that are technically "clean," tithed, dedicated to priests, and correctly slaughtered—apply to God's food as much as they apply to the foods an Israelite consumes. The Israelite priesthood, as reflected in the Torah, mediates this relationship by acting, as one scholar puts it, as "surrogate stomachs" for

God, "consuming the bounty of the earth on the altar fires so as to send its essence back up to the Creator as a 'pleasing fragrance' [*reach nikhoakh*]."[7]

At Qumran, this metaphor is extended to the entire community. The priests bless the food and the wine, consecrating the food so that it is fit for consumption as though it were being offered to God. In this sense the rituals of the table parallel, or even replicate, the sacrificial system in Jerusalem. At Qumran a priest needs to be present at meals: "In every place where there are ten men of the Community council, there should not be missing amongst them a priest" (1QS 6.3-4). Similarly, only fully initiated members of the group can take part in the communal meals. Sinners and newer initiates are excluded.

When we consider the Pharisees and their practices, the evidence is not nearly as clear. Although the Mishna contains 229 legal decisions coming from the houses of Shammai and Hillel about the ritual state of food—ranging from the state of cleanliness of people to agricultural rules concerning proper growing and tithing to implements for preparation—nowhere in these traditions do we find references to Pharisaic ceremonial meals or table fellowship. There are several references to the meetings of *havurot*, or fellowship groups, but it is not clear how these meetings were conducted or whether any kind of communal meal was involved.

When we get to New Testament accounts of the early Christian practice of communal meals—we won't call it communion yet because that implies the ritualized service that takes several centuries to develop—we find a similar ritual: The bread is blessed first, and then the cup, which may or may not be wine. In Paul's account, which he gives to remind the Corinthian church that they should share in the meal together, he says Jesus gave thanks for the bread before he broke it, and then, after the supper, he took the "cup" and blessed that as well (1 Cor 11:23–26). (We will examine the language of "body" and "blood" below.) In Mark's gospel, Jesus blesses a loaf of bread and gives it to the disciples while they are eating, and then seems to give the cup, after giving thanks, of course, immediately following (Mark 14:22–25). Mark adds that they sing a hymn before they go to the Mount of Olives. Matthew follows Mark closely (Matt 26:26–30). John's gospel does not have what are called the "words of institution" that appear in the Synoptic Gospels.

In the Gospel of Luke, the order of prayers is reversed. Jesus first takes a cup and gives thanks, and then shares it with the disciples; afterward he takes a loaf of bread and blesses it and gives it to the disciples. But then, after supper, he takes another cup and gives it to them (Luke 22:14–20). Some of the oldest texts lack the second blessing over the cup. In other words, the original of Luke probably had the reversed order, and some conscientious scribes inserted the second blessing later on to make Luke conform to Mark and Matthew. We do find a further example of blessing the cup before the bread, however, in the *Didache*, which spells out what to say for the Eucharist, saying "But concerning the Eucharist, after this fashion give thanks," and specifies the prayer to be said over the cup and then the prayer to be said over the bread.

If we were to be telling this history in the traditional way, we might assume that Luke and the Didache are following the Kiddush, the normal Jewish blessings said over feasts. In the Kiddush, the bread is kept covered while a prayer of thanksgiving is said over the wine. Then the bread is uncovered and another blessing is given. Nineteenth- and twentieth-century research on liturgy tended to assume that Christianity developed its liturgies from pre-existing Jewish ones or from a deliberate rejection of pre-existing traditions—as we saw above in the example on fasting from the *Didache*. Thus scholars assumed that the communion liturgy drew upon, and transformed, the Sabbath blessing. Today many liturgical historians would agree with Andrew McGowan, however, and say that it is probably best to think of traditions about meals as developing side-by-side, rather than sequentially, or before (or above) the other.[8]

The point we are trying to make here is that a foundational identity marker for a number of different groups exists in their practice of eating together. The book of Acts and the letters of Paul describe actual meals that are shared. Acts simply depicts the early community as eating meals together (Acts 2:42, 46; 20:7, 11). Post-biblical Christian literature also mentions "agapé" meals, or "love feasts," in which people share food. Writing in the early third century, Tertullian describes an agapé meal, in which the participants eat reclining, as was the custom at the time. They eat as much "as satisfies the craving of hunger; as much is drunk as befits the chaste" (*Apol.* 39). The meal begins and ends with a prayer, and after everyone has eaten and washed their hands, they stand and sing a hymn to God. A third-century sarcophagus depicts Christians engaging in a rowdy funeral banquet, a reminder that the catacombs were places Christians actually met to eat memorial meals in. Paul F. Bradshaw writes that there is no clear evidence of "institution narratives" (the body-and-blood language) used "until the fourth century, and then it has the marks of an innovation rather than a well-established custom."[9]

The Pharisees, in the meager sources we have about them, also seem to be concerned with certain activities surrounding food and meals, though there is little evidence to suggest that they have communal meals. We have already noted that the Pharisees are concerned with eating properly tithed food in a state of ritual purity. They extend the purity laws beyond the temple precinct. While temple priests are required, according to Leviticus, to be in a state of ritual purity in order to perform sacrifices and to consume food at the temple, the Pharisees seem to believe that these requirements should be followed outside the temple, in the home, and at every meal. As we have noted already, Pharisees behave a lot like priests. They are concerned with following priestly rites of purity in places that fall outside of traditional priestly purview. Eating food at one's own table, then, is no different than consuming a ritually clean, tithed, and slaughtered offering to God. If priests are God's "surrogate stomachs" in the temple, the Pharisees are as well, but outside the temple, in their homes, and anywhere else that food is consumed.

In sum, we find that a number of first-century groups do in fact eat together in ways that set out social boundaries and values. We can see that particular rituals—from simple rules of etiquette such as not belching at the table to reciting specific prayers—are observed. Charting the process by which these meals are eventually transformed into sacraments (for Christians) or religious obligations (for Jews) is a difficult task.

The Redefinition of Sacrifice

Traditionally, most studies and textbooks make a leap from temple sacrifices to Jewish prayer and Christian communion via the destruction of the second temple. Without a temple, but with the need for sacrifices (or communication with God) remaining, sacrifice is reinterpreted, or so the story goes.

Jews today would probably say that during the Babylonian Exile a synagogue system develops in the absence of the temple. The synagogue provides a sense of community for the Judahites displaced by deportation. On the Sabbath and other holy days, the deportees can get together for religious observances. Upon their return to Judea, according to the traditional story, they bring with them the concept of the synagogue. This institution coexists with the rebuilt temple and apparently serves as a worship center as well as the location for communal study and prayer. Along with a separate synagogue, the Pharisaic traditions of the elders provide the foundation for a new system once the second temple is destroyed. These two institutions—synagogues and traditions of the elders—provide for the continuation of sacrifice with a new understanding. As a result, rabbinic Judaism smoothly replaces sacrifice with prayer and transfers the services and rituals in the temple to the home and the synagogue, especially on the Sabbath. As one Jewish faculty member explained to us, when the temple is destroyed, "the altar moves from the temple into the home and becomes the table."

Christians today obviously tell a different story. They would say that Jesus challenges a corrupt temple system during his lifetime. Turning to Paul, they would say that Jesus' death abolishes the sacrificial system entirely. The New Testament reports that Jesus reads scripture in the synagogue and attends synagogue regularly on the Sabbath. But the synagogue is also corrupt, apparently degraded by hypocritical Pharisees who pray long and loud in public but who neglect the poor. Jesus dies a sacrificial death for our sins, according to Paul; later interpreters in the book of Hebrews go further and say that Jesus is both the high priest *and* the sacrifice, thus ending all further need for sacrifices since there will never be another priest or offering as unblemished as he is. Christians today celebrate communion by eating bread and drinking wine or juice, which are sacramentally Jesus' body and blood.

The process by which new understandings of sacrifice emerge, as readers will recognize by now, is not only vastly more complicated, but also quite a bit different from the way the respective faiths tell their stories and from the way scholars have traditionally described changing liturgies. For one thing, as we have noted, the sacrificial system does not abruptly end when the temple is destroyed. Similarly, there are groups both inside and outside of Jerusalem who either understand, or actually practice, sacrifice in a variety of ways even before 70 C.E. For another thing, there is little evidence outside the New Testament to indicate what exactly occurs in the synagogues. Many researchers today would challenge the notion that synagogues originally serve as houses of worship, although prayer and Torah study seem to take place there. Moreover, prior to 70 C.E. a number of first-century Judaic groups say prayers that are either the same, or are remarkably similar in language and structure. Clearly the Psalms are used—and some are even written—as types of prayers or are compiled into a hymn book. Alternatives to sacrifice, then, exist long before the late first century as the means by which to get close to God, if we remember the original meaning and purpose of sacrifices.

A number of scholars would argue that there is a great deal of interchange between the groups claiming to be Israel, especially regarding observance of festivals such as Passover and the practice of eating some sort of commemorative or communal meal together. Far from there being an orderly progression of Jews supplying Christians with their prayers and practices, it appears that there is dialogue between various communities, both friendly as well as polemical, which serves as a two-way street for mutual transformation. Perhaps most controversial of all current claims is that of Israel Yuval, who persuasively argues that the current Jewish Passover *Haggadah*, or narrative, arose in response to the Christian Haggadah provided in Melito of Sardis' Homily on the Passover in the late second century. This is just one example of many which seem to suggest that the development of liturgies and the reinterpretation of sacrifice is much more complicated than we might think.[10]

As we have stated, when the priesthood moves outside of the temple, its tasks do as well: Two of these are the reading and interpretation of Torah and the practice of sacrifice. So far we have shown that people do indeed read Torah outside of the temple and actually bring Torah into their homes via the mezuzot. We have also indicated that people are communicating with God (through prayer, blessings, hymns, and dance) in the sharing of bread. Although we see evidence of a "substitution" occurring prior to 70 C.E., it is clear that the definitive move from altar sacrifices to other types of sacrifices happens with the destruction of the temple. The route from one to the other is neither clear nor straight.

From Sacrifice to Prayer?

Prayer in the Hebrew Bible, if we have to generalize, for the most part consists of outbursts made by individuals, primarily in times of extreme crisis or extreme joy. Prayer does not appear to be offered at set points in the course of daily life, nor are there communal occasions specified at set times of the day or week. The prayers that are evidenced in the texts have no particular fixed structure. They are not said at any specific times or mandated occasions. Rather, they are innovative, spontaneous acts of human emotion, and no single place is specified as the locus of prayer. This might reflect the fact that until the construction of the temple in Jerusalem, there is no single place to conduct sacrifices either. The tabernacle is portable. Moreover, there are a number of significant "high places" mentioned in Torah, such as Peniel and Bethel, where some significant event occurs, and thus sacrifices are made on those spots.

The classic example of individual biblical payer in Tanakh is Hannah's prayer in 1 Samuel 2:1–10. But there are numerous other examples too. The sheer variety and spontaneity suggests a universal need to converse with God, which we see in the book of Psalms and the book of Daniel. Even before the incidents that modern readers would recognize as prayer, we find people "talking" to God, such as Adam conversing with God in the garden or Abraham and Sarah receiving instructions from God.

We see more textual evidence for prayers playing a liturgical role as we move closer to the Common Era. Daniel K. Falk has examined the prayers said at Qumran in great detail, differentiating between those said on a daily basis, those given on the Sabbath, and special festival prayers.[11] A comprehensive daily liturgy is found in the *Community Rule* (1QS 10), and the practice of praying appears to be public and communal, rather than individual and private. Important too is the fact that prayer, as it is depicted at Qumran, is not directly associated with the performance of sacrificial offerings. The *Community Rule* says: "[It will be] the most holy dwelling for Aaron with eternal knowledge of the covenant of justice and in order to offer a pleasant aroma; and it will be a house of perfection and truth in Israel in order to establish [. . .] a covenant in compliance with the everlasting decrees" (1QS 8.8–10, ellipses in original). The purity of the community serves as atonement for the land, and the group itself is the "most holy dwelling for Aaron."

It is not altogether clear whether prayer accompanies sacrifices at the temple. The second book of the Maccabees provides a prayer which the High Priest Jonathan gives over a temple sacrifice (2 Macc 1:24–31), but this is a relatively late document. Thus we do not know if the rich liturgical and prayer life of those living at Qumran—as indicated by the wealth of texts—suggests a departure from traditional practice or not.

We also can identify some important examples of Jesus praying and of Paul and others advising prayer. John 17 depicts Jesus making a long petition to God on behalf of his disciples. Matthew and Luke present the "Lord's Prayer" (Matt 6:9–13 // Luke 11:2–4), and Luke shows Jesus in frequent prayer (3:21, 6:12, 9:28, 11:1, 22:45). In Acts, Luke continues to present prayer as a part of the practice of the early church, as in Acts 1:14 where the disciples "were constantly devoting themselves to prayer, together with certain women, including Mary the mother of Jesus, as well as his brothers." The prayers in Acts often coincide with temple sacrifices: "One day Peter and John were going up to the temple at the hour of prayer, [at the ninth hour]" (Acts 3:1). Elsewhere Acts notes that "Cornelius replied, 'Four days ago at this very hour, [at the ninth hour], I was praying in my house.'" Cornelius sees a man in dazzling clothes who tells him, "Cornelius, your prayer has been heard and your alms have been remembered before God" (Acts 10:30–31). In one instance when Paul prays in the temple in Jerusalem, he falls into a trance and receives a vision of Jesus (Acts 22:17–21). There are several significant points in these passages. First, two disciples are going to the temple at the hour of prayer. Second, Cornelius keeps the ninth hour of prayer in his house. It seems that the hours and practice of temple prayer (if such occurred) have been brought into the home.

In the post-Pauline New Testament literature there are additional references to prayer. The letter of James advises prayer for the suffering and the sick, since "the prayer of the righteous is powerful and effective" (James 5:16). The letter notes the example of Elijah, who first prays that it might not rain, and then prays that it will rain: Both prayers are equally effective. The book of Revelation mentions the prayers of the saints (Rev 5:8, 8:3–4) as especially efficacious. 1 Peter mentions prayer several times (3:7, 4:7) and even cites Psalm 34:15, saying "The eyes of the Lord are on the righteous, and his ears are open to their prayer" (1 Pet 3:12).

Post-biblical Christian literature also indicates the importance of prayer in the life of the individual, and more significantly, the fact that prayer is prescribed for set times during the day, just as is noted in Acts. The *Didache* provides Matthew's version of the Lord's Prayer, with an addition at the end spoken in churches today: "For the power and the glory are yours forever." More importantly, however, the *Didache* says to "pray like this three times a day" (*Did.* 8:3). It also provides prayers to be said before, during, and after the thanksgiving meal, that is, communion.

Post-biblical Jewish literature reports in the Mishna a dispute between the rabbinic houses of Hillel and Shammai over how and when one should say the Shema (*m. Ber* 1), which is to be recited morning and night. Whether saying this prayer is a rabbinic innovation or simply a clarification of earlier practice is not at all clear. Indeed there is no consensus among scholars who study the origins of Jewish liturgy as to how and when the communal prayer service comes about. By the time the sages meet after the destruction of the second temple, they appear to argue for the *obligatory* nature of certain prayers.[12] Whether the obligation itself is novel or whether the entire liturgical practice is a later rabbinic innovation is an ongoing subject of scholarly debate.

The rabbis in the Gemara directly compare daily recitation of the *amidah* prayer (The Eighteen Benedictions) to the daily sacrifices offered while the temple was standing and explicitly state that prayer corresponds to sacrifice. Other rabbinic texts refer to prayer as the "sacrifice of the heart" (*y. Ber* 4:1, 7a; *b. Taanit* 2a). They also delineate that one should always face the direction of the holy of holies in the temple, if not physically, then at least in one's heart (*m. Ber* 4:5–6). In the Gemara there is little question that prayer is discussed as a suitable replacement of sacrifice such that when one prays correctly—according to rabbinic law—one sufficiently fulfills the biblical requirement of sacrifice (see *b. Ber* 14b–15a). The rabbis also pray for the reinstitution of sacrifice, which encompasses the rebuilding of the temple in Jerusalem. All of these texts are relatively late for our purposes, and it remains nearly impossible to discern to what extent rabbinic writings couch innovation in terms of accepted practice or vice versa.

Some scholars believe that by the end of the first century, prayer has become a more organized form of communication, with specific language and times mandated for the communication. The variety of liturgical texts from Qumran, as well as the times set aside for prayer in the *Didache*, suggests that several groups are saying prayer communally, in some sort of organized, and requisite, fashion. The Lord's Prayer given by Jesus also indicates a specific prayer is to be said by his followers. A number of groups seem to have been following, or developing, their own liturgies and prayers—from priests to Pharisees to those at Qumran or those in other Judaic groups.

These examples from the Hebrew Bible, Jewish Greek scriptures, Qumran, the New Testament, rabbinic literature, and post-biblical literature all show that prayer is already a part of the religious life of those belonging to the house of Israel. It is seen as a substitution for temple services even before 70 C.E. Eventually Jewish prayer becomes obligatory, with the times for prayer specified by the rabbis.

From Eating and Praying to Sacrifice: The Jewish View

With the destruction of the temple, the practices of eating together and praying together assume greater significance. What begins as a way to be priests outside of the temple—by maintaining purity and eating the appropriate foods in the appropriate manner—becomes a way to maintain sacrifice in light of a radically different environment. If the Pharisees consume meals at home as priests and the community at Qumran blesses the food as priests, the rabbinic material appears to take this one step further. Consider the following passage:

> "This is the torah of the burnt offering, the grain offering, the guilt offering . . ." Whoever engages in the study of the Torah portion on burnt offering is as if he sacrificed a burnt offering, the portion on grain offering as if he sacrificed grain offering, the portion on guilt offering as if he sacrificed guilt offering. (b. Men 110)

Similarly, in m. Abot 3:3:

> R. Simeon said, "Three who have eaten at one table and have not said words of Torah over it, it is as if they have eaten from sacrifices of the dead . . . But if the three have eaten at one table and have spoken over it words of Torah, it is as if they have eaten from the table of God, as it is written 'And he told me: This is the table that stands before the Lord.'" (Ezek 41:22)

The community at Qumran and the Pharisees conduct their daily meals as though they in some way parallel or replicate temple sacrifice—even before the destruction of the temple. But it is the rabbis who transform the act of sacrifice and of eating by stressing teaching, studying, and interpreting *about* biblical sacrifice, albeit at a meal, in place of the actual performance of the sacrifice.

> As it is written, "An altar of wood, three cubits high . . . He said to me, 'This is the table which is before the Lord.'" The verse begins with "altar" and ends with "table." R. Johanan and R. Eleazar both said, As long as the Temple stood the altar atoned for Israel, but now a man's table atones for him. (Berakhot 55a; Hagigah 27a; Menahot 97a)

As a result, the teachers or explicators of the laws of sacrifice replace or even supersede the priests who used to perform the rituals themselves. The Pharisees behave like priests outside of the temple in the absence of a hereditary claim. The rabbis redefine priestly qualifications altogether by stressing the ability to interpret oral and written Torah over the capacity to perform the ritual or lay claim to the hereditary claim. The ritual of the altar finds its way to the table. This occurs before the destruction of the temple at Qumran, and possibly with the Pharisees, and continues with great significance and intensity amongst the rabbis and the early Jesus Movement.

From Eating and Praying to Sacrifice: The Christian View

Most Christians would say that the sacrificial understanding of communion begins with Jesus and the last supper with the disciples. This may be true, although not necessarily in the way people think. To accept this view, we would first have to accept the historicity—that is, the historical nature of Jesus' sayings—of the "words of institution" we find in the Synoptic Gospels. This might be a case of reading history backward: What if the notion of sacrifice comes long after Jesus' death, and even long after the Gospels are written? Given the fact that Jesus has a reputation for being a "glutton and a drunkard" and that the Gospels show him eating in a variety of settings, and given the reality of communal eating in the early church, the idea of eating as a religious act begins to seem foreign.

Even if we accept the historicity of the account, we should think of it in the context of Jesus' life. He appears to be in conflict with religious authorities, and despite an ambiguous relationship with the temple regarding Torah observance, he seems to be claiming direct access to God via himself. What might Jesus be saying, then, when he equates bread and wine with body and blood? Bruce Chilton makes a compelling case for understanding the words of institution as follows: Jesus cannot mean that the bread and wine are his personal body and blood, but rather that bread and wine are alternatives to the flesh and blood sacrifices offered at the temple.[13] "In essence, Jesus made his meals into a rival altar," says Chilton. Thus, Jesus explicitly substitutes bread and wine for temple sacrifice—but not in a way that requires a sacrificial victim. Indeed, he rejects flesh and blood, which may make the claim that Jesus was a vegetarian plausible.

There are other ways to interpret the body-and-blood language, however, especially when we consider the Hellenistic context in which Paul is teaching and preaching a decade or so after Jesus' death. Paul needs to present the Eucharistic meals (rather than rituals) the early church is sharing in as an alternative to pagan sacrifices. His first letter to the Corinthian church clearly shows his concern about pagan practices, or rather, the concerns that the Corinthians have about them. Meat is routinely sacrificed to idols, and libations of wine are commonplace. Thus, flesh and wine strongly connote paganism. This may be one reason Paul and the Gospels use the "cup" language, rather than saying "wine." And it may be that the use of bread as a sacrifice, rather than flesh, avoids memories of pagan sacrifices. Paul uses body-and-blood language throughout the letter to emphasize the oneness of those at Corinth: with each other, with Jesus, with demons and prostitutes, with whomever or whatever one is united. A number of scholars believe he learns the tradition recited in 1 Corinthians 11 from Peter, for Paul does not reflect a Paschal (sacrificial) theology and actually attempts to reject it.

The New Testament book of Hebrews, however, unambiguously links Jesus' death with tabernacle sacrifices. Written at the end of the first century, Hebrews identifies Jesus as the high priest "who is seated at the right hand of the throne of the Majesty in the heavens, a minister in the sanctuary and true tent [tabernacle] that the Lord, and not any mortal, has set up" (Heb 8:1–2). The early sanctuary is but a pale comparison to the heavenly original, according to Hebrews. Moreover, "when Christ came as a high priest of the good things that have come, then through the greater and perfect tent [tabernacle] (not made with hands, that is, not of this creation), he entered once for all into the Holy Place, not with the blood of goats and calves, but with his own blood, thus obtaining eternal redemption" (Heb 9:11–12). The blood of Jesus provides more effective purification than that of goats, bulls, or heifers. Further, this blood inaugurates a new covenant: Just as the covenant with Moses was sealed with blood, the new covenant is sealed with Jesus' blood.

The Synoptic Gospels link Jesus' last meal to a Passover Seder, while John's Gospel suggests that Jesus *is* the Passover sacrifice, since he is executed on the day before Passover begins. The Passover Homily by Melito of Sardis, noted above, tends to cement the sacrificial interpretation of the Eucharist by comparing the story of Jesus with the story of Moses and the Exodus. Later on, the figurative interpretation of the body-and-blood language is replaced by fourth-century theologians' literal understanding. The Christian church in the West adopts the doctrine of transubstantiation in the early thirteenth century, and it is not until the sixteenth century that Protestant Christians claim a spiritual sense of the words of institution.

Conclusions

We have argued in this chapter that the sacrificial interpretation of table fellowship and the use of prayer as the means for communicating with God have their roots in the movement of the priesthood outside the confines of the temple. Various groups see themselves as being priests and, as a result, bring along with them a number of priestly practices, most specifically the public reading of Torah, the custom of prayer, and communal eating in a state of holiness or intentionality. Prayer and communion seem to become formalized, if not strictly ritualized, even before the destruction of the second temple. Moreover, a sacrificial interpretation attaches to them prior to 70 C.E., although this is developed more fully in the second century C.E.

A final note is the observation that as these groups move outside the temple—or more precisely, as they move the temple and its apparatus beyond the walls of Jerusalem—they also move the presence of God to new locations. Again, this movement predates the loss of the temple. And, again, the similarities among various groups are striking, as we see in the next chapter.

Suggestions for Further Reading

Paul F. Bradshaw. *The Search for the Origins of Christian Worship: Sources and Methods for the Study of Early Liturgy*, 2d. ed. New York: Oxford University Press, 2002.

Jonathan Brumberg-Kraus. "Meals as Midrash: A Survey of Ancient Meals in Jewish Studies Scholarship." In Leonard J. Greenspoon, Ronald A. Simkins, and Gerald Shapiro, eds. *Food and Judaism*, Vol. 15 of *Studies in Jewish Civilization*. Omaha: Creighton University Press, 2005, 297–318.

James H. Charlesworth, with Mark Harding and Mark Kiley, eds. *The Lord's Prayer and Other Prayer Texts from the Greco-Roman Era*. Valley Forge, Penn.: Trinity Press International, 1994.

Daniel K. Falk. *Daily, Sabbath, and Festival Prayers in the Dead Sea Scrolls*. Boston: Brill, 1998.

Gillian Feeley-Harnick. *The Lord's Table: The Meaning of Food in Early Judaism and Christianity*. Washington, D.C.: Smithsonian Institution Press, 1994.

Steven Fine, ed. *Jews, Christians, and Polytheists in the Ancient Synagogue: Cultural Interaction during the Greco-Roman Period*. London and New York: Routledge, 1999. Especially Lawrence Schiffman, "The Early History of Public Reading of the Torah," 44–56.

Ruth Langer. *To Worship God Properly: Tensions between Liturgical Custom and Halakhah in Judaism*. Cincinnati: Hebrew Union College Press, 1998.

Lee I. Levine. *The Ancient Synagogue: The First Thousand Years*, 2d. ed. New Haven: Yale University Press, 2005.

Andrew McGowan, "Food, Ritual and Power." In Virginia Burrus, ed. *Late Ancient Christianity*, Vol. 2 of *A People's History of Christianity*. Minneapolis: Fortress, 2005.

Heather A. McKay. *Sabbath and Synagogue: The Question of Sabbath Worship in Ancient Judaism*. Leiden: Brill, 1994.

Jacob Neusner. *From Politics to Piety: The Emergence of Pharisaic Judaism*. Englewood Cliffs, N.J.: Prentice-Hall, 1973.

Stefan Reif. *Judaism and Hebrew Prayer: New Perspectives on Jewish Liturgical History*. Cambridge, U.K.: Cambridge University Press, 1993.

Israel Jacob Yuval. *Two Nations in Your Womb: Perceptions of Jews and Christians in Late Antiquity and the Middle Ages*. Trans. Barbara Harshav and Jonathan Chipman. Berkeley and Los Angeles: University of California Press, 2006.

Tzvee Zahavy. *Studies in Jewish Prayer*. Lanham, Md.: University Press of America, 1990.

Notes

1. Tefillin, also called phylacteries, are little boxes containing scripture that are worn around the head by Jewish males, following the commandment in Deuteronomy 6:8.

2. Ben Zion Luria, "The Development of the Mezuzah," *Dor le Dor* 5:1 (1976): 11.

3. Luria suggests that originally, biblical passages may have been carved on the lintel of the doorpost itself as evidenced in a Jewish structure uncovered in Palmyra (10).

4 Martin S. Jaffee, *Early Judaism* (Englewood Cliffs, N.J.: Prentice Hall, 1997), 202.

5. Amy-Jill Levine, "Misusing Jesus: How the Church Divorces Jesus from Judaism," *The Christian Century* 123, no. 26 (26 December 2006): 21; excerpted from her book *The Misunderstood Jew: The Church and the Scandal of the Jewish Jesus* (San Francisco: HarperSanFrancisco, 2006).

6. Philo, *The Contemplative Life*, trans. F. H. Colson (Cambridge, Mass.: Harvard University Press, 1985).

7. Jonathan Brumberg-Kraus, "Meals as Midrash: A Survey of Ancient Meals in Jewish Studies Scholarship," in Leonard J. Greenspoon, Ronald A. Simkins and Gerald Shapiro eds., *Food and Judaism*, Vol. 15 of *Studies in Jewish Civilization* (Omaha: Creighton University Press, 2005), 309.

8. Andrew McGowan, *Ascetic Eucharists: Food and Drink in Early Christian Ritual Meals* (Oxford: Clarendon Press, 1999).

9. Paul F. Bradshaw, *The Search for the Origins of Christian Worship: Sources and Methods for the Study of Early Liturgy*, 2d. ed. (New York: Oxford University Press, 2002), 62.

10. Israel Jacob Yuval, *Two Nations in Your Womb: Perceptions of Jews and Christians in Late Antiquity and the Middle Ages*, trans. Barbara Harshav and Jonathan Chipman (Berkeley and Los Angeles: University of California Press, 2006), 56–91.

11. Daniel K. Falk, *Daily, Sabbath, and Festival Prayers in the Dead Sea Scrolls* (Boston: Brill, 1998), 237.

12. The Council of Yavneh, or Jamnia, is now considered to be a hypothetical construct designed to explain inclusion of the Writings (Ketuvim) in the Hebrew canon, although it was considered historical for most of the 1900s. What is certain is that sages did indeed discuss the nature of prayer at this time and throughout the first and second centuries C.E.

13. Bruce Chilton, "Ideological Diets in a Feast of Meanings," in *Jesus in Context: Temple, Purity, and Restoration*, ed. Bruce Chilton and Craig A. Evans (New York: Brill, 1997), 59–89.

Where Is God? Divine Presence in the Absence of the Temple

T HE AUTHORS OF THE HEBREW BIBLE deal with the issue of the so-called "dwelling place" of the God of Israel in a variety of ways. The idea of locating the deity within a specific space is key to the delineation of an ongoing and productive relationship between the Israelites and their god. The "location" of God, the physical place where one can find him, becomes the center for divine-human relations. Any change in the status of this space would in turn necessitate a theological reevaluation of this relationship and of the rituals and practices associated with it.

Just as the Israelites exiled to Babylon struggle with the problem of where God dwells after the destruction of the Jerusalem temple in 587/586 B.C.E., this issue is contemplated yet again when the second temple falls to the Romans in 70 C.E. Those who had been exiled by the Babylonians are reassured by Ezekiel (10:18; 11:22, 23), who writes that God leaves the temple and is not destroyed among the ruins. The prophet sees God return to "dwell" (literally, "to tabernacle") in the temple as part of his utopian vision (Ezek 43:7).

This chapter explores a variety of explanations as to where God "goes"—that is, the dwelling place of the God of Israel—after the destruction of the Jerusalem temple in 70 C.E. The identification of the location of God leads ineluctably to the development of different orientations to God, and as a result, to the rise of Christianity and rabbinic Judaism. Consequently, Jesus comes to be viewed as the locus for encounter with the divine for early Christians, while the Torah becomes the locus for the Jewish encounter with God. In addition, however, both groups believe that God dwells within the community of believers.

The Dwelling Place of God in Biblical Israel

As we discuss in chapter 2, the God of Israel as described in Tanakh dwells in the tabernacle and in the temple. Although none of the narrative books of the Hebrew Bible provide any information as to the fate of the tabernacle after Solomon, both Psalms and Lamentations suggest it is destroyed along with the temple in 587/586 B.C.E. "They made your sanctuary go up in flames; they brought low in dishonor the dwelling place of your presence," writes the Psalmist (Ps 74:7). Lamentations goes further:

> [The Lord] has broken down his booth like a garden, he has destroyed his tabernacle; the LORD has abolished in Zion festival and sabbath, and in his fierce indignation has spurned king and priest. The LORD has scorned his altar, disowned his sanctuary; he has delivered into the hards of the enemy the walls of her palaces; a clamor was raised in the house of the Lord as on a day of festival. (Lam 2:6–7)

What happens to the presence of God, given the fate of the temple and tabernacle?

Ezekiel's elaborate vision of God's departure from the Jerusalem temple shows that God has not perished along with his "house" (10:18–22). The "presence of the Lord" (Heb., *kavod*), a brilliant radiance or glory that indicates God's immanence, moves off the threshold of the temple. God, or rather God's glory, steps above a wheeled vehicle driven by cherubs, who carry God eastward out of the city to the Mount of Olives. (Biblical cherubs, by the way, are not winged angels exchanged at Valentine's Day, but rather are supernatural creatures that usually appear as hybrid animals, such as an eagle-winged, human-faced lion. They frequently are associated with the presence of God in the Hebrew Bible.) The theological implications of this vision are far-reaching and significant. God is not destroyed by the Babylonians in the Jerusalem temple, but survives and literally abandons the city to its fate. When Ezekiel is finally shown a vision of the future rebuilt temple, he sees the return of God to "dwell" in the holy of holies, expressly corresponding to the vision of God's departure (43:2–5).

The prophets Haggai and Zechariah seem to mirror the view of their predecessor Ezekiel by reiterating that God will return and inhabit a rebuilt temple:

> Go up to the hills and bring wood and build the house so that I may take pleasure in it and be honored (Hag 1:8).
> I will return to Zion and will dwell in the midst of Jerusalem (Zech 8:3).

The Dwelling Place of God:
587/586 B.C.E. to 70 C.E.

It is apparent that at least Israel's prophets active in Exile hope that the mortal return to Judah and Jerusalem and a new temple would accelerate and assure a divine return as well. With the rebuilding of the Jerusalem temple under Darius, it would seem that Ezekiel's visions are in fact realized. Though the plan of the second temple does not follow the prophet's blueprint, the return of God to Jerusalem may have been implicit in both the

renewed presence of the temple and the resumption of sacrificial offerings. We see in the Hebrew Bible an understanding of this return as a recapitulation of the Exodus, that is, a second exodus. Perhaps the earliest occurrence is in the book of Hosea, where, in the context of future restoration, the bride Israel will be refreshed "as in the time of her youth, when she came up from the land of Egypt" (Hos 2:15). Micah, in the face of the Assyrian crisis in the late eighth century B.C.E., foresees God's future redemption of Israel as a repeat of past miracles (Mic 7:14–15). Isaiah anticipates God's setting his hand a "second time" to recover his people from Egypt and Assyria (Isa 11:11). Jeremiah looks to the return of Israel's northern tribes with the reformulation of a traditional oath formula: "The days are surely coming, says YHWH, when it shall no longer be said, 'As YHWH lives who brought the people of Israel up out of the land of Egypt,' but 'as YHWH lives who brought the people of Israel up out of the land of the north and out of all the lands where he has driven them'" (Jer 16:14–15). This image would be further explored by Second Isaiah (Isa 40–55), which refers to the Exodus as a "former thing" to which the new "second exodus" will directly correspond (Isa 43:18–19).

The ark and the tabernacle, so essential to the first exodus as elements directly tied to God's presence, are missing from this second exodus. Their absence in the second temple suggests that, though the temple is quickly rebuilt, it is not necessarily a complete replacement for the first temple. This may lead various Judaic groups to redefine the temple and sacrifice and even to make the Jerusalem temple somewhat irrelevant. This is especially true when we see that these groups appear to "move" the dwelling place of God from the temple into different environments in which God's presence may be encountered. The rest of this chapter examines these other environments.

The Jesus Movement

The Jesus Movement offers a parallel track complementary to the Jerusalem temple. The Gospels depict Jesus in conflict with temple authorities, though whether this reflects historical events or retrojects tensions felt at the time of gospel composition is not entirely clear. They mention temple priests, including the high priest Caiaphas by name. Acts shows James, the brother of Jesus, as retaining ties with the temple and depicts Paul as frequenting the temple. The Gospels show Jesus teaching and healing in the temple (Mark 12:35, 14:49 // Matt 21:14 // John 7:28), and on one occasion he directs ten lepers to the temple, and they are healed en route

(Luke 17:14). (We will discuss the incident of Jesus overturning the tables of the temple money changers below.)

John the Baptizer and Jesus directly challenge the temple's program in one important regard. John offers forgiveness of sins, an act that bypasses the sacrificial system of the temple. Baptism serves as both the sign of a changed relationship with God and also as the very means of change, as it says in Mark 1:4–5: "John the baptizer appeared in the wilderness proclaiming a baptism of repentance for the forgiveness of sins." Although temple purification rites include washing, the system also requires presentation of offerings to priests, who serve as the intermediaries between the petitioner and God. Baptism eliminates offerings and intermediaries.

Jesus goes still further. By healing people by forgiving their sins (e.g., the healing of the paralytic in Mark 2:3–12), God's presence seems to move to Jesus himself. When the scribes ask, "Who can forgive sins but God alone?" (Mark 2:7), the author of Mark is suggesting the answer, namely, that God is with and in Jesus. The divine presence comes to Jesus at his baptism, when the Gospels say that the Holy Spirit descends upon him like a dove, and a heavenly voice announces that "you are my Son," or, "this is my Son" (Mark 1:10–11 // Matt 3:16–17 // Luke 3:21–22 // John 1:32–33). The fact that the Gospel writers show the Spirit coming upon Jesus suggests the presence of God in him. This is most fully developed in John's gospel.

The Qumran Community and the Pauline Churches

Another apocalyptic group, the community at Qumran, completely abandons the Jerusalem temple before 70 C.E., identifying it as corrupt and impure and therefore lacking the divine presence. The altar has been polluted, thus rendering sacrifices unclean. Because the priests fail to observe the commandments—sleeping with menstrual women, marrying nieces, defiling the holy spirit by expressing doubts—"whoever comes close to them will not be unpunished; [the more he does it], the guiltier he shall be" (CD-A 5.14–15). The only solution is to separate the community completely from the temple and its cultus, and this is exactly what the community at Qumran does.

God will build a renewed temple in some eschatological future; in the meantime, God has deserted the temple in Jerusalem, preserving a remnant, however, and providing them with a Righteous Teacher to guide the way (CD-A 1.3–11). (A number of texts from Qumran mention a

Righteous Teacher as a founder and exemplar for the group. Some historians estimate that the teacher lives around the time of the Maccabees. One of the teacher's primary roles is to explain how biblical prophecies refer to the group.) In terms of the temple, the community itself will temporarily function in that capacity. By virtue of its adherence to the law and its holiness, the community serves as the dwelling place of God, excluding anyone and anything that fails to meet the purity requirements of Leviticus 21:16–24 and 22:17–25 (1QSa 2.3–11).

A number of texts describe the group as a "house" or "house of truth." The *Community Rule*, for example, says:

> When these things exist in Israel the Community council shall be founded on truth, to be an everlasting plantation, a holy house for Israel and the foundation of the holy of holies for Aaron, true witnesses for the judgment and chosen by the will (of God) to atone for the land and to render the wicked their retribution. This (the Community) is the tested rampart, the precious cornerstone that does not [blank] whose foundations shake or tremble from their place. [blank] (It will be) the most holy dwelling for Aaron with eternal knowledge of the covenant of justice and in order to offer a pleasant [aroma]; and it will be a house of perfection and truth in Israel in order to establish [. . .] a covenant in compliance with the everlasting decrees. (1QS 8.5–10)

Chapter 5 of the *Community Rule* reiterates the purpose of righteousness:

> to lay a foundation of truth for Israel, for the Community of the eternal covenant. They should make atonement for all who freely volunteer for holiness in Aaron and for the house of truth in Israel and for those who join them for community, lawsuit and judgment, to proclaim as guilty all those who trespass the decree. (1QS 5.5–7)

All of the members of the community act as the temple, though only a few serve as priests. By living in purity and holiness until the eschatological world to come, they perform the atonement required by God. If the temple is the house of God, and the community at Qumran is serving as the temple, then God is present in the community. We have been unable to identify any texts that explicitly state that God dwells in the community, and so we essentially are extrapolating this view from the texts that speak about the holy house that has been created within and by the community.

In contrast, the apostle Paul explicitly says that "We are the temple of the living God," referring to believers (2 Cor 6:16). Despite this apparent distinction, there are more similarities than differences between the theology of Qumran and Paul. The apostle and his churches share a similar vision of the temple and the presence of God. Like the Qumran community, Paul writes that the faithful must separate themselves from the unclean, maintaining their purity and holiness apart from the defiling world:

> Do not be mismatched with unbelievers. For what partnership is there between righteousness and lawlessness? Or what fellowship is there between light and darkness? What agreement does Christ have with Beliar? Or what does a believer share with an unbeliever? What agreement has the temple of God with idols? (2 Cor 6:14–16)

Just as Qumran differentiates between the righteous and the unrighteous, light and dark, and idols and the true temple, so too does Paul make these distinctions.

Perhaps most interesting is the shared metaphor of constructing a building, which we find in 1 Corinthians 3 where Paul states that Jesus—rather than the community—is the foundation,[1] and concludes by saying, "Do you not know that you are God's temple and that God's spirit dwells in you? If anyone destroys God's temple, God will destroy that person. For God's temple is holy, and you are that temple" (1 Cor 3:16–17). It is important to note that Paul is referring to the entire congregation, and not to single individuals, for the "you" is plural.

The primary difference between Paul and the Qumran community is that Paul seems to think that the temple, already existing within and as the community, will not be replaced by a literal temple. Those in Qumran, however, believe that they are temporarily acting as the temple, until God builds a new one. A heavenly temple will come down and replace the earthly one. The Qumran community shares the idea apparent in the Hebrew Bible, in pseudepigraphical literature (such as 1 Enoch and Jubilees, which are discovered in the caves), and in Revelation, that God is to be found in heaven. It will only be in a future, messianic era that God will reconstruct a heavenly temple.

A further difference is in both communities' understanding of sacrifice. Those in Qumran write that they:

> atone for the guilt of iniquity and for the unfaithfulness of sin, and for approval for the earth, without the flesh of burnt offerings and without the fats of sacrifice—the offering of the lips in compliance with the decree will be like the pleasant aroma of justice and the perfectness of behavior will be acceptable like a freewill offering. (1QS 9.4–5)

Since the temple in Jerusalem is no longer holy, sacrifices performed there are inadequate. The community itself atones for Jerusalem's sins through prayer and righteousness.

Paul also rejects the sacrificial system of the Jerusalem temple by interpreting Jesus' death as an atoning sacrifice for all (Rom 5:6, 8; 1 Cor 15:3; 2 Cor 5:15; 1 Thess 5:10). While the community at Qumran believes that the obedience of the community serves a sacrificial function, Paul believes that Jesus' obedience to God is sufficient. In this way, Paul gives meaning to the death of Jesus and at the same time provides Gentile audiences an explanation for abandoning their own local temple sacrifices.

The Pharisees

Yet another model for encountering God exists before 70 C.E. The theology of the Pharisees seems to be founded upon the premise that the geographical separations envisioned by the priests at the temple cannot lead all Israel to holiness. They believe it is possible, and in fact necessary, to fulfill God's command to holiness in Lev 19:2 and to present themselves as holy before God no matter where or how they live. They strive to keep many purity laws—traditionally reserved for the temple priesthood—outside of the temple precinct. Holiness is not based on genealogy, but on following the traditions that have been handed down from the elders.

While the Pharisees do not oppose the temple or its priests, their adoption of the priestly rules of purity nevertheless undermines the authority and status of the temple. While New Testament evidence is problematic given the lateness of gospel composition, nevertheless the Pharisees play a large role when it comes to halakhic interpretation, once the provenance of the priesthood.[3] Josephus also attests to the importance of the Pharisees in his works. Holiness is extended to the world outside the temple. If God is holy, they can be holy. This means that the home is sanctified in a way similar to the temple: The altar becomes the table, as we discuss in chapter 5. The immanence of God in the home and in the lives of individuals becomes a real possibility and is not solely mediated by priests in a temple.

In addition, the Pharisees observe the Sabbath by gathering together in the synagogue. The New Testament provides abundant evidence for the existence of synagogues, although it is not entirely clear what goes on in them. Certainly attendance is not limited to Pharisees. Archaeological evidence is more suggestive than conclusive regarding first-century synagogues. The four gospels indicate that Jesus teaches or heals in a synagogue on more than a dozen occasions. At the same time, Jesus is shown in frequent conflict with the Pharisees over doing some type of work on the Sabbath. What is most striking is that in Galilee, where Jesus preaches and teaches, the temple is a distant institution, while the synagogue is local, immediate, and may be thriving.

In short, well before the destruction of the temple, a number of alternate dwelling places for God—and for God's glory, presence, and name—are in existence in well-developed or nascent form. Although they may not be conceived as alternatives, and certainly in the first century C.E. the synagogue is not seen as the locus for God's presence, they nonetheless develop in new, but not entirely surprising, directions after 70 C.E.

Where Does God Dwell after 70 C.E.?
The Presence of God in Torah

One response to the destruction of the second temple comes to us in a variety of later rabbinic writings edited and revised over hundreds of years. These sources indicate that for the early rabbis—who may have viewed themselves as the immediate successors of the Pharisees—the temple and, by extension, the divine-human encounter, need not be restricted to one specific geographic location. By focusing on interpretation of Torah commandments and by pushing the observance of these commandments outside the temple precinct, the descendants of the Pharisees are able to contend that, for them, the loss of the temple does not cut one off from God. Instead, the precursors to rabbinic Judaism meet God in Torah, as mediated by the sages rather than the priesthood.

The Torah is the record of the Israelite god's encounter with the people of Israel. The Torah presents the revelation of God to Israel, in word, nature, and history. The Pharisees and their successors do not understand this message as a series of events in the distant past, but rather read Torah as an ongoing encounter with God who reveals himself to all generations—past, present, and future. It is in this context that one can understand the opening tractate of *m. Abot*:

> Moses received the Law on Sinai and delivered it to Joshua; Joshua in turn handed it down to the Elders (not to the seventy Elders of Moses' time but to the later Elders who have ruled Israel, and each of them delivered it to his successor); from the Elders it descended to the prophets (beginning with Eli and Samuel), and each of them delivered it to his successors until it reached the men of the Great Assembly. The last, named originated three maxims: "Be not hasty in judgment; Bring up many disciples; and, Erect safe guards for the Law." (*m. Abot* 1)

As Jacob Neusner puts it, "study of Torah in the chain of tradition formed by the relationship of disciple to master, from the present moment upward to Moses and God at Sinai . . . affords that direct encounter with God through his revealed words that Judaism knows as revelation."[2]

Torah study then is, in essence, encounter with God. In this way Torah becomes more than a recollection of past events, but is instead an experience and opportunity for each person to encounter God in the present. Torah in this sense replaces the tabernacle as the dwelling place of God. It also replaces the word of God that comes through living prophets, by consigning prophecy to texts and their interpretation. Consider *m. Abot* 3:6:

> Rabbi Halafta of Kfar Hananiah says, "Among ten who sit and work hard on Torah study the Presence comes to rest, as it is said, 'God stands in the congregation of God' (Ps 82:1) . . . Whence do we know even by five? As it says, 'the foundation of his group is on earth' (Amos 9:6). When do we know even by the three? As it says, 'among the divine beings he pronounces judgment' (Ps 82:1). Whence do we know even two? As it says, 'Thus those who fear the Lord have conversed one with another and the Lord has heard and listened to it' (Mal 3:16). And how do we know that this is even so of one? Since it is said 'In every place where I record my name I will come to you and I will bless you' (Exod 20:24) and it is in Torah that God has recorded his name."

A similar concept is found in *b. Ber* 6a, where God's presence is said to dwell among ten men praying together, three who deliver judgment, and two who study Torah. So too in a midrash on Lamentations it says that one who sits in private study of Torah has God sitting with him.

Torah study among a community of devoted believers, even individual Torah study, is envisioned as occasioning the presence of God. There is a correlation between the name of God—in this case, the actual letters that make up the divine name, the tetragrammaton—the presence of God as symbolically located in Torah, and the Deuteronomic idea that God dwells in the sanctuary that bears his name (Deut 12:5, 14:23–24, 16:11). The following passage from *b. Sabbat* 63a illustrates a similar attitude:

> R. Abba said in the name of R. Simeon b. Lakish: "When two scholars pay heed to each other in halachah, the Holy One, blessed be He, listens to their voice, as it is said, 'Thou that dwellest in the gardens, The companions hearken to thy voice: Cause me to hear it.' But if they do not do thus, they cause the Shechinah[4] to depart from Israel, as it is said, 'Flee, my beloved . . .'"

Just as God is present, some would even say incarnate, in Torah and in discussions of Torah, so too can the presence of God be found in prayer. There are several rabbinic texts that suggest that Jewish prayer involves envisioning the presence of God within one's mind: "The one who prays must see himself as if the Shechinah were opposite him, as it says, 'I have set the Lord always before me' (Ps 16:8)" (b. Sanh 22a). This iconic image of God brings about God's presence in a real sense.

In rabbinic literature we also encounter the concept of the presence of God as the *Shekinah*. This term derives from the verb *skn* "to dwell" and is directly related to the etymology of the *mishkan*, the tent that is the dwelling place of God for the Israelites. Indeed the Shekinah initially refers to the dwelling place or abode of God and only gradually comes to refer to God himself. Numerous rabbinic texts reflect the difficulty in comprehending what happens to the Shekinah after its dwelling place—the Jerusalem temple—is destroyed:

> It has been taught: R. Simon b. Yohai said: "Come and see how beloved are Israel in the sight of God, in that to every place to which they were exiled the Shechinah went with them. They were exiled to Egypt and the Shechinah was with them, as it says, 'Did I reveal myself unto the house of thy father when they were in Egypt.' They were exiled to Babylon, and the Shechinah was with them, as it says, 'for your sake I was sent to Babylon.' And when they will be redeemed in the future, the Shechinah will be with them, as it says, 'Then the Lord thy God will return [with] thy captivity.' It does not say here and he shall bring back but and he shall return. This teaches us that the Holy One, blessed be He, will return with them from the places of exile."
>
> Where [is the Shekinah] in Babylon? Abaye said: "In the synagogue of Huzal and in the synagogue of Shaf-weyathib in Nehardea. Do not, however, imagine that it is in both places, but it is sometimes in one and sometimes in the other." (b. Meg 29a)

The rabbinic concept of Shekinah suggests that the early rabbis do not entirely abandon the idea of tabernacle, but in fact redefine it. The portable tent containing the presence of God becomes the portable presence of God himself. The skin-covered tabernacle of the Israelites grows into the skin-made parchment of the Torah scrolls. Tent becomes text, and God assumes flesh in the logos, the word of scripture.[5] At the same time the rabbis continue to hope for the restoration of the temple and its cult.

Where Does God Dwell after 70 C.E.?
The Presence of God in Jesus

In the Gospel of John, God assumes flesh in Jesus, whose body becomes the new temple and who himself serves as the tabernacle for the presence of God. John 1:1–3 identifies Jesus as the Logos of God. Logos is usually translated as "Word," though Logos in Greek thought suggests God's rationality, reason, and wisdom. Logos also refers to God's *davar*, or word spoken at creation, and thus John 1:1–3 shows Jesus—or rather, the Logos—as present and involved in creation.

> In the beginning was the Logos, and the Logos was with God, and the Logos was God. He was in the beginning with God. All things came into being through him, and without him not one thing came into being.

Not only was the Logos *with* God, but the Logos *was* God. Since the gospel narrates a life of Jesus, the redactor begins the work by establishing a clear relationship between Jesus and God. We see an identity between Jesus, the son, and his divine Father throughout John. For example, Jesus says, "If you know me, you will know my Father also. From now on you do know him and have seen him . . . Whoever has seen me has seen the Father . . . I am in the Father and the Father is in me" (14:7, 9, 10).

John explicitly links the divine Logos to the human Jesus. "And the Logos became flesh, and lived among us, and we have seen his glory, the glory as of a father's only son, full of grace and truth" (John 1:14). The Greek word that is translated variously as "lived" (NRSV), "dwelt" (RSV), and "made his dwelling" (New American Bible) is *eskenosen*, which comes from the Greek word for tent, or tabernacle. John is saying that the Logos "tabernacled" among us. Thus, the Logos of God is present to humanity in the flesh of Jesus.

The idea of God tabernacling with us on earth, rather than in heaven, appears throughout the Septuagint. Ezekiel reports God saying: "My tabernacle shall be with them: and I will be their God, and they shall be my people" (37:27 LXX). The prophet Joel states that "So you shall know that I, the LORD your God, tabernacle in Zion, my holy mountain. And Jerusalem shall be holy, and strangers shall never again pass through it" (3:17, 4:14). A third example comes from Zechariah:

> Sing and rejoice, O daughter of Zion! For, lo, I will come, and tabernacle in your midst, says the LORD. Many nations shall join themselves to the LORD on that day, and shall be my people; and I will tabernacle in your

midst. And you shall know that the LORD of hosts has sent me to you. (2:10–11, 2:14–15 LXX)

While it is possible that John 1:14 is alluding to these prophetic works, the evangelist also seems to be referring to the actual tent of meeting, or tabernacle, of the Israelites, which is described in great detail in the book of Exodus. When John uses the word "glory" two times in reference to the Logos "tabernacling" among us, he directs us to Exodus 40:34, when "the cloud covered the tent of meeting, and the glory of the Lord filled the tabernacle." God's "glory" appears elsewhere in Exodus when, for example, God tells Moses to hide in the cleft of a rock so that when the glory passes by, Moses will see it only from the back (33:17–23). In both Exodus and John, a theophany—or appearance of God—occurs.

John's discussion of the Logos tabernacling among us has echoes in both Hebrew and Greek texts. Proverbs 1–9 describes the figure of Woman Wisdom, Hokhmah, who is present with God at creation and who calls people to her.

> Wisdom has built her house, she has hewn her seven pillars . . . "Come, eat of my bread and drink of the wine that I have mixed. Lay aside immaturity, and live, and walk in the way of understanding. (Prov 9:1, 5–6)

Proverbs links Wisdom to the Torah when chapter 7 says:

> Keep my commandments and live, keep my teachings as the apple of your eye; bind them on your fingers, write them on the tablet of your heart. Say to Wisdom, "You are my sister." (Prov 7:2–4)

The deuterocanonical book of ben Sira, which was written in Hebrew before 180 B.C.E. and then translated and circulated in Greek, claims that Sophia (Greek for *Hokhmah*) "tabernacled" in the highest heavens and had a throne "in a pillar of cloud." She was also sent to earth to "tabernacle" among the people:

> Then the Creator of all things gave me a command, and my Creator chose the place for my tabernacle. He said, "Make your tabernacle in Jacob, and in Israel receive your inheritance." Before the ages, in the beginning, he created me, and for all the ages I shall not cease to be. In the holy tabernacle I ministered before him, and so I was established in Zion. (Sir 24:8–10)

Here the tabernacle may mean the literal tent of meeting; but it also can imply the presence of God among the Israelites. The reverberations of

Proverbs and Sira in the prologue to John is rather unmistakable, with references to Hokhmah/Sophia/Logos, creation, and tabernacling.

In addition to presenting Jesus as the tabernacle for the Logos, John's gospel also depicts the body of Jesus as the new temple. While all four gospels depict Jesus overturning the tables of money changers in the temple (Mark 11:15–17 // Matt 21:12–13 // Luke 19:45–47 // John 2:15–16), John's account of this event differs from the Synoptic reports in several key ways. The Synoptics place this event at the end of the Gospels—perhaps indicating that this is the way Jesus came to the attention of temple authorities. John locates it at the beginning of Jesus' ministry, as its inauguration. The Judeans ask Jesus what he thinks he's doing causing a ruckus, and he replies:

> "Destroy this temple, and in three days I will raise it up." The Jews then said, "This temple has been under construction for forty-six years, and will you raise it up in three days?" But he was speaking of the temple of his body. After he was raised from the dead, his disciples remembered that he had said this; and they believed the scripture and the word that Jesus had spoken. (John 2:19–22)

Unlike the Synoptics, John states explicitly that the temple is Jesus' body. Jesus may be referring to his resurrected body as the new temple, since there seems to be a difference between Jesus' body as the new temple (John 2:21) and Jesus' flesh as the tabernacle for the Logos (John 1:14). The tabernacle and the temple have different valences in the first century, especially in the New Testament, where the tabernacle generally is viewed positively, while the temple generally, though not always, is viewed negatively.

It seems to us that the temple of Jesus' body in John 2 implies a fixity that the concept of tabernacle undermines. While the temple is set on Mount Zion in Jerusalem, with God enthroned in heaven and on earth, the tent of meeting, or tabernacle, suggests God's portability and mobility, God's presence wherever we are. Propp calls Jesus the revived tabernacle, "God's temporary, soft, mobile presence on Earth," and this seems to be what John is implying.[6] At the same time, the perishable tabernacle of flesh is replaced by the imperishable temple of Jesus' resurrected body, according to John's gospel, just as Moses' tabernacle is replaced by the imperishable temple of Solomon, and eventually, the dwelling of God in Torah. But both earthly temples are perishable.

Tabernacle usually seems to refer to the immanence of God, while temple seems to intimate the priestly cultus, and thus, the separation from God that is overcome by sacrifice. In this respect, the tabernacle is "superior" and the temple is "inferior," especially after its destruction. We can see this in a number of New Testament texts, including the book of Acts. There the apostle Stephen indicts his Jewish listeners for building a temple rather than a tabernacle, arguing, "the Most High does not dwell in houses made with human hands" (Acts 7:48). In Luke's gospel the disciples are rebuked by a heavenly voice when they attempt to build tabernacles for Jesus, Moses, and Elijah (Luke 9:28–36). A voice came out of a cloud, saying, "This is my Son, my Chosen; listen to him." A final critique of temple-centered religion appears in John, when Jesus tells a Samaritan woman that "the hour is coming when you will worship the Father neither on this mountain nor in Jerusalem . . . The hour is coming, and is now here, when the true worshipers will worship the Father in spirit and truth" (John 4:21, 23).

The book of Hebrews—probably written after 70 C.E., though a few date it as early as 60—completely ignores the temple and focuses instead on the heavenly tabernacle and sanctuary that Jesus entered:

> When Christ came as a high priest of the good things that have come, then through the greater and more perfect tabernacle (not made with hands, that is, not of this creation) he entered once for all into the Holy Place, not with the blood of goats and calves but with his own blood, thus obtaining eternal redemption . . . For Christ did not enter a sanctuary made by human hands, a mere copy of the true one, but he entered into heaven itself, now to appear in the presence of God on our behalf. Nor was it to offer himself again and again, as the high priest enters the Holy Place year after year with blood that is not his own . . . But as it is, he has appeared once for all at the end of the age to remove sin by the sacrifice of himself. (Heb 9:11–12, 24–25, 26)

Jesus is the new, and greater, priest *and* sacrifice in Hebrews. The path to God comes through Jesus' blood, "by the new and living way that he opened for us through the curtain (that is, through his flesh)" (10:20). In the original tabernacle, access to the holy of holies is limited to the high priest; but in Hebrews, all now have access to the divine presence. As in John's gospel, Jesus' body is glorified and serves a salvific purpose, much as the tabernacle, priest, and sacrifice do in Israelite tradition.

Some final examples of the importance of the tabernacle in the New Testament come from the Apocalypse of John. Revelation 7:15 envisions God dwelling with the redeemed, in heaven:

> Therefore they are before the throne of God and worship him day and night within his temple, and the one who is seated on the throne will [spread his tent over] them.

In this passage, tent or tabernacle indicates God's protection. But the conjunction of temple and tabernacle in the same verse suggests something more, the push-pull of transcendence (God hidden in the holy of holies and enthroned in heaven) and immanence (God present in the tent of meeting). Revelation 21:3–4 uses the word "tabernacle" in the sense of the divine presence in the tent:

> And I heard a loud voice from the throne saying, "See, the tabernacle of God is among mortals. He will tabernacle with them as their God; they will be his people[s], and God himself will be with them [alt: and be their God].

Chapter 21 describes a new heaven and a new earth and a new Jerusalem coming down out of heaven in which no temple exists, "for its temple is the Lord God Almighty and the Lamb" (21:22). The figure of the Lamb alludes to Jesus' sacrificial death and indicates the resurrected Christ. Interpretations of the new Jerusalem vary: Some say it symbolizes the church. Our point, however, is that God dwells among the people and that the temple is no longer a fixed point on earth.

When Jesus dies in John's gospel, his followers face the same problem as those who suffer the destruction of the second temple: Where does the divine presence reside once the tabernacle or temple is gone? But the evangelist anticipates this predicament (writing after the events) and sets the stage throughout the gospel for the transfer of the divine presence from Jesus to the community surrounding him. At the Feast of Tabernacles in chapter 7, for example, Jesus promises his disciples "living water":

> On the last day of the festival, the great day, while Jesus was standing there, he cried out, "Let anyone who is thirsty come to me, and let the one who believes in me drink. As the scripture has said, 'Out of the believer's heart shall flow rivers of living water.'" Now he said this about the Spirit, which believers in him were to receive; for as yet there was no Spirit, because Jesus was not yet glorified (John 7:37–39).

This passage points to Jesus' promise of "another Advocate" (14:16–17), whom God the Father will give and whom the disciples will recognize "because he [the Advocate] abides with you, and he will be in [among] you" (14:17b). Jesus' followers move God from the temple into the community of believers both before and after the destruction of the second temple. Paul writes that believers are the new temple of the Spirit. John writes that God tabernacles in Jesus during his lifetime, but then comes to Jesus' followers in the life of the Spirit. The transfer of God's indwelling presence from Jesus into the community allows for the continuing encounter with God even after the death and resurrection of Jesus. God is not absent, no matter what.

Conclusions

The destruction of the second temple forces Judaic religions to reassess the locus of God's immanence. Yet even before the temple system collapses, various groups develop creative ways to "find God" and to offer sacrifices. The idea of tabernacle—the mobile divine presence traveling with a holy people—and the idea of temple—the fixed location for encountering the divine—lead to diverse explanations and interpretations of what these concepts might mean. The existence of a temple in Jerusalem does not negate the possibility of a human temple existing as community, as is seen in Qumran and the Pauline churches. The community at Qumran seeks God within its own geographical isolation, while the Pauline churches encounter God within the "temple" of the community. In addition, the Jerusalem temple does not preclude the existence of other temples outside Judea. Furthermore, the non-existence of a Jerusalem temple does not mean that God is absent.

With the temple destroyed, we find that different Judaic groups begin to use temple and tabernacle terminology as metaphors for the presence of God. That is, they redefine temple and tabernacle, interpreting them in creative ways to meet the demands of a new historical situation and to answer the pressing question of the whereabouts of God. The rabbis, for example, find God within the Torah itself, while some of the followers of Jesus identify God in Jesus and some find God in the community of followers.

God is present to the emerging Christian community in the word (scripture) about the Word (Jesus): "If two of you agree on earth about anything you ask, it will be done for you by my Father in heaven," Matthew quotes Jesus as saying. "For where two or three are gathered in my name, I am there among them" (18:19–20). God is present to the emerging Jewish community also in the word (Torah): As Rabbi Halafta said, "The Shechinah dwells amongst ten men who sit together occupied with the Torah" and even among a single one, for as Exodus 20:24 says: "In every place where I cause my name to be mentioned I will come to you and bless you" (m. Abot 3:7).

Both communities envision a divine body, though the substance of that body differs. For Jews, the divine "body" exists in the letters and words of the Torah scrolls, which are "dressed" in the vestments of priests, and which "walk" in the midst of the congregation. The rabbi removes the Torah scroll from the ark and processes through the congregation. The Torah has a decorative covering that includes a breastplate and crown, reflecting the biblical attire for priests. For Christians the divine "body" exists in Jesus, and we see a similar pattern in the centrality of the cross (and for Catholics, the crucifix) in the architecture of the church: The cathedrals of Europe are built in the shape of a cross. In addition to the presence of God in the Logos, however, God exists in scripture for Christians, just as God exists in scripture for Jews.

Moreover, the community is the "body" of God for both groups. This body houses the divine presence. Paul states this explicitly when he tells the Corinthian church, "You are the body of Christ and individually members of it" (1 Cor 12:27). Torah study for Jews houses the presence of God, so that the "body" has its home within the community of interpreters.

In this sense, "what the Torah is for Jews, Jesus is for Christians."[7] Both provide for the encounter with God in the present, and both establish the immanence of God in the congregation of believers. The different locations for finding God affirm the basic fact of God's ongoing presence to Christians and Jews.

We see, therefore, how different interpretive communities address the presence of God in the first century, especially after the temple is destroyed. The concepts of tabernacle and temple remain. But they are redefined to meet the new historical situation.

Suggestions for Further Reading

Ronald E. Clements. *God and Temple*. Oxford: Blackwell, 1965.

Mary L. Coloe. *God Dwells with Us: Temple Symbolism in the Fourth Gospel*. Collegeville, Minn.: Liturgical Press, 2001.

J. Frey. "Temple and Rival Temple—The Cases of Elephantine, Mt. Gerizim, and Leontopolis." In *Gemeinde Ohne Temple/Community without Temple*, ed. Beate Ego, Armin Lange, and Peter Pilhofer, with Kathrin Ehlers. Tübingen: Mohr Siebeck, 1999.

B. Gärtner. *The Temple and the Community in Qumran and the New Testament: A Comparative Study in the Temple Symbolism of the Qumran Texts and the New Testament*. Cambridge: Cambridge University Press, 1965.

Michael M. Homan. *To Your Tents, O Israel! The Terminology, Function, Form, and Symbolism of Tents in the Hebrew Bible and the Ancient Near East*. Leiden: Brill, 2002.

Alan R. Kerr. *The Temple of Jesus' Body: The Temple Theme in the Gospel of John*. Sheffield: Sheffield Academic Press, 2002.

R. W. Klein. "Back to the Future: The Tabernacle in the Book of Exodus." *Interpretation* 50, no. 3 (1996): 271.

Jacob Neusner. "Judaism in a Time of Crisis: Four Responses to the Destruction of the Second Temple." *Judaism* 21, no. 3 (1972): 317.

_____. *The Incarnation of God: The Character of Divinity in Formative Judaism*. Philadelphia: Fortress, 1988.

William H. C. Propp. *Exodus 19–40: A New Translation with Introduction and Commentary*. New York: Anchor Bible, 2006.

Lawrence Schiffman. "Community without Temple: The Qumran Community's Withdrawal From the Jerusalem Temple." In *Gemeinde Ohne Temple/Community without Temple*. ed. Beate Ego, Armin Lange, and Peter Pilhofer, with Kathrin Ehlers. Tübingen: Mohr Siebeck, 1999.

Elliot Wolfson. "Iconic Visualization and the Imaginal Body of God: The Role of Intention in the Rabbinic Conception of Prayer." *Modern Theology* 12 (1996): 139–140.

Notes

1. Additional references in the New Testament also point to Jesus as the foundation (Rom 15:20, Eph 2:20).

2. Jacob Neusner, *Judaism in the Beginning of Christianity* (Philadelphia: Fortress, 1984), 16.

3. Halakah, also spelled halachah, can refer to a particular covenantal law in Judaism or it can refer to the entire Jewish legal system. In this quotation it designates a discussion about law occurring between two persons.

4. The Shekinah, also spelled Shechinah, is God's presence in the world. See below.

5. We thank William H. C. Propp for clarifying this connection.

6. William H. C. Propp. *Exodus 19–40: A New Translation with Introduction and Commentary* (New York: Anchor Bible, 2006), 391.

7. L. Kravitz, "The Torah and Jesus," *Living Pulpit* 6, no. 4 (1977): 26.

"By What Authority Do You Say This?" Interpretation, Authority, and the Claim to Israel   7

T HE QUESTION OF WHO HAS THE RIGHT to interpret scripture is debated within and across the groups who lay claim to being Israel,
the people of God. Although sacred texts are used to justify the
claim, differing hermeneutical lenses—that is, ways of reading scripture—
allow for widely divergent understandings and thus varying practices. Because all hermeneutics can, in theory, be equal, the question of authority
becomes crucial because only proper authority can dictate the correct interpretation. The authors of the Pseudepigrapha, for example, ground
their literary works on the name recognition of biblical figures such as
Adam, Enoch, Abraham, and Moses. Similarly, later New Testament literature gains status with the cachet of apostolicity, such as the pseudony-
mously written letters of James and 2 Peter and the Pastoral Epistles (1 and
2 Timothy and Titus, supposedly written by Paul). Claiming apostolicity
or antiquity provides a measure of bona fides. Revising biblical works, as
those at Qumran do, also imputes authority to the new work by relying
upon the legitimacy of the original. Another way to elevate one's own status is to attack the opposition by questioning its ethics and integrity, as the
members of the Qumran community do when they write about the im-
moral practices of the Jerusalem priesthood. Yet another claim to certainty
is to appeal to ancient traditions. In short, the authority of the interpreters
preserves the claim to legitimacy.

In our literate, eye-centered culture in which the television screen,
computer monitor, and movie theater have replaced storytelling, in-person
visits, and live performance, it is difficult for us to understand oral societies.
In order to comprehend the nature of the conflict and debate among the

various groups claiming to be Israel, it is necessary to set aside our preconceptions about the way people learn, the way they think, and the way they communicate. While texts are used to transmit cultural values and customs, they are secondary to the oral traditions. Even after something is committed to writing—an epic poem, for example, or a long story—people continue to repeat the narratives orally and to receive them aurally. We need to jump into oral culture, then, to appreciate the significance of tradition and how it not only shapes the debates about who is Israel, but also how tradition serves as the basis for redefining and rewriting the texts themselves.

Each group that stakes a claim to Israel draws its ultimate authority from God, whose will is revealed in the Torah, through an unbroken succession of interpreters. The Righteous Teacher of the Dead Sea Scrolls, for example, is divinely anointed to explicate biblical mysteries. The Jerusalem priesthood has a hereditary claim—instituted by God and revealed in the Torah—to run the temple. Although little is known about the Pharisees, it seems evident that they rely upon an authority they refer to as the "traditions of the elders." Jesus has a charismatic authority unlike the scribes and Pharisees, according to Mark 1:22, 27 (// Matt 7:29), but like the Righteous Teacher, he seems to be inspired by God. Jesus' followers claim to receive his teachings from him directly or from others who are eyewitnesses or to receive their own revelations from God, as we see in Paul's letters.

While we might think of texts as something fixed and static, unchanging and unchangeable, the reality is that they are adaptive, mobile, and dynamic, which means they can be reinterpreted to serve the present. This is especially true of the cultures of late antiquity where written texts coexist alongside oral tradition, but where speech is privileged over writing. "Writing" is dictating to a scribe, "reading" is speaking or hearing, and texts are eminently alterable. Writing merely supplements, rather than supplants, oral teachings. The oral version is generally preferred to the written because people can see and hear the one speaking. In a society in which few have access to written texts, orality is trusted, writing is distrusted. Thus, reading is not a solitary pursuit, but a collective endeavor. Even when things are written down, they continue to be performed orally in group settings. For example, a number of scholars believe the Gospel of Mark begins as an oral gospel, and, even after it is written down, it continues to be performed orally.

We need to remind ourselves that no one in the first century C.E. has a Tanakh or Bible on their nightstand. Scripture is written down on huge scrolls made of animal skins and is not readily accessible to the masses. Certainly the Qumran community has scrolls. But most people, including learned sages and their schools of disciples, would learn scripture by heart, committing it to memory.

Just as scripture itself is heard, not read, so also is a group's or community's commentary. The fact that people learn scripture by hearing it clarifies some of the inconsistencies we find in our various interpreters. It explains the inventiveness with which those at Qumran unlock the mysteries of scripture, the liberties Paul takes "quoting" scripture, the allusions the Evangelists make to scripture, and the freedom the sages adopt in interpreting scriptures. If a text is the source of authority, it is clearly the interpreter of the text who wields power by explicating the text's true meaning. In that way, texts come to symbolize authority. Appeals to scripture are not a type of fundamentalism, but rather an invocation of the heritage of Israel. In the first centuries before and after the turn of the Common Era, teachers, inspired interpreters, sages, and scribes replace the prophets in bringing the "word of God" to the people. Thus, the question of their authority to interpret becomes paramount.

When interpretation and tradition are eventually committed to writing, these new texts acquire sanctity, at least for the communities from which they emerge. In the case of Qumran, the *pesharim*, the biblical commentaries produced by the group, assume eminence within the group. For those in the Jesus Movement, the teachings of Jesus, along with traditions about his life, are compiled into gospels that eventually supersede the texts of Torah and the Prophets. The teachings of first-century sages are assembled at the end of the second century into the Mishna, which gathers all the authoritative opinions of various teachers together in one place.

Considering that a variety of different groups compile their own authoritative traditions, how do we judge whose tradition is most faithful, authentic, and reliable? How did they judge back then? Each group finds it necessary to proclaim the inherent truth of its beliefs and practices by establishing the source as being linked directly to God. Of course, the very sources upon which the groups rely for authority become subject to debate and challenges from other groups.

This chapter examines different interpretive styles and considers various claims to authority in the Second Temple period by focusing on several groups, including Qumran, the Sadducees and Pharisees, the Jesus Movement, Paul, the rabbis, and the early church. It particularly analyzes the shift from prophetic and charismatic authority in the Righteous Teacher and Jesus to the weight of scripture for the Sadducees to the influence of tradition in the Pharisees and Paul. It then takes up the parallel developments of the idea of the chain of tradition in what becomes rabbinic Judaism and the creation of the concept of apostolicity in Christianity.

Both the chain of tradition and apostolicity serve as constructs to justify the authority of specific groups by identifying them as the *true* bearers of the *correct* tradition, especially the proper interpretive tradition.

Interpretation at Qumran

We begin with the method of interpretation found in the texts from Qumran. These writings depict a righteous community living in expectation of God's ultimate redemption. Principles and precepts are not derived from scripture, but rather are revealed to the leaders and then to the community. This view legitimizes the role of the leader as an interpreter who can explain scripture for the current situation of crisis. Such a vision allows not just for the reinterpretation of ancient texts, but their actual rewriting and revision so that new texts replace ancient writings. One example of this is the *Temple Scroll* (11QT), which is essentially rewritten Torah in which God speaks directly to Moses in the first person.

Thus, the role of the Righteous Teacher is not only to carry on the work of the biblical prophets, but to surpass them in the eyes of his followers because he is able to correctly interpret the mystery of their oracles. The community at Qumran believes that its teacher is the sole source for prophetic interpretation: Not even the original biblical prophets completely grasped the full import of the words that they spoke. God communicated the mysteries to the prophets, but the interpretation is made known by God only to the divinely anointed interpreter. We see evidence for the Teacher's divinely granted authority in a number of texts:

> And God told Habakkuk to write what was going to happen to the last generation, but he did not let him know the consummation of the era and as for what he says [Hab 2:2] "so that may run the one who reads it." Its interpretation concerns the Teacher of Righteousness, to whom God has made known all the mysteries of the words of his servants the prophets. (1QpHab 7.1–5)

The Damascus Document also describes the authority given to the Righteous Teacher to interpret: "God appraised their deeds, because they sought him with an undivided heart, and raised up for them a Teacher of Righteousness, in order to direct them in the path of his heart. And he made known to the last generations what he had done for the last generation, the congregation of traitors" (CD-A 1.10–12).

Though scripture—and this includes many more books than appear in the canonical Hebrew Bible—is authoritative, it only exercises that influence insofar as it applies to the community's beliefs and practices in its adherence to the instructions of the Righteous Teacher. Texts serve as the point of departure from which new interpretations assume centrality, which in turn allows the texts to be rewritten. The interpretation's influence is tied to the authority of the individual who provides the interpretation, an individual who in turn acquires his legitimacy through the authentication of the original text. This is a logical and foolproof system of interpretation, but only if there is faith on the part of adherents.

The interpretive vision at Qumran grants status to contemporary writings that accurately describe the present or foretell the future with the assurance of victory for the community. The texts preserved at Qumran rationalize the authority of the teachings and traditions of the community. They are not mere interpretations of biblical literature, although some are in the form of commentaries, but rather they extend the period of ancient Israel into the present and serve as a competing form of religious authority—just one among many.

Interpretation in Paul

Just as the Qumran community accepts the authoritativeness of the Law, the Prophets, and Writings, so too does Paul; just as the group feels free to reinterpret ancient truths for the present time, so also does Paul; just as the Qumran texts demonstrate a belief in an imminent eschatological judgment by God, so too do Paul's letters. Both seem to exhibit dualism in their writings, with Paul seeing a sharp contrast between life in the "flesh" and life in the spirit, and the Qumran community contrasting their righteousness with that of the evildoers in Jerusalem and the Kittim, who most scholars think are the Romans. Both believe in the power of an inspired teacher, a righteous man who dies before the end of the current evil age. In fact, we see a number of literary parallels and similarities that may be attributed to common sources and currents running throughout the contemporary groups identifying themselves as Israel.

While the Qumran writers express themselves in a variety of genres— hymns, rewritten Torah, commentaries, guidelines—Paul relies on a single written form, the letter. Paul begins his career by teaching in the churches he established or visited, presenting the "good news" orally rather than in writing. It is only later that Paul relies upon texts to communicate the gospel in a peculiarly oral form of writing, that is, letters intended to be read out loud in local churches. Paul cites scripture directly in his letters, highlighting specific citations with formulas such as "it is written" (Rom 14:11, citing Isa 45:23) or "Moses says" (Rom 10:19, citing Deut 32:21). Half of all overt references to scripture appear in the letter to the Romans, with 80 percent of Paul's citations coming from either the Pentateuch, Isaiah, or the Psalms.

In addition to directly quoting scripture, however, Paul alludes to it indirectly, as in the echo of Job 13:16 (LXX) that appears in Philippians 1:19, or the reverberation of the Exodus account in Paul's claim that "a hardening has come upon part of Israel" (Rom 11:25b), which suggests that, just as God hardened the heart of Pharaoh for some larger soteriological purpose, God may also have deliberately hardened the hearts of the Jews. Paul incorporates scripture into the text quite naturally, writing for example that "not all of Abraham's children are his true descendants, but it is through Isaac that descendants shall be named for you" (Rom 9:7, alluding to Gen 21).

While the Qumran community believes that God will fulfill historical prophecies in the near future, Paul believes that the coming of Jesus Christ fulfills God's plan of drawing Gentiles into the covenant with Israel's God. The process will not be complete until the Gentiles have been evangelized and Jesus returns. Nevertheless, believers live in the new eschatological reality of "spirit" when they put aside "flesh." The clearest indication of the new reality appears in 2 Corinthians 3, with its strong statement that Christ provides the new, and surpassing, interpretive key to understanding the Law:

> Since, then, we have such a hope, we act with great boldness, not like Moses, who put a veil over his face to keep the people of Israel from gazing at the end of the glory that was being set aside. But their minds were hardened. Indeed, to this very day, when they hear the reading of the old covenant, that same veil is still there, since only in Christ is it set aside. Indeed, to this very day whenever Moses is read, a veil lies over their minds; but when one turns to the Lord, the veil is removed. (2 Cor 3:12–16)

In other words, Paul believes that one cannot understand scripture correctly unless one lives in the spirit of Christ. Those who do not have this spiritual experience are only able to read the text literally and, as a result, misread its meaning. Paul defends an interpretive strategy that employs allegory, typology, metaphor, figure, and other non-literal means. A spiritual interpretation of the text supersedes the literal reading, because Jesus' death and resurrection makes the hidden sense of scripture plain.

A Word about Philo of Alexandria

The allegorical interpretation of scripture is conceived in the union of Hellenistic and Judaic cultures, and emerges in Alexandria, Egypt, in the hands of Aristobulus (*Explanations of the Book of Moses*) and Pseudo-Aristeas (the so-called *Letter of Aristeas to Philocrates*). Judaic allegory comes to full flower in the writings of Philo (ca. 20 B.C.E.–ca. 50 C.E.), who lives during the time of both Jesus and Paul. Hellenistic Judeans seek to demonstrate the antiquity, and thus the superiority, of their traditions to those of the pagan world, and one way to do this is to interpret texts allegorically rather than literally, a technique already in use within Hellenistic culture. Just as Paul reads scripture through a Christological hermeneutic, Philo reads all of scripture through the lens of Moses' original Torah.

Abraham is just as important to Philo as Moses is, however, and the patriarch also appears in the Pseudepigrapha (Jubilees and the *Apocalypse of Abraham*) and in Paul as a major, even surpassing figure. He looms large in later Christian writings that serve to "disinherit the Jews" (in Jeffrey Siker's language) and appears throughout Philo's works, often symbolizing the soul's journey to truth. For Philo, Abraham is a paradigm of the "wise man," someone who can appeal to Gentiles as well as to Jews, and thus Philo's use of Abraham may have served an apologetic purpose. For Paul, Abraham serves as a model of obedience (though this trope occurs in Philo as well), and equally important is Abraham's relevance to Gentile converts.

A significant difference between Paul and Philo, however, is that despite his allegorical flights of fancy, Philo continues to believe that the Mosaic Law must be observed. The Alexandrian uses allegory to justify and defend the Law, not to abolish or abandon it. While there is diversity of opinion on Paul's view of the Law, especially regarding its continued practice by those born into the Israelite covenant, it seems clear that he does not want to impose certain rituals upon Gentiles. Thus, it is not allegory as such that differentiates various Judaic groups, but rather it is the interpretive lenses by which allegory is read that create the separation. When Moses is the key, interpretation leads in one direction; when Jesus is the key, it leads in another.

The Law and the Prophets in the Gospels

In the Gospel of Luke, the risen Jesus meets with some of his followers, shares a meal with them, and then proceeds to instruct them in how to read the Law, the Prophets, and the Writings:

> "These are my words that I spoke to you while I was still with you—that everything written about me in the law of Moses, the prophets, and the psalms must be fulfilled." Then he opened their minds to understand the scriptures, and he said to them, "Thus it is written, that the Messiah is to suffer and to rise from the dead on the third day, and that repentance and forgiveness of sins is to be proclaimed in his name to all nations, beginning from Jerusalem. You are witnesses of these things." (Luke 24:44–48)

While we will never know whether Jesus actually said this, we do know that his followers believe that their scriptures—the Law, the Prophets, and the Writings—do indeed speak of Jesus, from beginning to end. Moreover, they are fulfilled or completed in his life, death, and resurrection. When he begins to preach in Galilee, Jesus reads Isaiah (Isa 61:1–2), and after rolling up the scroll and sitting down, he announces to the congregation of the synagogue, "Today this scripture has been fulfilled in your hearing" (Luke 4:21). All of the Gospels describe the death of Jesus by weaving together material from the Prophets and the Psalms to show that the prophecies have come true. The New Testament—especially the Gospels—tells the story of Jesus with texts that are familiar to its audience. The prophetic writings are read in the context of Jesus' arrival, rather than in the historical context in which they are written. The authors of the Gospels and Acts accept the sacred texts of Israel as authoritative, normative, and essential for understanding Jesus as the messiah promised by God and predicted by the prophets.

Because the accepted messiah seems to be a king of the Davidic line (though there are exceptions, in Daniel, as well as in Qumran literature), New Testament writers have to defend their conviction, or that of Jesus, that he is the messiah by a number of scriptural means: Mere assertion does not suffice. Therefore we see the interpretation of Isaiah's servant songs (Isa 42:1–4, 49:1–6, 50:4–9, 52:13–53:12) as referring to Jesus (Matt 12:18–21, 8:17; Acts 32–33; 1 Pet 2:22–25). When an Ethiopian eunuch reads the words "Like a sheep he was led to the slaughter, and like a lamb silent before its shearer" and asks "About whom, may I ask you, does the prophet say this?" the apostle Philip "began to speak, and starting with this scripture, he proclaimed to him the good news about Jesus" (Acts 8:32–35). Jesus' silence before Pilate in the passion narratives also reflects this interpretation of the Servant Songs. Luke goes to great pains to get Joseph and Mary to give birth in Bethlehem, the city of David's origins, so that the prophecy of the Davidic descendant may be fulfilled (Luke 2:1–7); Matthew solves the problem by having Mary and Joseph living in Bethlehem (no birth in a stable), fleeing to Egypt to escape Herod's slaughter of baby boys (in a reversal of the Exodus account), and then moving to Nazareth, where fairly solid tradition locates Jesus.

This Christological conviction drives all reading of sacred texts, and we can assert with confidence that the authors of the Gospels and the Acts of the Apostles—as well as twenty-first-century Christians—read all previous scripture as being about Jesus the Messiah. The first half of Acts is a veritable pastiche of quotations, all intended to prove to the religious establishment in Jerusalem—and more importantly, to the Gentile reader of Acts—that the new community established by Jesus is the continuation of Israel, all according to God's plan. In his gospel, Luke has Jesus say of John the Baptist, "This is the one about whom it is written, 'See, I am sending my messenger ahead of you, who will prepare your way before you'" (Luke 7:27, citing Exod 23:20, Mal 3:1).

Just as those in Qumran believe that the scriptures are describing their community and their life situation; and as Paul believes that scriptures, rightly interpreted, describe the new situation of Gentiles in relation to Israel's God; and as Philo believes that the scriptures, understood allegorically, point to a divine wisdom that surpasses that of Hellenism; so the Gospel writers believe that the scriptures describe Jesus' life, predict his death, and foretell his resurrection.

The Written Torah and the Pharisees

While a wealth of written materials from Qumran and the New Testament indicate the various hermeneutical "glasses" that people are wearing as they write commentaries, letters, and "good news," we have a singular dearth of information regarding the Pharisees. To date, we do not have a single document written by a Pharisee that expresses what they believe or what their attitude is toward the interpretation of Torah. As a result, any information that we can piece together about this group comes from reports about them from a variety of others, each coloring its report according to its own particular agenda. None of our main sources for examining the traditions of the Pharisees—several scrolls from Qumran, selected material from the New Testament, the writings of Josephus, and information contained in the Mishna—provides an unbiased, objective historical account of the group.

The Dead Sea Scrolls never directly mention the Pharisees as a group, but scholars have traditionally connected this group with references in the scrolls to the "Expounders of Smooth Things" or "those looking for easy interpretations," mentioned in the Damascus Document, the pesharim of Isaiah and Nahum, and the Thanksgiving Scroll. The Damascus Document, for instance, refers to a group "seeking easy interpretations." They are rebuked by the authors of this text as people who preferred:

> illusions, scrutinized loopholes . . . acquitted the guilty and sentenced the just, violated the covenant, broke the precept, banded together against the life of the just man, their soul abominated all those who walk in perfection, they hunted them down with the sword and provoked the dispute of the people. (CD-A 1.18–21)

The presumably Pharisaic interpretive method goes against the revelatory method revered by the people at Qumran. There remains a considerable amount of debate concerning just what type of interpreting the Pharisees are doing that so angers the various scroll authors. Some evidence suggests that the people at Qumran associate the Pharisees with oral interpretations that conflict with their community's understanding of its authoritative texts.

The Gospels identify the Pharisees as observers of the Law who, along with the scribes, seem to act as interpreters of Torah. They provide numerous instances of the Pharisees fasting and being concerned about food and purity; they also indicate a Pharisaic concern with proper observance of the Sabbath. The Pharisees ask Jesus his opinion on various legal matters, such as whether divorce is lawful, if one can heal on the Sabbath, or whether one should pay taxes to the emperor. Matthew's gospel also identifies some Pharisees as hypocritical, observing the Torah with their actions but not their hearts (see chapter 4 for more on the Pharisees).

Based on these sources, the most we can say is that the Pharisees seem to lay claim to an ancestral tradition that guides their customs. We know virtually nothing about what is contained in this tradition, but we do know that they have specific practices regarding Sabbath observance, hand washing, festivals, dietary concerns, tithes, and purity. Rabbinic Judaism—which emerges later—seems to embrace at least some Pharisaic teachings as its own, such as practices guiding ritual purity. By the time the rabbis identify the Pharisees as their predecessors, the "ancestral tradition" can no longer be separated from Torah itself. Both written and oral religious teachings are equally authoritative when the Mishna is compiled around 200 C.E., and both embody for rabbis the essence of their understanding of the inheritance of Israel.

It is probably fair to assert that the pre-rabbinic Pharisees practice a variety of rituals and customs that are not spelled out directly in Torah, but which they nonetheless interpret as fulfilling the intention of God's will. The community at Qumran, the followers of Jesus, and even the priests at the temple would undoubtedly disagree, however, and would see their behavior as idiosyncratic and not sanctioned in Torah.

But Which Interpretation Is Right?

We have looked at some of the ways that several first-century groups read scripture. There are other ways of reading, of course, such as the apocalyptic visions expressed in the Pseudepigrapha and the allegorical readings of Philo of Alexandria. All of these contradictory interpretations lead to a serious problem: Which interpretation is correct? The answer depends upon the authority of the interpreter. Once that can be established, then one can make the claim of being a true descendant of Israel. We find both similarities and differences in the arguments that various groups make to defend their claim as we examine conflicting assertions of authority.

Authority in Paul

Paul seems to face challenges to his authority wherever he goes. He continually must defend his legitimacy as an apostle in light of his early career as a persecutor of the movement and in the face of rival teachers and apostles. Paul justifies his authority in five main ways: by referring to teachings of Jesus, by turning to scripture, by appealing to traditions which he has been taught, by citing heavenly revelations he receives, and by pointing to his exemplary lifestyle.

Paul names Jesus as the source of his teachings and distinguishes between those of the Lord, and those which he, Paul, gives:

> To the married I give this command—not I but the Lord (1 Cor 7:10)
> To the rest I say—I and not the Lord (1 Cor 7:12)
> This is my rule in all the churches (1 Cor 7:17)
> Now concerning virgins, I have no command of the Lord, but I give my opinion as one who by the Lord's mercy is trustworthy (1 Cor 7:25)

In 1 Corinthians 9, Paul defends his and Barnabas' behavior, not on "human authority," but rather on both scripture and the Lord's command, "that those who proclaim the gospel should get their living by the gospel" (1 Cor 9:14). In 1 Thessalonians, Paul also turns to Jesus when he states, "For you know what instructions we gave you through the Lord Jesus" (4:2) and "For this we declare to you by the word of the Lord" (4:15). Thus Paul contends that he is relaying the teachings and commands of Jesus.

The apostle's use of the authority of scripture is evident throughout his letters, perhaps most clearly in the letter to the Galatians. There he points to Abraham as a model of faithfulness (3:6–9); to the Law and Prophets to lift up faith and denigrate the commandments (3:10–14); and to Sarah and Hagar as an allegory of slavery and freedom (4:21–31). In chapters 9–11 of the letter to the Romans, Paul relies upon scriptural authority to underscore his arguments about the role of the Law and the future of Israel. He cites the Law (Leviticus, Numbers, and Deuteronomy), the Prophets (Hosea, Isaiah, Jeremiah, and Joel), and the Psalms.

Moreover, Paul appeals to the traditions he receives and which he passes along to the churches he founds. Two examples of this appear in 1 Corinthians. In chapter 15, he repeats an early creed regarding the resurrection of Jesus, prefacing his remarks by saying "For I handed on to you as of first importance what I in turn also received" (15:3). In chapter 11, Paul instructs the members of the divided Corinthian church in the proper observance of the Lord's Supper, reminding them of his previous instruction when he writes, "I received from the Lord what I also handed on to you" (11:23). The Greek words he uses for "received" and "handed on" (*parelabon* and *paredoka*) reflect the Hebrew terms that Judeans would use to signify the transmission of tradition (*l'qabel* is to receive and *l'msor* is to pass on). When Paul says he receives the teaching from the Lord, then, he does not mean he had a revelation, but rather that the tradition begins with Jesus. He identifies himself as a link in the tradition, but not as the source.

In addition to relying upon teachings of Jesus, scripture, and tradition, Paul claims divine revelation is the source of his authority. Chapter 1 of Galatians begins with Paul saying that he is an apostle "sent neither by human commission nor from human authorities, but through Jesus Christ and God the Father, who raised him from the dead" (Gal 1:1). Then he goes on to assert that:

> The gospel that was proclaimed by me is not of human origin; for I did not receive it from a human source, nor was I taught it, but I received it through a revelation of Jesus Christ. (Gal 1:11–12)

Paul makes a point of declaring his independence from the disciples in Jerusalem (Gal 1:16–19) and at the same time notes their affirmation of his mission to the Gentiles (2:2–9). He also implies an equality between himself and Peter, balancing his own mission to the uncircumcised against Peter's apostolate to the circumcised. Thus, Paul's divine call to preach to the Gentiles receives the seal of approval from church leaders. In this way he is doubly legitimated, by both God and humans.

A final source of authority for Paul is the witness his own life makes. His willingness to endure imprisonment and beatings is a testament to the dependability of his message. Paul's biography describes someone who can be confident in his worldly credentials, yet the apostle emphasizes that his knowledge of Christ and his imitation of the Lord's sufferings surpass previous accomplishments. "I press on to make [the goal] my own, because Christ Jesus has made me his own" (Phil 3:12). In other words, Paul's authority comes by belonging to Christ and by sharing in his sufferings. Similarly, in 2 Corinthians, Paul declares that "our competence is from God" (3:5). While his life, therefore, is exemplary, whatever value the model has comes solely from God.

The same can be said for Paul's other claims to authority: They come from God, either through the teachings of Jesus, the scriptures, the traditions of the apostles, or divine revelations. They come "from" Paul only insofar as he is "in Christ."

The Authority of Jesus

Given the fact that wonder-workers and magicians, sages and prophets are prevalent in first-century Judea, what makes Jesus different? H. C. Kee's description of charismatic authority provides a partial answer:

> Charisma lacks any abstract code and any formal means of adjudication. Its principles emanate concretely from the highly personal experience of heavenly grace and from the personal power of the leader, which derives from the gods. It rejects ties to external order, transvalues everything, calls for a break with traditional norms, and settles disputes by prophetic revelation or oracle.[1]

Charisma is one explanation for understanding Jesus' *exousia*, or authority. The Gospels and their interpreters identify Jesus as an eschatological prophet inspired by God, a righteous teacher who is the new Moses, a blameless messiah who fulfills the scriptures, and the Word of God who is in close communication with the Father. In one way or another, Jesus seems to draw his power directly from God. Certainly we cannot discount the fact that the Gospels, our sources for studying the authority of Jesus, are written in a polemical environment, a time that witnesses competing claims of various groups to be the bearers of tradition, properly interpreted. We also cannot discount the possibility of intragroup conflict, that is, debate over which commandments were still in effect for those proclaiming Jesus as the messiah.

All of the Gospels show Pharisees, Sadducees, and others questioning Jesus about his authority. When he goes to his hometown, his neighbors wonder, "Where did this man get all this? What is the wisdom given to him?" (Mark 6:2). When he teaches in the temple, the chief priests and elders ask him, "By what authority are you doing these things, and who gave you this authority?" (Matt 21:23). It seems evident that the Gospels attempt to establish the authority of Jesus in order to ensure reading texts in and through him. The Evangelists resolve the question of the source of Jesus' authority in remarkably different ways.

Mark 1:14–3:6 addresses the issue of authority at the outset. John the Baptist announces the coming of Jesus, and after he baptizes Jesus, Jesus "saw the heavens torn apart and the Spirit descending like a dove on him. And a voice came from heaven, 'You are my Son, the Beloved; with you I am well pleased'" (Mark 1:10–11). When Jesus goes into the wilderness, "angels waited on him"; when he calls Simon and Andrew, they drop what they are doing to follow him; he teaches in the synagogue and astounds people with his teaching, "for he taught them as one having authority [Greek: *exousia*]" (1:22); they repeat their amazement after he performs an exorcism, saying, "what is this? A new teaching—with authority! He commands even the unclean spirits, and they obey him" (1:27). Jesus continues to heal people and conduct exorcisms, and people flock to him "from every quarter" (1:45) so that he cannot go about unnoticed.

While Mark portrays Jesus as an itinerant healer and prophet attested to by miracles, healings, and exorcisms, Matthew depicts Jesus himself as the new Moses. The evangelist begins by having the Holy Family (Joseph, Mary, and Jesus) flee to Egypt because Herod plans to kill all of the boy babies in Judea. This reverses Moses' flight out of Egypt, but nevertheless sets the stage for identifying Jesus as the prophet revisited. Matthew puts together a collection of sayings in what is called the "Sermon on the Mount" (Matt 5–7) because Jesus goes up to a mountaintop to receive and deliver Torah. In this sermon, Jesus presents the written Torah—the Ten Commandments—and then gives out new, oral Torah. For example, after he says "You have heard that it was said to those of ancient times, 'You shall not murder,'" he then says that anyone who is angry or insulting is liable to judgment (5:21–26). When he states, "You have heard that it was said, 'You shall not commit adultery,'" he adds that anyone who looks upon another with lust in his or her heart has already committed adultery (5:27–30). For Matthew, Jesus is the *interpreter* of Torah *par excellence* and indeed, is the *giver* of Torah as well.

The author of Luke understands Jesus as fulfilling the promises of scripture, thus his authority comes from his divine appointment according to God's plan. He begins his ministry by reading Isaiah and then announces, "Today this scripture has been fulfilled in your hearing" (Luke 4:21, citing Isa 61:1, 58:6, 61:2). When John the Baptist sends his disciples to find out if Jesus is the one prophesied or not, Jesus points to his many miracles and tells them to report to John what they have seen and heard: "The blind receive their sight, the lame walk, the lepers are cleansed, the deaf hear, the dead are raised, the poor have good news brought to them" (Luke 7:18–23). People identify Jesus as the expected prophet, and he is linked with Elijah and Elisha, as well as to Moses. In a post-resurrection appearance, Jesus instructs his disciples in how to read scripture in order to find where it speaks of him, as we have noted.

Volume Two of Luke's two-part work, the Acts of the Apostles, continues to present Jesus as the fulfillment of the promises made to Israel. But Luke also appears to claim that the story of Israel now exists in the life of the early church. The authority Jesus had is transferred to the disciples with the descent of the Holy Spirit at Pentecost. Just as the Jewish festival of Shavuot memorializes Moses' receipt of Torah, the new Pentecost remembers the receipt of the Holy Spirit by the apostles. (The Acts narrative may be the earliest witness to what becomes standard in rabbinic Judaism.) The risen Christ tells them that they will "receive power when the Holy Spirit has come upon you; and you will be my witnesses in Jerusalem, in all Judea and Samaria, and to the ends of the earth" (Acts 1:8). Even Peter notes that "the scripture had to be fulfilled, which the Holy Spirit through David foretold concerning Judas" (1:16). After the Holy Spirit fills people of various nations, Peter explains the event by invoking Joel's prophecy of God pouring out the spirit and enabling men, women, and even slaves to receive it and to prophesy (Acts 2:1–21, quoting Joel 2:28–32). When the religious leaders in Jerusalem ask Peter and John, "'By what power or by what name did you do this?' Then Peter, filled with the Holy Spirit, said to them . . . 'Let it be known to all of you, and to all the people of Israel, that this man is standing before you in good health by the name of Jesus Christ of Nazareth'" (Acts 4:7–11). The direct authority of Jesus, who fulfills the scriptural promises, moves to the apostles, who teach, preach, and heal in his name.

Finally, John's gospel identifies Jesus as the Word, or Logos, of God: "In the beginning was the Word, and the Word was with God, and the Word was God" (John 1:1). It would be difficult to have more authority than God Almighty, and John's gospel presents many ironic situations in which people do not understand who Jesus is, or who ask him about his identity. When Jesus tells Nicodemus that he must be born anew (or "born from above"), Nicodemus doesn't understand. Jesus asks him, "Are you a teacher of Israel, and yet you do not understand these things? Very truly I tell you, we speak of what we know, and testify to what we have seen; yet you do not receive our testimony" (John 3:1–15). This is a sharp slap at those who are "teachers of Israel" but who still do not "receive our testimony." Elsewhere Jesus bears witness to himself and says that the Father also bears witness to him (John 8:18). An extended story about the healing of a blind man points out the blindness of the Judeans who do not "see" Jesus. When the Judeans wonder at Jesus' teaching and ask, "How does this man have such learning when he has never been taught," Jesus proclaims that "My teaching is not mine, but his who sent me. Anyone who resolves to do the will of God will know whether the teaching is from God or whether I am speaking on my own" (John 7:14–18). In John's gospel, Jesus derives his authority directly from God. If people do not recognize this, then they are blind.

Rabbinic Sacred History and the Chain of Tradition

Jesus is interpreting Torah for his audience, but there are others doing exactly the same thing. Usually they are referred to as "rabbis," but to avoid confusing them with later rabbinic Judaism, we refer to them as "sages." Like Jesus, the sages have disciples, issue opinions that their disciples find authoritative, and engage in discussions within their own group and with others about how Torah should be understood and practiced.

The book of Acts mentions one such sage, a Pharisee named Gamaliel, who is also mentioned in the Mishna (*m. Abot* 1:16). Acts 5:34 explicitly says he was a Pharisee, a teacher of the Law, and a member of the temple council. The Mishna portrays him as a skeptic regarding priestly observance of regulations and an influential transmitter of ancient tradition. Josephus and the Mishna mention Simon, or Simeon, son of Gamaliel (*m. Abot* 1:17–18). Josephus says that this Simon is from an illustrious family and that he came into conflict with the Sadducees over observance of the Sabbath (*Vita* 190–91).

Josephus also describes Pollion and Samaias (*Ant.* 15, 379–71), two Pharisees who are in conflict with Herod. These two enigmatic figures may also be mentioned in chapter one of *Pirke Abot*. Some scholars have proposed that these alliterative names point to Hillel and Shammai, the first century B.C.E. sages whose disciples may have been engaged in disputes with Jesus. Some have even argued that Jesus himself is a disciple of Hillel, because his liberal interpretation of Torah seems to parallel that of Hillel. Jesus' explication of the "Golden Rule" ("Do unto others as you would have them do unto you") echoes Hillel's own advice to "not do to others what you do not want done to yourself." The schools of Hillel and Shammai are important, not because they are necessarily Pharisees, but because they represent different interpretive schools at the end of the first century B.C.E.

As they are depicted in the Mishna, these first-century sages and others discuss and formulate opinions regarding proper observance of Torah. For example, Hillel and Shammai argue over the nature of rituals involved in Sabbath observance. In particular, they disagree over how the Sabbath meal should be sanctified. Though the Torah commands that the Sabbath should be made holy, there is nothing in the text that explains how this holiness should be achieved. The tradition of sanctification of the day is a ritual performed over a cup of wine at the beginning of the meal. It also occurs in the middle blessing of the Sabbath and festival *amidah* that precedes this meal. All of these discussions are attributed to Hillel and Shammai (*m. Ber* 8). None of these practices are found in the Torah and must have originated later. Sages such as Hillel and Shammai issue decisions and make claims about practices that are not explicitly mandated in Torah, and therefore they must appeal to some other form of authority. Some scholars consider Hillel and Shammai to be Pharisees because of the similarity of what they are doing in regard to the "tradition of the elders." These traditions are associated with the Pharisees by Josephus and the New Testament, prior to compilation of the Mishna.

The rabbis of the Mishna clearly associate themselves with these early sages and engage in discussions and disputes over ritual practice and observance, the details of which are either not specifically spelled out in the Torah or in their time—after the destruction of the second temple—can no longer be followed. For example, they are concerned with ritual observance in the home and with the organization of liturgy, both necessitated by the destruction of the temple and the cessation of the sacrificial cult. As Martin Jaffee states:

> If God required absolute obedience, and if the destruction of the Temple made many of his commandments impossible to fulfill, then it was only

through traditions preserved outside the textual confines of scripture that Jews could begin to reconstruct their covenantal relationship with the god of Abraham, Isaac and Jacob.[2]

As we see in chapter 4, the Pharisees attempt to legitimize their particular practices and beliefs by asserting themselves as the transmitters of an authoritative body of teaching that exists in addition to the Written Torah, namely the "traditions of the elders." While the temple priesthood can claim the right to explicate Torah by virtue of its ancestry, and while the community at Qumran believes its teacher has access to "privileged revelations," the Pharisees assert an ancestral tradition that in their minds is equally authoritative, equally binding, and equally ancient. By the period of the Mishna, the sages make the same claim but attribute the source of these traditions as God's revelation to Moses at Sinai.

The Rabbinic Chain of Tradition

1. Moses received Torah from Sinai and passed it on to Joshua, and Joshua to the Elders, and the Elders to the Prophets, and the Prophets passed it on to the men of the Great Assembly. They said three things: Be careful in giving judgement, raise up many disciples, and make a fence around the Torah.

2. Simeon the Just was one of the last members of the Great Assembly. He used to say: Upon three things the world stands—on the Torah, on the Temple service, and on acts of kindness.

3. Antigonus of Sokho received Torah from Simeon the Just. He used to say: Do not be like slaves who serve their master only in order to receive their allowance, but be like slaves who serve their master with no thought of receiving an allowance; and let the fear of heaven be upon you.

4. Yose ben Yo'ezer of Zeredah and Yose ben Yohanan of Jerusalem received Torah from them. Yose ben Yo'ezer says: Let your house be a meeting-place for the Sages; sit in the dust of their feet and drink in their words thirstily.

12. Hillel and Shammai received Torah from them. Hillel says: Be one of Aaron's disciples, loving peace and pursuing peace, loving mankind and bringing them near to the Torah.

13. He used to say: He who promotes his own name, destroys his name; he who does not increase decreases; he who does not learn deserves death; he who exploits the crown [of the Torah] to his own advantage perishes.

14. He used to say: If I am not for myself, who, then, is for me? And when I alone am for myself, what am I? And if not now, when?

15. Shammai says: Make your study of the Torah a fixed habit; say little and do much, and greet everyone with a cheerful look on your face.

16. Rabban Gamaliel says: Provide yourself with a teacher and remove yourself from doubt, and do not get into the habit of tithing by guesswork.

17. Simeon his son says: All my days I grew up among the Sages and I have found nothing better for a man than silence. Expounding [the Torah] is not the chief thing, but fulfilling [it]. Whoever multiplies words occasions sin.

18. Rabban Simeon ben Gamaliel says: On three things the world stands: on justice, on truth and on peace, as it is written: "Execute the judgement of truth and peace in your gates" (Zechariah 8:16). (*m. Abot* 1)

Source: Philip Alexander, *Textual Sources for the Study of Judaism* (Chicago: University of Chicago Press, 1984).

The "Chain of Tradition" from *Pirke Abot* links the revelation at Sinai through various personalities in the biblical text all the way through to the sages of the late second and early third centuries. Thus, the rabbis see themselves as part of a long line of authorities, originating with Moses at Mount Sinai, who develop observances that may not appear in the Torah, but which nevertheless possess the same legitimacy because of their direct connection to their forebears.

What follows is what some call "dual Torah." There is a Written Torah, given to Moses at Sinai, which Jews today know as Tanakh; but there is an Oral Torah as well, just as authoritative and binding, that was also given to Moses at Sinai. In this way, the judgments of the rabbis are not mere conjecture or opinion, but are divinely revealed, though notably distinct from the Written Torah.

As we can see from the boxed quotation from *Pirke Abot*, one of the very first things that is passed along is the command to "make a fence around the Torah." Most scholars understand this "fence" as referring to an interpretive net cast over the Torah by the rabbis. In other words, the Chain of Tradition limits who has the authority to interpret Torah. An interpreter would have to show some connection to the individuals on the official list of the Chain of Tradition, either by ability, social status, or birth. Tradition passed on as Torah by rabbis, therefore, begins with Moses and remains intact for more than 1,000 years. Moreover, tradition is Torah if and only if it is transmitted by a rabbinic sage. Furthermore, and most important, the tradition transmitted in rabbinic teaching is nothing less than Torah itself. Other groups can and do put forward their own interpretations of Torah, but by the mid–third century, the rabbis exclude all other interpretations save their own, perhaps responding to the early Christian interpretations of the same texts.

Of course, the question of what rabbis transmit is quite complex. They certainly pass on minority traditions that are not determinative of halakah. While there is some exclusion of what goes on beyond the walls of the academy, there is no exclusion of disagreements inside the walls. They also preserve disputes with certain outsiders, refuting their interpretations explicitly.

Christian Sacred History and Apostolicity

Just as the rabbis of early Judaism want to define the boundaries of Israel by establishing a retroactive and authoritative chain that goes back to Moses and, ultimately, to God, so too the bishops of early Christianity seek to limit the acceptable bounds of Christianity by identifying a "chain" that goes back to Jesus and, ultimately, to God. By the end of the first century, the church at Rome faces a number of theological challenges. Gnostic Christians such as Valentinus preach a version of Christianity that is both more egalitarian and more hierarchical, in which Jesus is the heavenly messenger of divine truths about our true nature. Ebionite Christians continue to observe the Torah, and yet proclaim Jesus as the Messiah, while Marcionite Christians reject the God of the Old Testament, even excising all Hebrew writings from their unofficial canon of literature. These various forms of early Christianity—normative within their geographic places and in particular periods—are labeled as heresies by those who seek to maintain the hegemony of the church in Rome by claiming to be the recipients of a pure and unadulterated doctrine.

The church also faces the opposition of Judaic groups that assert an equally venerable and even more ancient tradition. Church leaders remain unmoved, however, by these groups' competing claims to authority and the "traditions of the elders." Paul's own interpretive strategies skip over Moses, Aaron, and the commandments, and jump back to Adam, Abraham, and the promises. The Gospels provide a new way of reading old texts, and the Mount of Beatitudes (Mount Eremos in the Galilee) replaces Mount Sinai as the site of divine revelation. In the second century, Justin Martyr's *Dialogue with Trypho* "constructs" Judaism, according to Daniel Boyarin, by specifying exactly what "Judaism" believes and does not believe, most especially what it does not "believe" about the Logos. "In essence," Boyarin writes, "the *Dialogue* is part of Justin's overall project of inventing orthodoxy as the form and structure of Christianity and, as such, demonstrates the intimate role that producing a non-Christian Judaism plays in the project."[3]

The path from the teachings of an itinerant "Jewish Mediterranean peasant," in the words of John Dominic Crossan, to the interpretation of those teachings by an urban, elite group of religious authorities is neither straight nor true. The Gospels and the book of Acts provide the narrative from which the early church eventually creates its own chain of tradition. Jesus of Nazareth personally commissions his earliest followers, sending them out two-by-two with next to nothing (Mark 6:7–13 // Matt 10:5–15 // Luke 22:35–36). The risen Jesus then tells the disciples to go and preach the gospel throughout the world (Matt 28:19). In Acts, the Holy Spirit provides charismatic authority to leaders of the early church, so that they can perform miracles and healings in the name of Jesus. The post-resurrection Jesus tells them, "you will receive power when the Holy Spirit has come upon you; and you will be my witnesses in Jerusalem, in all Judea and Samaria, and to the ends of the earth" (Acts 1:8). While the early church is somewhat egalitarian—for example, selecting Judas Iscariot's replacement by casting lots (Acts 1:23–26)—Paul nevertheless notes a preliminary hierarchy of authority in which God appointed apostles first, then prophets, teachers, "then deeds of power, then gifts of healing, forms of assistance, forms of leadership, [and] various kinds of tongues" (1 Cor 12:28).

The New Testament generally does not yet recognize the preeminent authority of bishops, and so their importance in church administration seems to come relatively late. Paul identifies Jesus' immediate followers as apostles rather than disciples, probably in order to suggest parity between himself and eyewitnesses to Jesus of Nazareth. But New Testament texts and later literature are used to shape a view of the past that claims that the instructions of Jesus pass from disciples to apostles to church leaders such as elders and deacons, and ultimately to bishops in a divinely directed way. Several key texts foster this particular historiography.

The Pastoral Letters, for example—1 Timothy, 2 Timothy, and Titus—focus on doctrine rather than scripture, and they subordinate both Israel and Jesus Christ to the preservation of a body of teachings. The bishop is charged with safeguarding this tradition, since he "must have a firm grasp of the word that is trustworthy in accordance with the teaching, so that he may be able both to preach with sound doctrine and to refute those who contradict it" (Titus 1:7–9). The author advises the reader to "[p]ay close attention to yourself and to your teaching; continue in these things, for in doing this you will save both yourself and your hearers" (1 Tim 4:16). And later:

> Teach and urge these duties. Whoever teaches otherwise and does not agree with the sound words of our Lord Jesus Christ and the teaching that is in accordance with godliness, is conceited, understanding nothing, and

has a morbid craving for controversy and for disputes about words. (1 Tim 6:2b–4)

It is clear that oral traditions given *by* Jesus, especially concerning interpretation of Torah, and oral traditions given *about* Jesus have hardened. The fluidity and differing viewpoints of the decades immediately preceding and following his death have frozen into a singular doctrine which must be shielded from opposition.

An extra-biblical letter attributed to Clement, bishop of Rome (ca. 90–100 C.E.), shows this consolidation further by discussing how God has delegated authority to bishops, priests, and deacons. The substance of his letter is remarkably similar to the Chain of Tradition, in that it specifies who exactly is the legitimate bearer of tradition and has the authority to interpret it.

Clement of Rome on Apostolic Succession

The Apostles were entrusted with the gospel for us from the Lord Jesus Christ; Jesus Christ was sent from God. Christ, therefore, is from God and the Apostles from Christ. Both, accordingly, came in proper order by the will of God. Receiving their orders, therefore . . . they went forth announcing the gospel, the kingdom of God that was about to come. Preaching, accordingly, throughout countries and cities, they appointed their first-fruits, after testing them by the spirit, to be bishops and deacons of those who were about to believe. (1 Clement 42:1–4)

The purpose of this hierarchy is to protect and promote the purity of Jesus' teachings, which have become church doctrine rather than mere textualized oral traditions. This succession from God to Jesus to the Apostles to their "first fruits" becomes the necessary link between first-century apostles and second-century bishops. So it is that Clement of Rome is believed to be a disciple of Peter (as is the evangelist Mark). Irenaeus in the mid–second century has two degrees of separation from Jesus, through Polycarp, a disciple of John; and Clement of Alexandria in the third century believes that his teachers received training personally from Peter, James, John, and Paul.

While Clement of Rome provides the justification for granting bishops and deacons authority, Ignatius of Antioch places supreme power with the bishop. Martyred sometime during the reign of emperor Trajan (r.

98–117), Ignatius imputes a divine hierarchy on earth as it is in heaven. The bishop supervises priests and deacons, ensures the validity of sacraments of Eucharist and baptism, and is responsible for church harmony, sound doctrine, and human welfare. Because the bishop represents the one God to his congregation, he is owed the same obedience as is due God. A major task of bishops is to teach and interpret scripture.

The conflict between authority and interpretation in the early church is best illustrated in the antagonism that heresy hunters, or heresiologists, feel toward Gnostic Christians. The Gnostics in Rome seem to practice a democratic form of worship, celebrating communion without benefit of a bishop. They select leaders at each meeting by drawing lots. But if God is one, then the church is one, and according to Irenaeus, there can only be one leader and one teaching. Thus, the Gnostics do not have the authority to offer alternative interpretations of scripture or to develop competing doctrines. Despite the names of apostles attached to them, the Gnostic gospels deviate from accepted truths. The Gnostics, however, feel they must reject the authority of a centralized church in order to read the scriptures according to their hermeneutic of saving gnosis offered through Jesus Christ. For some, this means abandoning the teachings of apostolic doctrine, or Christian Oral Torah.

It is easy to see how second-century heresiological texts consolidate the power of bishops as "overseers" of all liturgical, pastoral, and instructional life in the churches by naming, constructing, and characterizing the "other." Not only are heresies defined, but so too is Judaism. Just as Irenaeus, Tertullian, and others fashion heresies by excluding alternative ways of understanding scripture and creating centralized structures of authority within the church, Justin Martyr invents Judaism as a theological system in opposition to the church rather than a competing method of interpretation. Boyarin calls the "double construction of Jews and heretics—or rather Judaism and heresy—effected through Justin's *Dialogue*" the means by which Christians secure a religious identity.[4]

The process of self-definition through constructing heresy and Judaism continues in succeeding centuries. The power of bishops grows, and in the third century, the *Apostolic Tradition*, attributed to Hippolytus (d. 236), indicates that bishops are the successors of the apostles. Authority shifts from the individual himself (as we see in the Pastoral Letters) to the office of the bishop. Later documents such as the *Didascalia* and the *Apostolic Constitutions* continue this process. The Pastoral Letters, probably written in the early second century C.E., are used in many treatises on ecclesiastical leadership because they provide apostolic support in the voice of Paul for claiming greater authority and power.

Thus we see how the idea of apostolic succession arises from disputes within the Pauline churches, and later on between competing claims about the right to interpret scripture, both among those who claim to be followers of Jesus and against those who claim the heritage of Israel. How can Christians such as the Gnostics, and other forms of Israel, like the "Jews," be excluded from the interpretive role except by establishing limits on who has the right to interpret scripture?

Conclusions

The development of the concepts of the chain of tradition and apostolic succession serve extremely useful purposes, however we regard the historicity of such claims. They allow a single group to become the dominant, and eventually the only, voice, thus ensuring the long-term survival of Judaism and Christianity. Had Christianity not created the idea of apostolic succession, it might have remained a collection of competing sects and groups, each with its own scriptures, beliefs, and practices, which might have gone the way of the mystery religions of late antiquity: interesting historical artifacts, but no longer relevant. Had Judaism not created a chain of tradition that legitimizes the teachings of Oral Torah, it might not have survived the destruction of the temple in 70 C.E. and the interpretive challenges presented by Christianity. The emergence of these defined paths guarantee the continued existence of Christianity and Judaism beyond their twin births in the early centuries of our era.

What is most significant is not how these two paths differ, however, but rather how very similar they are. From establishing limits as to who has the right to interpret scripture by inventing a sacred trajectory from God into the present, to valuing traditions as much as texts for the same reason—their transmission is supervised by the divine—what ultimately become Judaism and Christianity grow out of parallel concerns.

Suggestions for Further Reading

Paul Achtemeier. "'Omne Verbum Sonat': The New Testament and the Oral Environment of Late Western Antiquity." *Journal of Biblical Literature* 109, no. 1 (1990): 3–27.

Hugh Anderson. "Jesus: Aspects of the Question of his Authority." In *The Social World of Formative Christianity and Judaism*. Jacob Neusner, Peder Borgen, Ernest S. Frerichs, Richard Horsley, eds. Philadelphia: Fortress, 1988.

Daniel Boyarin. *Border Lines: The Partition of Judaeo-Christianity*. Philadelphia: University of Pennsylvania, 2004.

_____ . *A Radical Jew: Paul and the Politics of Identity*. Berkeley and Los Angeles: University of California Press, 1994.

Bruce Chilton and Jacob Neusner. *Types of Authority in Formative Christianity and Judaism*. London: Routledge, 1999.

Michael Fishbane. "Use, Authority and Interpretation of Mikra at Qumran." In *Mikra*, ed. Martin Jan Mulder. Philadelphia: Fortress, 1988.

Martin S. Jaffee. *Torah in the Mouth: Writing and Oral Tradition in Palestinian Judaism*. New York: Oxford University Press, 2001.

Jacob Neusner. *Oral Torah: The Sacred Books of Judaism: An Introduction*. San Francisco: Harper and Row, 1986.

W. Sibley Towner. "Hermeneutical Systems of Hillel and the Tannaim: A Fresh Look." *Hebrew Union College Annual* 53 (1982): 101–35.

Notes

1. H. C. Kee, *Understanding the New Testament,* 4th ed. (Englewood Cliffs, N.J.: Prentice-Hall, 1983), 395, discussing Max Weber, "The Sociology of Charismatic Authority," in *From Max Weber: Essays in Sociology*, trans. and ed. H. H. Gerth and C. Wright Mills (New York: Oxford University Press, 1946), 245–48.

2. Martin S. Jaffee, *Early Judaism: Religious Worlds of the First Judaic Millennium,* 2d. ed. (Bethesda, Md.: University Press of Maryland, 2006), 78.

3. Daniel Boyarin, *Border Lines: The Partition of Judaeo-Christianity* (Philadelphia: University of Pennsylvania Press, 2004), 28.

4. Boyarin, *Border Lines*, 39.

The Question of the Messiah   8

T HUS FAR WE HAVE EXAMINED A NUMBER of concepts central to Israelite religion and looked at how they are reevaluated in light of
changing historical realities. The covenantal relationship between
God and Israel remains, but the nature of Israel itself changes to include or
exclude various factions. Priesthood and sacrifice continue, but in new
forms that literally move the temple into the life of the community and
into the home, where alternative ways of sacrifice occur in prayer and
sanctified meals. Throughout this transformative era, Torah persists as the
key to creating an identity for different groups.

The one concept that stands out as causing an unbridgeable chasm is
that of "messiah." It is on this apparently troublesome notion that we will
conclude by showing that it need not continue as a point of contention between Jews and Christians today.

The Meaning of "Messiah"

We might hear a Christian assert that though the Jews expected an earthly
messiah in the form of a political or religious leader, God sent a spiritual
or heavenly king. A Jew, on the other hand, might argue that Jesus could
not possibly have been the messiah, because he did not institute a period
of peace and justice on earth. The question of whether or not Jesus was
the Messiah expected by first-century Judeans has proven to be one of the
most divisive questions, if not *the* most divisive issue, to exist between the
descendants of the interpretive communities we examine in this book.
Modern Jews point to the fact that there are dozens, if not hundreds, of
messianic claimants in the first century. These kingly aspirants promise

relief from Roman oppression and the restoration of Israel as a nation among the nations. Jews today say that Christians, not God, redefine the meaning of the word *messiah*. Christians, on the other hand, understand the concept of messiah differently from Jews, drawing their understanding of kingship from the model of the suffering servant in Isaiah (42:1–4, 49:1–6, 50:4–9, 52:13–53:12) and the heavenly "son of man" in the book of Daniel (7:13–14; see also Mark 13:26–27).

Paradoxically, both claims have some truth. Jews are correct in their interpretation of messiah as meaning a political ruler. The word *mashiach* in the Hebrew Bible literally means "the poured one," that is, the one who is anointed with oil, an action meant to designate God's selected one, a person set apart or consecrated for a particular role or task. The term *mashiach* would have in this sense described all the kings of Judah and Israel. As we have noted earlier, this word is translated as *christos* in Greek and initially lacks the exalted meaning it has today. The biblical text also refers to the anointing of priests. The high priest in Leviticus 4:3 and 4:5 is referred to as *hakkohen hamashiach*, "the anointed priest," though many scholars suggest that the practice of anointing priests was eventually replaced by bestowing the special priestly garments upon them.

In the first century, technically speaking, there was no anointed one of Israel. Kingship had long since disappeared, and the high priest was ceremonially appointed in a different manner.

But traditional Christian theology stands on firm ground as well—at least from an interpretive perspective—when it asserts that Jesus was a heavenly redeemer sent by God to save God's people. Far from being an innovation, the understanding of messiah as much more than an earthly king comes directly from the period we have been studying: 200 B.C.E. to 200 C.E. The pseudepigraphical texts composed at this time are full of angels, saviors, and heavenly beings, all come to save Israel in one way or another. They are called messiahs, and their rule extends throughout the cosmos, on earth as it is in heaven.

Thus, the differing interpretations of messiah have more to do with the historical realities of which texts various interpretive communities use than with polemical disputes between subsequent Christians and Jews. Long neglected as a legitimate source for understanding first-century Judaic thought, a number of texts from the intertestamental period clarify how those in the Jesus Movement, and those writing after his execution, begin to understand him as a heavenly redeemer. We will take a look at some of the texts that indicate the great diversity of views on the messiah, and which explain how later Jews and Christians can be both right and wrong.

Two Messiahs

While messiah, or *mashiach*, specifically refers to the king, it also generally refers to anyone who is anointed, and in the Hebrew Bible this includes, as we have seen, priests and prophets. The book of Numbers describes the lineage of Aaron and Moses, saying "these are the names of the sons of Aaron, the anointed priests, whom he ordained to minister as priests (3:3; see also Num 35:25, Lev 8:12, 16:32). In fact, we can state that before the institution of the monarchy, the primary persons anointed are priests and prophets. In later biblical texts we see kings and priests anointed together. The prophet Zechariah, for example, refers to someone called "the Branch," undoubtedly a descendant of David, and his counselor, a priest (Zech 3:8, 6:12), who sits beside the throne. In another vision, Zechariah mentions "two sons of fresh oil," that is, literally two "anointed ones."

We find clear evidence of a two-messiah theology at Qumran: the anointed of the House of Aaron—a priest—and an anointed of Israel from the line of David—a king. Both are described in detail when the *Community Rule* discusses a Council of Holiness of those who walk in the way of perfection, who will atone for the sins of unfaithfulness "without the flesh of burnt offerings and without the fats of sacrifice" (1QS 9.4). The text then goes on to predict that they "shall be ruled by the first directives which the men of the Community began to be taught until the prophet comes, and the *Messiahs* of Aaron and Israel" (1QS 9.10–11, our emphasis). The Damascus Document also mentions a messiah of Aaron and of Israel (at least five times!) and states that God "raised from Aaron men of knowledge and from Israel wise men, and made them listen" (CD 4.2–3).

Although the messiah of Israel is connected directly to the line of David in the Scrolls—4QFlorilegium describes a "shoot of David" who will appear at the end of days—this king exists alongside a "teacher of Torah," undoubtedly a priest. The *Community Rule* clearly delineates a hierarchy of sorts between these two anointed ones in the meeting of the community council at the end of days:

> At [a ses]sion of the men of renown, [those summoned to] the gathering of the community council, when [God] begets the Messiah with them: [the] chief [priest] of all the congregation of Israel shall enter, and all [his] br[others, the sons] of Aaron, the priests [summoned] to the assembly, the men of renown, and they shall sit be[fore him, each one] according to his dignity. After, [the Mess]iah of Israel shall [enter] and before him shall sit the heads of the th[ousands of Israel, each] one according to his dignity, according to [his] po[sition] in their camps and according to their marches. (1QSa 2:11–16)

In the biblical sources it is more common for lay leaders to precede the priests; this order is reversed at Qumran, both in the here and now, and at the end of days.

Additional examples of the dual messiahs appear in the Pseudepigrapha. The *Testament of the Twelve Patriarchs*, a pseudepigraphical work from the second century B.C.E., states that "the Lord will raise up from Levi someone as high priest and from Judah someone as king" (*Test. Simon* 7.2). The book of Jubilees, written about this same time, also identifies both a priest and a prince as rulers of Israel and the nations. It may not be coincidental that this ideal picture of Judean leadership hearkens back to the period of the early monarchy as depicted in the biblical text, where king and priest assumed roles of considerable power in their respective different realms.

A final example of the priest-king motif can be seen in the mysterious figure of Melchizedek, who appears in the Hebrew Bible, the New Testament, and the Pseudepigrapha. In Genesis, Melchizedek blesses Abram after Abram's military victory:

> King Melchizedek of Salem brought out bread and wine; he was priest of God Most High. He blessed him and said, "Blessed be Abram by God Most High, maker of heaven and earth; and blessed be God Most High, who has delivered your enemies into your hand." And Abram gave him one tenth of everything. (Gen 14:18–20)

In a psalm used by later Christian writers, the author promises that God will overcome the enemy and exercise judgment among the nations, sending "out from Zion your mighty scepter." The psalmist says, "The Lord has sworn and will not change his mind, 'You are a priest forever according to the order of Melchizedek'" (Ps 110:4). The pseudepigraphical work Jubilees features Enoch in the beginning, but spends the second half on Melchizedek. Finally, the book of Hebrews in the New Testament provides a rather lengthy interpretation of this key priest-king, comparing him to Jesus. It repeats the Genesis story, elaborating upon the meaning of the name "Melchizedek" and the significance of Salem. The purpose of introducing Melchizedek is to note how great he is, how unique he is, and by extension, "accordingly Jesus has also become the guarantee of a better covenant" (Heb 7:1–22, esp. 22).

The idea of two messiahs, therefore, seems to be a commonplace among certain apocalyptic groups. Indeed, the thesis of James Tabor in *The Jesus Dynasty* is that Jesus of Nazareth intends to be a royal messiah, while his cousin John the Baptist plans to be a priestly messiah.[1] In other words, Jesus plans a political restoration of Israel under the reign of God, according to Tabor. Certainly the Romans, as depicted in the New Testament, see the Jesus Movement as a political threat and execute Jesus as "King of the Judeans," a messianic title.

Heavenly Messiahs

In addition to the prevalence of a belief in two messiahs at this time, we find a number of heavenly "redeemer" figures. In the Hebrew Bible, it seems clear that God is the redeemer of Israel, with numerous references in evidence. "I will redeem you with an outstretched arm and with mighty acts of judgment," God tells the Israelites in Exodus (6:6). "Is there another nation on earth whose God went to redeem it as a people?" asks 2 Samuel (7:23). The Psalms name God the redeemer of Israel in several places, and call upon God to redeem Israel (Ps 25:22; 26:11; 69:18; 77:15; 119:134, 154; 130:8). In other words, redemption—which has multiple meanings—is an important role God plays in the Hebrew Bible.

Redemption moves into the angelic realm in the Pseudepigrapha and the Dead Sea literature. Angels, archangels, and other spirits seem to be working on behalf of humanity (1 Enoch 20; Song of the Sabbath Sacrifice; throughout 1QM, the *War Scroll*; and Jubilees). The *War Scroll* describes the archangel Michael as leader of the heavenly host in the battle against the Children of Darkness (1QM 17.6–7). 1 Enoch describes an Elect One, a Son of Man, who is going to help humanity in its struggle against evil forces (1 Enoch 71:14–17). We cite these examples as ways to understand how heavenly forces begin to supplant human kings in the apocalyptic worldview prevalent in the Second Temple period. As we note in chapter 3, which discusses apocalypticism, earthly subjugation leads the oppressed to look for divine salvation, or in traditional language, redemption. Even the book of Daniel alludes to an unnamed "prince" in chapter 9, and then a named prince—the archangel Michael—in chapter 12 (12:1).

Prophetic Messiahs

A final messianic figure we want to note is the prophet. "The spirit of the Lord God is upon me, because the Lord has anointed me," Third Isaiah begins (Isa 61:1). The prophet describes his task to proclaim good news as a God-given appointment, or anointment. The Hebrew prophets frequently say "the Lord put out his hand and touched my mouth," or, "the word of the Lord came to me" (Jer 1:9, 2:1). Ezekiel says that God told him to prophesy to a field of dry bones (37:4). He does so, and God puts flesh on the bones and breathes life into them. The book of Hosea begins: "The word of the Lord came to Hosea son of Beeri . . . When the Lord first spoke through Hosea, the Lord said to Hosea . . ." (1:1, 2). Deuteronomy speaks of God raising up for them a prophet, and "I will put my words in the mouth of the prophet, who shall speak to them everything that I command" (Deut 18:18, cf. Acts 3:22).

Prophets play an important role in Israelite religion. This is apparent in the prominence they hold in the Tanakh, which devotes a section to prophetic works, the Nevi'im. Just as kings exercise political power and priests exercise religious rule, prophets exercise moral authority, calling the Israelites to account time and again. Indeed, inclusion of the prophetic works in the biblical canon provides a counterweight to narratives that justify the political and religious status quo by presenting a self-reflexive critique of the nation's history.

Moses is the central prophet of Israelite religion, the one who encounters God directly and brings God's commandments to the Israelites. He is a unique prophet, however, in that he does not predict future events—like Isaiah or Amos or Hosea—but acts as a military, spiritual, and political leader. Elijah plays a bigger role in Judaic eschatological thought, however. He is mentioned by name in the Qumran literature at least three times, and a number of scholars think that the community sees him as a model eschatological prophet and priest. That is certainly the case in later rabbinic literature. The Gospels shows people wondering if John the Baptist or Jesus is Elijah (Matt 16:14; Mark 6:15, 8:28; Luke 9:8; John 1:21, 24–25). The Synoptic Gospels remold a story about Elijah resurrecting a dead child in the account of Jesus raising Jairus' daughter (Mark 5:41–42, Luke 8:49–56). And finally, Moses and Elijah both appear with Jesus on a mountain, bathed in glory (Matt 17:4, Mark 9:5, Luke 9:30). The Gospels include the "Transfiguration" narrative to show that Jesus surpasses these two great prophets of Israelite history, suggesting that Jesus is also a prophet, and more than a prophet.

Jesus in Context

This discussion about biblical and extra-biblical interpretations of anointing and messianism lays the historical and theological groundwork for understanding New Testament assertions that Jesus is the messiah foretold in scripture. Placed in this context, Jesus is clearly a type of messiah that first-century Judeans might recognize: political or heavenly, priestly or prophetic, or all of the above. When the magi present the infant Jesus with a gift of myrrh, the writer of Matthew wants readers to know that Jesus will be anointed as a king (Matt 2:11). When Jesus reads from Isaiah 61:1–2 and announces that "Today this scripture has been fulfilled in your hearing," the author of Luke wants readers to know that Jesus is a prophet. When Mark refers to Daniel 7 and says that "Then they will see the Son of Man coming in clouds with great power and glory," he wants readers to know that Jesus is a heavenly redeemer figure (Mark 13:26). All four Gospels say that the inscription under Jesus' cross says "The king of the Judeans," indicating his political kingship. All four Gospels depict the reenactment, or fulfillment, of Zechariah's prophecy, when Jesus enters Jerusalem riding a donkey:

> Rejoice greatly, O daughter Zion! Shout aloud, O daughter Jerusalem! Lo, your king comes to you; triumphant and victorious is he, humble and riding on a donkey, on a colt, the foal of a donkey. (Zech 9:9)

The lowly king, then, is not something invented by the Evangelists, but something they find in their interpretive tradition—like everything else they find and use to develop their claim that Jesus fulfills biblical prophecy.

Subsequent historians and theologians of Christianity interpret Jesus' messianic role in a variety of ways. James Tabor sees Jesus as a failed messiah, a political aspirant who is killed before he can achieve his goals. Albert Schweitzer, writing in 1906, understands Jesus to be an eschatological prophet, preaching the imminent end of the age and the coming reign of God. Dietrich Bonhoeffer, a twentieth-century Christian martyr who died at the hands of the Nazis, probably categorizes Jesus as the suffering servant of Isaiah, the one who "comes and bids us die" in service to others. Most Christians today believe that Jesus is God's divine son and that his kingship is both spiritual and temporal. They take their cues, in part, from Paul's description of the last judgment:

> Then comes the end, when he hands over the kingdom to God the Father, after he has destroyed every ruler and every authority and power. For he must reign until he has put all his enemies under his feet. (1 Cor 15:24–25)

Those Christians for whom the book of Revelation is central see Jesus as a future king, come to rule, avenge, battle, and ultimately triumph over all earthly, and unearthly, forces.

In short, the New Testament does not provide a single interpretation of messiah but instead reflects the diversity of first-century Judaic thought. Traditional scholarship has tended to identify Hellenistic influences on Christian messianism, and it may be fair to say that images of the Messiah as healer, giver of eternal life, or divine son may indeed come from pagan sources. These explanations ignore the fact, however, that New Testament messianism generally has its roots in the Judaic thought and expectations of its day. It is only neglecting literature from Qumran and the Pseude- pigrapha, as well as the Tanakh itself, that allows Jews and Christians to conclude that New Testament views are a departure.

Who Is Right?

It should be clear by now that Jews and Christians both stand on solid ground when they make claims about what constitutes a messiah. Biblical and extra-biblical sources give us many ways to approach first-century mes- sianism. Indeed it is nearly impossible to speak of a single coherent mes- sianic expectation from the sources of this period. To limit the image strictly to political kingship ignores a large store of competing texts. To claim that God "reinterpreted" the meaning of messiah spiritualizes histor- ical realities and expectations. Neither contemporary Jews nor Christians may accept this paradox, however. An incident from one of our classes il- lustrates this. After we carefully articulated these arguments about messian- ism in a course on Jewish and Christian origins, a student came up after class and asked "Why don't Christians realize that the messiah was supposed to be a king?" Only if we discount a large amount of data can we make the claim that there is only a single type of messiah: a royal one. Unfortu- nately, this is eventually what happens in the history of Jewish and Chris- tian relations.

Those who pave the way for the development of Christianity adopt the theme of heavenly and spiritual redemption, which clearly exists in a wealth of Judaic texts and traditions, as we have shown. Jesus' followers un- derstand him through the interpretation of these texts. At the same time, the Gospels depict Jesus as preaching an earthly reign of God, coming in the here and now. The early church has to deal with the fact that its mes- siah has not completed the work of redemption and so must come back in order to finish the job. Thus we see the theology of a "second coming," in which the messiah returns. Redemption occurs in this world and the next.

Those who pave the way for the development of rabbinic Judaism adopt the theme of political and earthly redemption, as outlined in the He- brew Bible and other extra-biblical writings. Jews use the same texts that Christians employ, but obviously read them non-christologically, that is, without using Jesus as the hermeneutical key for interpretation. Jewish messianic expectations continue after the destruction of the second temple in Jerusalem, and even give rise to a second Jewish war in 132–135 C.E. This war, as the first, attempts to establish an earthly kingdom. It is only after the failure of the bar Kokhba revolt, as this war is called, that we begin to observe a shift in Jewish thinking. This shift is noticeable in the Mishna, composed around 200 C.E., which emphasizes priesthood and priestly practices over kingship and messianism.

What most Jews and Christians share today is a belief in the futurity of the messiah. That is, the messiah will come—or will come again, for Christians—at some point in the future. The work of redemption is postponed to a time we cannot currently see. Jews throughout history have adopted various leaders as their messiahs. These figures—who range from political and military to spiritual, mystical, and theological leaders—are not divine, but are thought to introduce a new and better reality for Jews. Today, the personal messiah has been replaced, or perhaps reinterpreted is a better word, by the theology of a messianic age in Reform Judaism: a time in which peace and justice exist on earth and righteousness prevails. Conservative Jews may believe in an actual messiah or in a messianic age, but Orthodox Jews believe an actual earthly, kingly figure will emerge. Some Orthodox Jews even want to rebuild the temple in Jerusalem to precipitate the arrival of this messiah. For the most part, however, modern Judaism sees the messiah as a goal and a hope rather than a reality or a necessity, though there are exceptions among the most apocalyptic of Jews.

Christians have also provided messianic interpretations of events and history throughout the ages. As early as the second century, some believe that Jesus' arrival is imminent. The Middle Ages in Europe see widespread messianic expectations, and during the Reformation, radicals establish millennial kingdoms in the hope that Jesus is returning. During the nineteenth century, millennialism—the belief that Jesus is coming soon to inaugurate a new age—spreads across the United States, and we see the development of a number of new Christian denominations, such as the Seventh-day Adventists; the Church of Jesus Christ, Latter-day Saints; and the Jehovah's Witnesses. These are exceptions, however, to the generally amillennial (or non-millennial) nature of Christianity for two thousand years. For the most part, modern Christianity sees the second coming of the Messiah—that is, the Christ—as a goal and a hope rather than a reality or a necessity, though of course there are exceptions among the most apocalyptic of Christians.

What Jews and Christians Can Agree On

What we have tried to communicate in this volume is how much Jews and Christians have in common, and have had in common, right from the beginning. Their religions develop at the same time, out of the same "cultic milieu" (to draw upon the expression coined by Colin Campbell). Using the same texts and traditions, the ancestors of Christians and Jews, as well as a number of other groups that either die out or are killed off, all conceive of a god whose presence extends beyond the boundaries of a single location. This deity can be experienced in the community of believers—whether in the home, at the dining table, in worship together, or in the study of scripture. This god can be encountered in the reading of Torah or in the worship of the Incarnation. Most importantly, this portable god can be found in spiritual communities and individuals, who serve as the new temple for the divine presence.

It is ironic that two groups that have so much in common can believe they are so far apart on so many issues. For Christians, the idea that God could take on the form of a human is articulated best in the Word becoming Flesh. For Jews, at least from the rabbinic period on, it seems to work, as Lawrence Kushner notes, in the other direction. In the desire to raise humanity to the holiness inherent in the Torah's teaching, the flesh is transformed into word.[2]

The predecessors of today's Jews and Christians debated with each other; they defined themselves, and their opponents, out of these debates. Working with the same raw materials or words they constructed very different institutions. That much is a historical given, the datum of where we have come from. It need not dictate where we must go, however, nor should it. By understanding the past we can direct the future. "What is past is prologue," said Shakespeare. While the prologue helps us to understand the present, it is not the whole story. That remains to be written.

Suggestions for Further Reading

Beatrice Bruteau, ed. *Jesus through Jewish Eyes: Rabbis and Scholars Engage an Ancient Brother in a New Conversation*. Maryknoll: Orbis, 2001, 120.

J. Charlesworth, H. Lichtenberger, G. Oegema, eds. *Qumran-Messianism: Studies on Messianic Expectations in the Dead Sea Scrolls*. Tübingen: Mohr Siebeck, 1998.

Dan Cohn-Sherbock. *The Jewish Messiah*. Edinburgh: T&T Clark, 1997.

Ed Condra. *Salvation for the Righteous Revealed: Jesus amid Covenantal and Messianic Expectations in Second Temple Judaism*. Boston: Brill, 2002.

J. Neusner, W. S. Green, E. Frerichs, eds. *Judaisms and Their Messiahs at the Turn of the Christian Era*. Cambridge: Cambridge University Press, 1987.

K. E. Pomykala. *The Davidic Dynasty Tradition in Early Judaism: Its History and Significance for Messianism.* Atlanta: Scholars Press, 1995.

James D. Tabor. *The Jesus Dynasty: The Hidden History of Jesus, His Royal Family, and the Birth of Christianity.* New York: Simon and Schuster, 2006.

James VanderKam. "Messianism in the Scrolls." In Eugene Ulrich and James VanderKam, *The Community of the Renewed Covenant: The Notre Dame Symposium on the Dead Sea Scrolls.* Notre Dame: University of Notre Dame Press, 1994, 211–34.

Notes

1. James D. Tabor, *The Jesus Dynasty: The Hidden History of Jesus, His Royal Family, and the Birth of Christianity* (New York: Simon and Schuster, 2006).

2. Lawrence Kushner, "My Lunch with Jesus," in *Jesus Through Jewish Eyes: Rabbis and Scholars Engage an Ancient Brother in a New Conversation* ed. Beatrice Bruteau (Maryknoll: Orbis, 2001), 120.

Glossary

Aggadah. Heb., "narration" or "recital." The term for the writings that illustrate and interpret non-legal portions of the Torah. The *Haggadah* is the Passover liturgy, or story, which elaborates on the account of the Israelites' exodus from Egypt (Exod 12–16).

Ahura Mazda. A wholly good and completely just god, described by Zoroaster, a Persian prophet ca. 1400–1200 B.C.E. Ahura Mazda wages cosmic war with Angra Mainyu on a battleground that includes heaven and earth. Zoroaster prophesies that eventually Ahura Mazda will prevail over Angra Mainyu, but in the meantime, the evil spirit will corrupt and degrade the world that Ahura Mazda created perfect and good.

Akiba, Rabbi. (50–135 C.E.) Second-century revered sage, martyred during the Second Jewish War, who identified Simon bar Kosiba as the messiah.

Alexander the Great. (d. 323 B.C.E.) Macedonian military commander who successfully spread Greek civilization throughout the Mediterranean world and far beyond to the east.

Aliyah. Heb., literally "to ascend." The practice of Jews from around the world to emigrate to Israel and settle there. Also refers to being called up to bless the Torah during Torah reading in synagogue services.

Amidah. Central Jewish prayer, which, according to the rabbis, was instituted as a replacement for daily temple offerings.

Amillennial. The non-millennial outlook of Christianity historically, in contrast to the millennialism of early Christianity and certain contemporary Christian groups.

Amoraim. Aram., "speakers" or "expounders." The sages in Babylonia and in Israel whose activities began after the redaction of the Mishna (200

C.E.) and continued to the final compilation of the Babylonian Talmud in 500 C.E.

Angra Mainyu. An evil spirit who is wholly wicked and completely destructive, locked in battle with Ahura Mazda, in Zoroastrian religion.

Antiochus III. Seleucid ruler in charge of Judea (r. 223–187) who adopted a liberal policy with the Judean residents.

Antiochus IV. Seleucid ruler in charge of Judea (r. 175–164) who adopted a policy of forced Hellenization, which led to the Maccabean revolt.

Apocalypse. A literary genre in which divine mysteries are revealed to human visitors to heaven.

Apocalypticism. A belief that develops during times of intense oppression that God is going to intervene militarily to right the wrongs of the earth. Usually armed conflict between the forces of good and the forces of evil is involved, with battles fought on earth as well as in heaven.

Apocrypha. A body of literature written in the period 250 B.C.E. to 200 C.E. that is not canonized in either the Hebrew Bible, the Old Testament, or the New Testament. *See also* Pseudepigrapha.

Apostle. Gr., literally, "one sent out." Apostle refers to missionaries in the early church, including, but not limited to, Jesus' twelve disciples.

Apostolic Constitutions. Early Christian collection of ecclesiastical regulations on discipline, worship, and doctrine from late fourth century.

Apostolic Tradition. The belief in Christianity that a body of doctrine originating in the teachings of Jesus Christ has been preserved intact by apostles, who have faithfully and accurately passed the tradition along.

Aquila. Gentile translator of Hebrew Bible into Greek before 177 C.E. who converted to Judaism, possibly a disciple of R. Akiba.

Aramaic Targumim. *See* Targums

Aristobulus, Judas. Hasmonean king of Judea (r. 104–103 B.C.E.) who promoted Hellenism. The first of the Hasmoneans to adopt the title "king."

Ark of the Covenant. In the Hebrew Bible, the container in which the tablets of the law are preserved and maintained in the holiest part of the Jerusalem temple.

Atonement. The process by which reconciliation between God and humanity occurs. Atonement requires a sacrifice in Jewish and Christian teaching.

Babylonian Exile. *See* Exile

Bar Kokhba. *See* Simon bar Kosiba

B.C.E. Before the Common Era. The designation used by biblical scholars to denote the period in the Christian calendar known as B.C. *See also* C.E.

Bethel. Literally, "house of God." Ancient site associated with Abraham and Jacob. Under the divided kingdom, Jeroboam I built a shrine there; the prophet Amos denounced another prophet at the sanctuary there (Amos 7:10–17).

Boethusians. A schismatic Judaic group probably related to the Sadducees, with family members serving as high priests during the era of Herod the Great.

Caligula (Gaius Julius Caesar Germanicus). Brutal Roman emperor (r. 37–41 C.E.) who offended the Judeans of Jerusalem by planning to place a statue of himself in the temple.

Canon. The official list of books considered to be holy scripture.

C.E. Common Era. The designation biblical scholars use to indicate the period called A.D. (Anno Domini) in the Christian calendar.

Chain of Tradition. The belief in Judaism that oral teachings God gave Moses at Mount Sinai have been preserved intact by sages, who have faithfully and accurately passed the tradition along.

Christology. In Christianity, the doctrine of Christ's identity, which answers the question "Who is Christ?" New Testament sources give a variety of answers.

Circumcision. The removal of the foreskin of a man's penis; the sign of the covenant God made with Abraham (Gen 17:9–14) and the sign of male membership in the covenant God has with the Israelites.

Clement, Bishop of Rome. Roman bishop (ca. 90–100 C.E.) who authored a letter that described the process by which God delegated authority and instruction from Jesus to apostles, bishops, and deacons.

Clement of Alexandria. Hellenized Christian of Alexandria (ca. 150–ca. 215) who drew upon Greek philosophy and Philo of Alexandria to develop a Christian "philosophy."

Community Rule. 1QS, a scroll found at Khirbet Qumran near the Dead Sea that presents the strict rules of the community apparently living there.

Copper Scroll. 3Q15, perhaps the most puzzling of all the Dead Sea Scrolls. Inscribed upon a sheet of copper and written in twelve columns, the text cites some sixty-four locations where over 100 tons of gold, silver, scrolls, and priestly items were supposedly hidden.

Covenant. A contract or binding agreement made between two parties in which both agree to do something. In the Hebrew Bible, the covenant

between God and the Israelites specifies that God will protect the Israelites, and they in turn will observe the commandments.

Cultus. The religious practices of a group, usually priests, in dealing with
its deity.

Cyrus the Great. Persian emperor (ca. 590 or 576–529 B.C.E.) noted in the
book of Isaiah (44:28, 45:1, and 45:13) who crushed the Babylonian
Empire and allowed the Israelites to return from their exile in Babylon.

Deacons. Gr., literally, "servants." An office in the early church in which
the officer had teaching functions. This office still exists today.

Dead Sea Scrolls. A large body of literature discovered in 1945 in the
Judean Desert near the Dead Sea. The majority of scrolls come from an
area called Khirbet Qumran, near the site of a first-century religious
group, which archaeologists have excavated.

Decalogue. *See* Ten Commandments

Deuterocanonical Texts. The books of the Christian Old Testament that
are considered sacred by Catholic and Orthodox Christians but are excluded by Protestant Christians. These texts include Ben Sira, Wisdom
of Solomon, Tobit, Judith, and others.

Deuteronomist Source. The Torah source that today is represented by the
book of Deuteronomy, authored by the Deuteronomist (D), an unknown writer who compiled and edited this work.

Dialogue with Trypho. A dialogue created by Justin Martyr (d. ca. 163) in
which Justin purportedly has a discussion with a Jew. This work begins
to delineate clear differences between Christians and Jews.

Diaspora. Literally, "scattering." Judeans who lived outside the land of Israel in the period 250 B.C.E. to 200 C.E., and today, Jews who live
outside of Israel.

Didache. A type of instruction manual providing guidelines for rituals and
practices for the early Christian community, dated to between 100 and
120 C.E., although the material it contains may be much older.

Didascalia. A lost, third-century Christian instruction manual outlining regulations for church life.

Dualism. A belief in the radical opposition of good and evil, especially as
part of apocalypticism.

Elephantine. A diaspora community of Judeans in Upper Egypt on the
Nile (ca. 495–399 B.C.E.) that had its own temple and continued a sacrificial system outside of Jerusalem. Known chiefly through the papyri
documents it generated and through archaeological excavations.

Elohim. One of the Hebrew words for God used in the Hebrew Bible.

Elohist Source. Scholarly term designated for one of the Pentateuchal sources (E). The name arose from its characteristic use of "Elohim" to denote the name of God.

Enoch. In Genesis 5:21–24 Enoch does not die but ascends into heaven. In the period 250 B.C.E. to 200 C.E., Enoch is a major figure in pseudepigraphical literature and the hero of apocalypses.

Enochic Judaism. Judaic group presumed to have existed from 300 B.C.E. to 200 C.E. that takes the pseudepigraphical book of 1 Enoch as its primary text. A heavenly redeemer plays an important role in other texts used by Enochic Judaism.

Eschatology. The doctrine of last things. Judaic eschatology in the period 250 B.C.E. to 200 C.E. was the apocalyptic precursor to the later Christian theology of a heavenly event, such as a final battle between good and evil. Eschatology may also be an earthly reality, such as the presence of the reign of God.

Essene. A "philosophy," described by Josephus and Philo, which seemed to follow ascetic practices. The Essenes have been linked to the documents found at Qumran, and many scholars believe they composed them.

Eucharist. Also known as communion, the Lord's Supper, the Mass, and the liturgy, Eucharist is the ritual taking of bread and wine practiced by Christians.

Exile. The period from 587/586 B.C.E. to 539 B.C.E. in which Judahites were deported from Judah to Babylonia. The time in which much of the Torah was composed.

Exousia. Gr., "power." A charismatic type of power and authority, which prophets, including Jesus, seemed to exert.

Ezra. A priest in post-Exilic times who read the Book of the Law to the Judahites who returned to Judah after the Exile.

Fertile Crescent. The geographic region between the Tigris and Euphrates Rivers, now modern-day Iraq, in which agriculture and early civilizations appeared to develop.

Galilee. Rural hill country to the northeast of Jerusalem; the region where Jesus grew up.

Gamaliel I. Patriarch of the Sanhedrin, grandson of Hillel, mentioned twice in the New Testament (Acts 5:34, 22:3). Reputed teacher of Paul, exponent of the liberal wing of the Pharisaic party.

Gemara. Commentary on the Mishna. Mishna and Gemara combined make up the Talmud.

Gentiles. English word for *goyim*, or nations. In the period 200 B.C.E. to the present, it refers to non-Jews.

Gospel. Literally, "good news." The four New Testament gospels—Matthew, Mark, Luke, John—give accounts of Jesus' life and teachings.

Hadrian, Publius Aelius. Roman emperor (r. 117–138 C.E.) who banned circumcision; Second Jewish War resulted. He razed Jerusalem and built a pagan city on its ruins, called Aelius Capitolina.

Haftarah. Selections from the prophetic books of the Bible recited after the Torah reading at Sabbath morning services and on festivals.

Haggadah. See Aggadah

Halakah. The body of rabbinic literature that deals with religious obligations as interpreted from Torah laws and commandments.

Hannah's Prayer. Prayer of thanksgiving given by the barren wife of Elkanah (1 Sam 2:1–10) after she gives birth to the prophet Samuel.

Hasmonean Period. The period ca. 140–63 B.C.E. in which the Hasmonean family controlled the priesthood and military/political power. The Maccabees come from the Hasmonean family.

Hebrew Bible. The name given to the text shared by Jews, Christians, and Muslims. Jews also know this text as Tanakh, while Christians know it as the Old Testament.

Hellenism. A complex of mores and values that promoted a global and universalist culture. It began with Alexander the Great (ca. 333 B.C.E.) and continued as a widespread worldview into the Roman period.

Heresiologists. Theological "heresy hunters" in early Christianity. They studied heresies, gathered information on them, and wrote treatises describing and denouncing non-orthodox Christian beliefs and practices.

Hermeneutical Lenses. Hermeneutics refers to methods of interpretation. Hermeneutical lenses refers to the methodological approach one takes to the Bible or other texts. One might adopt a feminist hermeneutic, a fundamentalist hermeneutic, a Jewish hermeneutic, and so on.

Herod the Great. Idumean ruler of Judea under the Romans (r. 37–4 B.C.E.) who enlarged the temple complex in Jerusalem. Herod was a Hellenizer who wanted the rest of the Mediterranean world to see Judea as a sophisticated and cultured place.

High Priest. Heb., *kohen gadol*. Chief among the priests, descended directly from Aaron. Only priest to wear the ephod and breastplate and the only one who could enter the holy of holies.

Hillel. Sage (ca. first century B.C.E.–C.E.) who provided relatively "liberal" interpretations of halakah.

Hippolytus. Second-century Christian antipope who nevertheless was well respected as a prolific writer after his martyrdom, with numerous commentaries and refutations of heresies.

Hyrcanus, John. A member of the Hasmonean family, Simon's son, John Hyrcanus was a high priest and commander of the army in Judea, 134–104 B.C.E.

Ignatius of Antioch. Christian bishop (d. ca. 110 C.E.) martyred during the rule of Emperor Trajan (r. 98–117 C.E.). He might be called the first Christian, because he used the term to describe himself.

Immanence. God's closeness, or nearness, in the world; as opposed to transcendence.

Incarnation. The "enfleshment" of the Logos of God, in John 1:14. This refers to God becoming human in the person of Jesus.

Ioudaismos. The cultural, ethnic, geographic, and political values of Judeans living within Hellenistic society; a precursor to Judaism, but not Judaism as it is understood or practiced today.

Irenaeus. Christian bishop and heresiologist (ca. 125–ca. 202 C.E.) who wrote treatises condemning Gnostic Christianity.

Israel. A word denoting a number of different concepts: the name adopted by Jacob after wrestling with an angel (Gen 32:22–28); the collective name of Jacob's sons; the name of the northern kingdom; the name of a people who make a covenant with God at Mount Sinai; a modern nation created in 1948.

James, brother of Jesus (d. ca. 62 C.E.). Leader of the church in Jerusalem. Maintained traditions and customs of Judeans.

Jamnia. *See* Yavneh

Jannaeus, Alexander. Son of John Hyrcanus, brother of Aristobulus, a high priest and king in the Hasmonean dynasty (r. 103–76 B.C.E.).

Jesus Movement. The term scholars use to describe the followers of Jesus and those in the early church; preferable to the term "Christians," which was not in common usage until the second century C.E.

Jewish War, First. Revolt against Roman imperial rule in Judea, 66–73 C.E. The Romans destroyed the temple in Jerusalem in 70 C.E. Rebels held out at Masada until 73 C.E.

Jewish War, Second. A second revolt against Roman imperial rule, 132–135 C.E. Led by Simon bar Kosiba, there is some indication that it was inspired by interest in rebuilding the temple in Jerusalem.

Johannine Literature. New Testament books that seem to share common themes; these include the Gospel of John; 1, 2, and 3 John; and Revelation.

John of Patmos. Presumptive author of Revelation. It is not entirely clear who he was historically. Some scholars say that he was a bishop of Ephesus.

Jonathan ben Uziel. One of eighty Tannaim who studied under Hillel, he is known as the author of the Targum Jonathan.

Jonathan, High Priest. High priest and commander of the army of Judea, 152–143 C.E.

Josephus, Flavius. (37–ca. 100 C.E.) Judean military commander and cultural interpreter whose works—*The Jewish War, Antiquities of the Jews,* and *Life*—provide historians a great deal of information about first-century Judean culture.

Judah, Judahite. A son of Jacob/Israel; the name of the southern kingdom after the Assyrian invasion of the northern kingdom; a geographical region. A Judahite is a person from Judah. The name Judah becomes Judea in the Hellenistic period.

Jupiter Capitolinus. Statue honoring the Greek god Jupiter placed in the Jerusalem temple in the Seleucid period, which helps ignite the Maccabean Revolt.

Justin Martyr. (ca. 100–ca. 165 C.E.) Christian philosopher of the second century who explained Christianity to a Hellenistic audience. Wrote an important tract, *Dialogue with Trypho*, which outlined what he saw as the key differences between Christianity and Judaism.

Kavod. Heb., the presence of God; literally, "glory." God cannot be seen, but God's glory can. This glory signifies God's presence.

Kiddush. Blessing said over wine and bread at the Sabbath meal.

Korban. Heb., sacrifice; literally, "to get close to." Something is korban when it is offered to God.

Leontopolis. A temple was built in Leontopolis in Lower Egypt ca. 163–145 B.C.E. as part of a political conflict between the Ptolemaic and Seleucid dynasties.

Levites. Sons of Levi, a son of Jacob. Levites are priests who perform various functions at the temple.

Logos. Gr., "word," "reason," or "rationality" of God. In Greek philosophy, applied to God's power in creation. In Christian theology, refers to God's presence in Jesus, as when the Logos of God takes up residence in the flesh of Jesus (John 1:1–4, 14).

Lord's Prayer. Prayer said by Jesus (Matt 6:9–13 // Luke 11:2–4), recited in churches today. It has elements similar to Jewish prayers.

Maccabean Revolt. Rebellion against Seleucid domination and corrupt priesthood, 152–143 B.C.E. Led by Judas Maccabeus ("The Hammer") who is a member of the Hasmonean family.

Mashiach. *See* Messiah

Melchizedek. Gentile priest and king who met with Abraham (Gen 14:18) and is noted in Psalm 110:4. Jesus is compared to Melchizedek (Heb 5:10; 6:20; 7:1, 10–11, 15, 17).

Melito of Sardis. (d. ca. 180 C.E.) Second-century Christian bishop in Asia Minor whose *Pascal Homily* interprets Passover as describing the passion of Jesus. This work may have inspired Jews to revise their own Passover Haggadah, according to Israel Yuval.

Menelaus. One of the corrupt temple priests who served under Antiochus IV in the Seleucid period.

Messiah. Heb., anointed one; literally, "poured-over one." Generally refers to kings in the Hebrew Bible, although priests and prophets are also anointed and called messiahs. The Hebrew Bible and Dead Sea Scrolls describe a future rule of two messiahs: a priest and a king. Messiah takes on soteriological meaning in the first centuries B.C.E. and C.E., and especially with Christian interpretations of the messiah as a savior figure.

Mezuzah, mezuzot (pl.). A small container that holds a biblical text, such as Deut 6:4, placed on the doorpost of a Judean family home. A sign of the presence of God, as well as a Judean identity marker.

Midrash. Rabbinic commentary and elaboration on biblical stories.

Millennialism. Initially, the Christian belief in Jesus Christ's thousand-year reign on earth before the final defeat of Satan, based on an interpretation of Revelation. Currently, any belief in a better, brighter future that is brought about by heavenly beings, human action, or both.

Mishna. A collection of legal opinions made by sages from the second century B.C.E. to the second century C.E. Compiled by Judah ha-Nasi (the "Prince") ca. 200 C.E. The Mishna serves as the foundation of textualized Oral Torah.

Mount Sinai. The location in Exodus where Moses encountered God and received commandments for the Israelites to follow in order to maintain their covenant with God (Exod 19). In Deuteronomy, it is called Mount Horeb (Deut 1).

Nebuchadnezzar. Babylonian king and general whose armies invaded Judah in the sixth century B.C.E. He destroyed the temple in Jerusalem in 587/586 B.C.E. and deported the Judahites to Babylonia.

Old Testament. Collection of texts primarily in Hebrew that Christians incorporate into their Bible. The Protestant Old Testament contains the books of Tanakh, while the Catholic and Orthodox Old Testaments also contain books from the Septuagint.

Onias. Judean high priest under reign of Antiochus IV (r. 175–164 B.C.E.) who was replaced by Jason, another corrupt priest of the era.

Onkelos. *See* Targums

Paschal Theology. In Christian theology, the understanding of Jesus as the "paschal," or sacrificial lamb, whose death atones for the sins of humanity.

Passover. The Jewish festival that commemorates the deliverance of the Israelites from Egyptian slavery (Exod 12–16). The week-long observance begins with a seder, a special meal, in which the Passover Haggadah recounts the story of the flight from Egypt.

Pastoral Letters. In the New Testament, 1 Timothy, 2 Timothy, and Titus are attributed to Paul, though scholars question Pauline authorship because of different vocabulary and theology.

Patriarch. The patriarchs in the Hebrew Bible are the ancestors of the Israelites, usually identified as Abraham, Isaac, and Jacob. In a later era, the Jewish Patriarchs are leaders of the synagogue in Jerusalem, or synagogues in the Diaspora. In modern Christianity, Patriarchs are the religious leaders in Orthodox churches.

Paul the Apostle. Also known as Saul of Tarsus, Paul had a revelation of Jesus (Acts 9:1–9, 22:6–11; Gal 1:11–16) that sent him on a mission to Gentiles to bring them the good news of Jesus' triumph over death in the resurrection. Instrumental in founding many churches, his teachings serve as the foundation for subsequent Christian doctrine, especially regarding observance of Judaic practices.

Peniel. The place where Jacob wrestled with a divine being (Gen 33:22–33). One of many sacred sites mentioned in the Hebrew Bible.

Pentateuch. The first five books of the Hebrew Bible: Genesis (Bereshit), Exodus (Shemot), Leviticus (Vayikra), Numbers (Bemidbar), and Deuteronomy (Devarim). Also called the five books of Moses. Called the Torah in Judaism.

Pentecost. Also known as the Feast of Weeks (Exod 34:22; Deut 16:10). In Hebrew, Shavuot, originally a harvest festival, later an observance of the giving of the Torah at Mount Sinai, celebrated 50 days after Passover. Christians observe Pentecost as the descent of the Holy Spirit and the birth of the church (Acts 2:1–41).

Pesher, Pesharim (pl.). Biblical commentary and interpretation, especially that instituted by the Righteous Teacher at Qumran. Numerous pesharim are found among the Dead Sea Scrolls.

Pharisees. One of the four philosophies identified by Josephus. Pharisees have a reputation for observing traditions and customs handed down by the elders. They are known for their attention to sabbath, tithing, hand washing, and dietary restrictions.

Philo. Alexandrian Judean (20 B.C.E–50 C.E.) known for integrating Hellenistic philosophical and rhetorical concepts into his explanation of the customs of the Judeans.

Pirke Abot. Also known as Chapters of the Fathers, a work dated to the mid–third century, which now constitutes the first chapter of the Mishna. A collection of sayings emphasizing the importance of Torah study and religious observance. The first two chapters of the work describe a "chain of tradition" extending from Moses to the schools of Hillel, Shammai, and Gamaliel.

Polycarp. Christian bishop and martyr (ca. 70–ca. 155 C.E.). He makes up an element of Apostolic Tradition in Christianity.

Pompey (Gnaeus Pompeius Magnus). Roman general (106–48 B.C.E.) who took Jerusalem in 63 B.C.E. and initiated Roman rule of Judea.

Pontius Pilate. Roman Prefect (r. 26–36 C.E.) of Judea, described by his contemporaries as "greedy and cruel." Sentenced Jesus of Nazareth to death.

Priestly Source. Priestly Pentateuchal source (P), consisting of genealogical, statistical, and legal material; major sections occur at the end of Exodus, the first twenty-seven chapters of Leviticus, and the first ten chapters of Numbers.

Prophets. Heb., navi. Truth-tellers, advisors, and social critics who preach the word of God, the Hebrew prophets predict the future, but primarily as a way to exhort people to change before it is too late. A prophet in Israelite religion was viewed as divinely inspired.

Proseuche. Gr., "house of prayer." Philo describes proseuche as locations where Judeans gather weekly to study Torah and listen to its interpretation.

Proto-Orthodox. The designation given to the type of Christianity that ultimately prevailed at the Council of Nicea in 325 C.E.

Pseudepigrapha. A body of literature that purports to have been written at an earlier time, usually by a biblical figure, such as Adam, Moses, or Enoch.

Pseudo-Aristeas. Author of a pseudepigraphical work, the Letter of Aristeas. He describes the translation of the Septuagint, as well as customs of Judeans in Alexandria.

Ptolemy I (Soter). Egyptian general (ca. 367/366–283/282 B.C.E.) who took Judea from the Greeks and began Ptolemaic empire.

Ptolemy II (Philadelphus). Egyptian king of Ptolemaic Dynasty (r. 285–246 B.C.E.) who authorized Greek translation of Hebrew scripture.

Pythagoras. Greek mathematician (570–ca. 500 B.C.E.) who Philo claims was influenced by Moses.

Qumran. Also known as Khirbet Qumran. The site near the Dead Sea in Israel where hundreds of scrolls were found, as well as the ruins of a first-century C.E. community. Scholarly consensus is that the people living in the community produced the scrolls, but it is not definite whether they can be identified as Essenes.

Rabbinic Judaism. Judaism that developed after the period of the second temple. After the destruction of the Jerusalem temple in 70 C.E., a group of teachers, called rabbis (Heb., "master" or "teacher") collected the teachings of sages and committed them to writing.

Redaction. The process of editing. In biblical studies, redaction refers to the process by which different traditions are compiled into a single narrative.

Reformation. The movement within Christianity in the sixteenth century that called for sweeping reforms of the church. It led to the split between Protestant and Catholic Christians.

Sadducees. One of Josephus' four philosophies, the Sadducees may be aligned with the priesthood. They seemed to be the wealthy, upper class. Little is known about them or their beliefs other than the fact that they rejected the idea of Oral Torah or traditions outside the Written Torah.

Samaritans. Descendants of the group formed by the mixture of Israelites remaining in the northern kingdom of Israel with others settled there by the Assyrians after 722 B.C.E. They have their own holy mountain, Mount Gerizim, and a temple in their holy city of Schechem. Judahites, and then Judeans, looked down upon Samaritans as unclean. The Samaritans accept the laws of the Torah but reject other books of the Bible and the Talmud.

Scripture. Sacred texts that a particular group finds holy or extremely significant. Most of the world's religions have scripture, but attitudes toward it vary, with some people reading scripture very literally and
others reading it metaphorically.

Sectarian. Referring to sects, this term suggests taking a religious, or even
biased, approach to a subject. In religious studies it is contrasted with
an academic or scholarly approach, which purports to be neutral.

Sectarian Scrolls. In the Dead Sea literature, texts that describe the rules of
the community at Qumran or indicate the beliefs of the community, as
opposed to biblical texts or interpretations of texts.

Secular. A modern concept that divides the world into religious and non-
religious arenas. The secular arena is considered non-religious. In the
ancient world, this division does not exist.

Seleucid dynasty. Syrian rulers who dominated Judea (201–152 B.C.E.)
and precipitated the Maccabean Revolt by their forced Hellenization of
the culture.

Septuagint. Oldest extant Greek translation of Hebrew scripture, made
during the rule of Ptolemy II (r. 285–246 B.C.E.); contains a number
of books not in today's Jewish or Protestant canons, but included within
the Old Testament of Catholic and Orthodox Christians.

Shammai. A sage (ca. 50 B.C.E.–30 C.E.) whose interpretations of halakah
tended to be stricter than those of his contemporary, Hillel. His opinions are recorded in the Mishna.

Shavuot. *See* Pentecost

Shekinah. Heb., "presence." Refers to the presence of God.

Shema. Heb., "hear." From Deut 6:4, "Hear O Israel, the Lord is our God,
the Lord alone." The basic statement of faith for Jews. Scrolls containing the shema are found in *mezuzot* from the first century C.E.

Simon bar Kosiba. Also known as Simon bar Kokhba, leader of the Second Jewish Revolt (132–135 C.E.); captured Jerusalem, minted coins,
and may have attempted to rebuild a temple; considered the messiah by
R. Akiba.

Soteriology. In Christian theology, the doctrine of how Jesus saves; what
Jesus does that brings salvation.

Supersessionism. The belief among some Christians today, and within
Christianity historically, that Christianity supersedes Judaism as God's
plan of salvation for people.

Symmachus. (late second century C.E.) Translator of Hebrew Bible into a
Greek version that more faithfully represents the original Hebrew.

Synagogue. Gr., "meeting," or "assembly." Initially referred to a congregation of people, and apparently served as a community center for

Judeans living in Diaspora. In the first century C.E., it became associated with a building. It is not entirely clear what goes on in a synagogue at this time, but it appears that Torah study and commentary occur.

Synoptic Gospels. The gospels of Matthew, Mark, and Luke, which share many similarities because Matthew and Luke appear to rely upon Mark for the basic story outline. The Synoptics depict Jesus as a preacher, teacher, and healer, in contrast to John's gospel, which shows Jesus as a heavenly figure who reveals God before returning to heaven.

Tabernacle. A sanctuary in which the ark of the covenant is housed; in Israelite religion, the tent of meeting that is the "dwelling" place of God.

Talmud. A body of literature in rabbinic Judaism that includes the Mishna and extensive commentary upon the Mishna (the Gemara).

Tanakh. Jewish scripture, which includes the Torah, the Prophets, and the Writings. The acronym Tanakh comes from Torah, Nevi'im, and Ketuvim.

Tannaim. Aram., "teachers." Rabbinic sages of the oral law who taught in the first century (20–200 C.E.). Their immediate predecessors were Hillel and Shammai. Responsible for the compilation of oral law into the Mishna, the Tosefta, the Baraita, and the Midrash Halakah. More than 120 Tannaim are cited in the Mishna.

Targums, Targumim. The Targums are Aramaic translations of Hebrew scripture, with commentary added. The Targum Onkelos is dated to second century C.E. and ascribed to the proselyte Onkelos. The Targum Jonathan is the targum to the Prophets, and is attributed in the Talmud to Jonathan ben Uziel.

Teacher of Righteousness. Also known as the Righteous Teacher, this mysterious figure is apparently the founder of the community at Qumran. Scrolls from the Dead Sea refer to this person as an inspired interpreter of scripture who teaches his followers how to read and understand Torah and Prophets.

Tefillin. Also called phylacteries. Small, quadrangular, black leather boxes containing four biblical passages that are worn around the head by observant Jewish males following the commandments in Exodus 13:1–10, 11–16 and Deuteronomy 6:4–9, 13–21 to bind the law onto their arms and wear it on their foreheads to keep God's commandments ever in mind.

Ten Commandments. The commandments from God that Moses brought to the Israelites at Mount Sinai (Exod 20:1–17, Deut 5:6–21).

Tertullian. (ca. 160–225 C.E.) Important Christian theologian in the early church; one of the heresiologists concerned about correct doctrine.

Theodicy. A theology that vindicates the goodness of God in the face of suffering and injustice.

Theodotion. (late second century C.E.) A Jew who translated Hebrew scripture into Greek, following the idiom of the Hebrew text and transliterating some Hebrew words into Greek. Christians widely adopted his translation, as did Jews.

Theology. The study of doctrines about God; more generally, the examination and systematization of religious beliefs.

Theophany. Gr., from the word meaning "appearance of God" (to a person). A manifestation, or appearance, of the divine. The appearance of God in the burning bush to Moses (Exod 3) is a theophany.

Therapeutae. Ascetic Judaic group in Egypt described by Philo of Alexandria, with some qualities similar, though not identical, to the Essenes.

Thummim. See Urim and Thummim

Titus Flavius Sabinus Vespasianus. (39–81 C.E.) Roman general who sacked Jerusalem and destroyed the temple there in 70 C.E. Son of Vespasian; tenth Roman Emperor (r. 79–81 C.E.). The Arch of Titus in Rome commemorates Titus' victory over the Judeans.

Torah. Heb., "instruction." Torah is the first five books of the Hebrew Bible. It also refers to the entire body of scripture for Jews. More generally, it means instructions from God.

Tosefta. In rabbinic literature, additions to the Mishna compiled ca. 300 C.E.

Tractate. In Judaism, a chapter in a work of rabbinic literature.

Trajan, Marcus Ulpius. Roman emperor (r. 98–117 C.E.) who ordered the execution of Ignatius of Antioch.

Transcendence. The distance of the divine from human and earthly concerns; the opposite of immanence.

Transubstantiation. The belief in Catholic Christianity that the bread and wine of communion become the body and blood of Jesus.

Twelve Tribes of Israel. The tribes descended from the twelve sons of Jacob, who is also called Israel (Gen 32:28). The sons are Reuben, Simeon, Levi, Judah, Zebulun, Issachar, Dan, Gad, Asher, Naphtali, Joseph, and Benjamin. Joseph later divided into the tribes of Manasseh and Ephraim.

Tzitzit. Fringes worn by observant Jewish males on the edge of their prayer shawls, based on the commandment in Numbers 15:38.

Urim and Thummim. Dice, straw, or other form of lots thrown in order to determine the will of God in ancient Israelite religion.

Valentinus. (ca. 100 C.E.–ca. 155 C.E.) A popular Gnostic Christian teacher, almost elected bishop of Rome, frequently at odds with Roman proto-orthodox authorities.

Vespasian, Titus Flavius. (9–79 C.E.) Roman general who defended Roman rule in Judea during the First Jewish War and destroyed the Jerusalem temple in 70 C.E. Ninth Roman emperor (r. 69–79 C.E.)

War Scroll. 1QM, an apocalyptic text found among the Dead Sea Scrolls that describes a heavenly battle between the children of light and the children of darkness in great detail. Fragmentary portions are 4Q491–496.

Way, The. Members of the early Jesus Movement called themselves followers of The Way (Acts 9:12; 19:9, 23; 22:4, 14).

Writings. A body of texts included in Tanakh that comprises psalms, proverbs, stories, and histories. *See also* Tanakh.

Yahwist Source. The name scholars give to the anonymous writer of the "J" document, the oldest source in the Pentateuch. Refers to the God of Israel as YHWH.

Yavneh. Also called Jamnia, the location of a hypothetical council held by Judean, or Jewish, leaders at the end of the first century that outlined the canon of scriptures Jews would consider authoritative. Scholars today consider the council a nineteenth-century explanation for the inclusion of the Writings (Ketuvim) in the Hebrew canon and doubt the historicity of such a council.

Yehudi, Yehudim (pl.). A resident of Yehud, that is, Judah. A word that is translated both as Judahite and Jew.

YHWH. The tetragrammaton, the sacred four consonants in the name of God. The acronym for the name of the god worshipped by the Israelites. Biblical historians sometimes spell this word as Yahweh, but Jews today would never pronounce this word or call God Yahweh.

Zadokite Fragments. Priestly instructions discovered at Qumran from caves 4 and 5 that replicate a text called the Damascus Document (CD) found in a Cairo genizah in the nineteenth century. These fragments refer to a Righteous Teacher.

Zadokite Priests. Priests descended from Zadok, one of David's two priests and the priest who anoints Solomon at David's request. After the Exile, Zadokites control the temple priesthood. Some scholars claim that the Qumran community was founded by disaffected Zadokite priests. Ezekiel regarded Zadok's descendants as the only legitimate priests.

Zealots. Josephus' fourth philosophy, a group of radicals who recognized no king but God. They rose to prominence just prior to the First Jewish War and had a reputation for being the equivalent of first-century terrorists.

Zoroastrianism. The religion of Zoroaster, a second-millennium B.C.E. Persian prophet who saw the world divided between good and evil, with a dualistic belief in a cosmic power struggle. It is one of the oldest monotheistic religions; its members worship a supreme creator God, Ahura Mazda, who is locked in battle with Angra Mainyu, an evil spirit in charge of violence and death. Before Ahura Mazda finally triumphs, those who die under evil circumstances are resurrected.

Index

Aaron, 40, 83–84, 167
Abraham, 22, 33–34, 68, 110;
    circumcision, xii; as first Jew,
    21–22; pseudepigrapha, 8, 145
Abram, 168. *See also* Abraham
Acts (book), 83, 101–6, 110–11, 122,
    133, 146, 153–54; chain of
    authority, 159; interpretation of
    texts, 147
Adam, 110; as first Jew, 21–22
adaptation, 15
adultery, 153
Aelia Capitolina, 71
Agrippa, 23
Akiba (rabbi), 71
Alcimus, 53
Alexander the Great, 46, 50
Amos, 170
Andrew, 152
Antiochus III, 69
Antiochus IV, 69
Apocalypse of John, 133. *See also*
    Revelation
apocalypses, 47
apocalyptic thinking, 63, 66–67, 71,
    149
apocalypticism, 47–48

apocryphal texts, 5, 7–8; Dead Sea
    Scrolls, 9
Apostolic Constitutions, 161
apostolic succession, 159–62
Apostolic Tradition, 161
apostolicity, 158
archaeology, 29
Aristobulus, 145
ark, 122
Armageddon. *See* apocalyptic thinking
Assyrian Exile, 58
Athanasius, 14
Authentic Fakes, 8
authority, God-given, 139–40
authorship, 10–11

Babylonian Exile, 14, 45–46, 107
bar Kokhba, Simon. *See* bar Kosiba,
    Simon
bar Kosiba, Simon, 70–71
Ben Sira, 98, 131–32
Ben Uziel, Jonathan, 99
Bethel, 109
Bethlehem, 147
Bible. *See* Bible study; biblical studies;
    Hebrew Bible; *individual books*; New
    Testament; Old Testament; Torah

Bible study, 1–2; vs. biblical studies, 1
biblical studies, 1, 2, 19; vocabulary, 2;
    vs. Bible study, 1
Boccaccini, Gabriele, 76–77
Boenhoeffer, Dietrich, 171
Boethusians, 74
Boyarin, Daniel, 60, 158, 161
Bradshaw, Paul F., 106–7

Caiaphas, 122
calendars. *See* dates
canon, 7
Catholicism, xv, 53; and the Bible,
    5
Chain of Tradition, 156–57, 160,
    162
Chilton, Bruce, 114
Christianity: accounts of beginnings,
    xi–xii; anti-Judaism, xiii; chain of
    authority, 158; commonalities with
    Judaism, xvi, 174; conflict with
    Judaism, xi; identity, 21; origins of
    term, 23–24
Chronicles (book), 4, 65
circumcision, 34, 54, 60, 76, 101; ban,
    70–71
Claudius, 23
Clement, 160
"Clement's First Letter," 23
Colossians, 10
commandments, 99. *See also* halakah
commentary, 9, 141
communion, 99; formalization,
    115–16; as sacrifice, 108; vs.
    Sabbath blessing, 106
Community Rule, 7, 9–10, 103–4, 110,
    124, 167
The Contemplative Life, 104
Corinthian Church, 23
Corinthians: 1 Corinthians, 58, 90,
    114–15, 125, 150; 2 Corinthians,
    90, 144, 151
Cornelius, 110–11

covenant, xiv, 17, 33–35, 43, 62–63;
    new, 115; study of, xv; wide view,
    xvi. *See also* Israel
Crossan, John Dominic, 158–59
Cyrus (Persian ruler), 3, 46

Damascus Document, 10, 61, 143,
    148, 167
Daniel (book), 67, 110; apocalypse in,
    67–69; as pseudepigrapha, 8
Darius, 121
dates, notation, 2–3
David (king), 18, 34–35, 42, 65, 167
Dead Sea, 77; map, 10
Dead Sea Scrolls, xiv, 7–9, 84, 140,
    148, 169; apocalypse in, 68; and
    Hebrew Bible, 17
deuterocanonical texts, 5, 8
Deuteronomist, 4
Deuteronomy, 17, 36, 83, 97, 99, 128
deutero-Pauline texts, 10, 62
Dialogue (Justin), 161
Dialogue with Trypho, 158
Didache, 102, 106, 111–13
Didascalia, 161
dietary laws, 60, 101. *See also* food
divine kingship. *See* kingship, divine

"Early Judaism," 57
Ecclesiasticus. *See* Sirach
Egypt, 79, 82
Elephantine Judeans, 82
Elijah, 66, 111, 170
Elohist, 4
Enoch, 66; 1 Enoch, 76–77, 125,
    169; 2 Enoch, 77; pseudepigrapha,
    8
Enochic Judaism. *See* Judaism
Ephesians, 10, 62
Epiphanius, 13
Epistle to Diognetus, 23
Essenes, 73–77, 79
Esther, 5

Eucharist, origins, 105–6. *See also* communion
Exodus (book), xiv, 17, 36, 80, 90–91, 122, 131, 135; on temple, 95
Explanations of the Book of Moses, 145
extra-biblical sources, 18, 160
Ezekiel, xiv, 61–62, 66, 82, 119, 130
Ezra, 3, 81–82, 96; language, 5

fakes. *See* apocryphal texts
Falk, Daniel K., 110
fasting, 101–2. *See also* dietary laws; food
First Jewish War, 18, 57
food, 101–3; in the Bible, 102; and Christianity, 114. *See also* dietary laws; fasting; table fellowship
fornication, 101
Fraade, Steven, 81–82

Gabriel, 68
Galatians, 150
Galilee, 127
Gamaliel, 154
Geertz, Clifford, xi
Gemara, 15–16; prayer in, 111–12
Genesis, 32, 34, 101
Gentiles, 89, 91, 144
globalization, 49–50
Gnostics, 13–14, 161
God: attributes, 32–33; in Jesus, 130–32; location, xv, 119–21, 125–27, 134–36; names for, 32–33; "portable," xiv, 132; present in Torah, 127, 129. *See also* Shekinah
Gospel of Mary, 13
Gospels, 12, 63, 77–78, 102; on food, 105–6; historicity, 87; interpretation of texts, 146–47; narrative, 159; on priests, 87. *See also individual gospels*; Synoptic Gospels

Hadrian (emperor), 70–71
haftarah, 98
Hagar, 150
Haggai, 120
Halafta (rabbi), 135
halakah, 12, 126
Hanukkah, 56
Hasmonean Revolt. *See* Maccabean Revolt
Hasmoneans, 70. *See also* Maccabees
Hebrew Bible, 3–4, 29, 120, 143; misrepresentation, xiii; vs. Old Testament, 5. *See also* Torah
Hebrews (book), 14, 90–91, 108, 115
Hellenism, 47–51, 79; conflict with Judaism, 60; and the Eucharist, 114; as globalization, 49; resistance to, 53–57; responses to, 52–53, 57
Hengel, Martin, 51
heresiologists, 13, 161
Herod the Great, 56, 70, 147, 154–55
Hezekiah (king), 42
Hillel, 18, 78, 87, 155
Hippolytus, 161
historicity, 18
Hokhmah (Woman Wisdom), 131–32
holocausts. *See* sacrifice
Holy Spirit, 159
Hosea, 122, 169–70
Hyrcanus, John, 86

idols, 56
Ignatius of Antioch, 23–24, 160–61
Infancy Gospel of Thomas, 13
Ioudaismos, 57–58, 60. *See also* Judaism
Irenaeus, 13, 160–61
Isaiah, 66, 101, 122
Israel, 17, 66, 98, 148, 153, 169; interchange between groups, 109; and Judah, 24, 26; key beliefs, 32; map, 25; meanings of term, 22; stories of, 29–31; as term of identity, 21–22, 61–63, 73

Jacob, 22
Jaffee, Martin S., 28, 100, 155–56
James, 101, 111, 122
Janneus, Alexander, 86
Janneus, Alexandra, 86–87
Jason, 53
JEPD. *See* sources
Jeremiah, 80, 122
Jesus: charismatic authority, 140, 151–52, 159; conflict with Jewish authorities, xi–xii; depictions of, 12–13; extra-biblical sources, 18; as first Christian, 23; historicity, 18; as institution, 91; as interpreter, 153; as logos, 154; as messiah, xiii, 146, 170–71; oral traditions, 14; and prayer, 110; presence of God, 130–32; as priest, 90–91; as sacrifice, 133; study of, xiv–xv. *See also* New Testament
Jesus ben Sira. *See* Sirach
The Jesus Dynasty, 168–69
Jesus Movement, xv, 52, 74, 89, 122–23, 166; temple, 95; as threat to Romans, 169
Jewish Antiquities, 52, 59, 74–75, 97
The Jewish War, 52, 74–75
Job, 8, 64–65
John (book), 12–13, 57, 90–91, 132, 152; on Judeans, 59; tabernacle, 130–31. *See also* Gospels
John of Patmos, 90
Joseph, 8, 27, 147
Josephus, 18, 52, 58, 63, 74–76, 80–82; on food, 104; on *mezuzot*, 99; on Pharisees, 126; on priests, 84–87; reading of Torah, 97–98
Joshua (book), 37
Josiah (king), 37, 42
Jubilees (book), 77, 125; apocalypse in, 67

Judah: in Diaspora, xiv; invasion by Babylonians, 45; and Israel, 24–26; map, 25. *See also* Judea
Judaism: accounts of beginnings, xii; commonalities with Christianity, xvi, 174; conflict with Christianity, xi–xii; democratization, 81; Enochic, 76; identity, 21; modern connotations, 57; rabbinic, 57, 119, 154; transformation, xiii; unified, 91–92. *See also* Ioudaismos; "Middle Judaism"
Jude (letter), 68
Judea, 56; ethnic significance, 58–60; occupied by Rome, 56–57, 70; under Seleucid dynasty, 69–70. *See also* Judah
Judges (book), 22
Jupiter Capitolinus, 71
Justin Martyr, 158, 161

Kiddush, 106
Kings (book), 4, 28
kingship, divine, xvi, 41–42, 166
Kodshim (Holiness), 15
korban. *See* sacrifice
Kushner, Lawrence, 174

labels, 21
Lamentations, 46, 120, 128
languages, 7–8, 50–52, 56
Law, 4, 143. *See also* Torah
Left Behind, 63
Leontopolis, temple of, 82
Letter of Aristeas to Philocrates, 99, 145
Levi, 84
Levine, Amy-Jill, 100
Levites, 40, 84–85
Leviticus (book), 17, 83, 89, 98, 101
Life of Adam and Eve, 8
logos, 130–32, 136, 154
Lord's Prayer, 111

Lord's Supper, 150
Luke, 12, 98, 133, 153, 170–71. *See also* Gospels

Maccabean Revolt, 8, 18, 46, 53–56, 70, 81, 83
Maccabees, 5, 46, 57, 83; 1 Maccabees, 58, 61, 63, 80, 83; 2 Maccabees, 54–55, 69, 98, 110
Manual of Discipline. See Community Rule
Mark, 12, 152, 171; apocalypse in, 67; as oral text, 140. *See also* Gospels
Mary, 147
Mattathias, 56
Matthew, 12, 170–71. *See also* Gospels
McGowan, Andrew, 106
Melchizedek, 89, 168
Melito of Sardis, 109, 115
Menelaus, 53
messiah: definition, 165–66, 169, 172–73; two-messiah concept, 167–68
mezuzot, 99–100, 109
Micah, 122
Michael (angel), 67–68, 169
"Middle Judaism," 57, 76–77
millennialism, 64
Mishna, 15–16, 78–79, 84, 87, 149, 154; historicity, 17; prayer in, 111
Moed (Times), 15
monotheism, 60
Moses, 33–35, 66, 88, 131, 145, 157, 167; as first Jew, 21–22; Mosaic Law, 145; pseudepigrapha, 8; and the Torah, xii, 14
Mount Sinai, xii, 14, 35–36, 157
Mount Zion, 132

Nahum, 148
Nashim (Women), 15
Nazareth, 98, 147

Nebuchadnezzar, 8
Nehemiah, 80, 96–97; language, 5; reading of Torah, 97–98
Neo-Nazism, 63
Neusner, Jacob, 28, 79, 128
Nevi'im. *See* prophets
New Covenant, 4–5. *See also* New Testament
new Jerusalem, 134
New Testament, 10; apostolicity, 139; canon, 14; in church administration, 159; and Hebrew Bible, 17; prayer in, 111; reading of Torah, 98; sacrifices, 108; temple, 133. *See also* New Covenant
Nezikim (Damages), 15
Nicodemus, 154
Niditch, Susan, 29–30
Noah, 33, 101
Numbers, 17, 100, 167

Old Covenant, 4–5. *See also* Old Testament
Old Testament, 4; people of, 22; vs. Tanakh, 5. *See also* Old Covenant
On Dreams, 98
Onias, 69
Onkelos, 99
oral society, 139–41
orthodoxy, xv, 5, 53

paganism, xiii, 91
Passover, 109, 115
Pastoral Letters, 10
Paul, 63, 91, 124–25; authority, 159; commentary, 141; on communion, 114–15; conflicts with Judaism, xii; deutero-Pauline texts, 10; as first Christian, 23; on food, 105–6; Hellenization, 52; identity, 23; interpretation of texts, 143–45; on Israel, 62; on Judeans, 58; letters,

10; on location of God, 136; on priests, 89; religious authority, 144, 149–51; temple, 95, 126. *See also individual books*

Peniel, 109

Pentateuch, 17, 109. *See also* Torah

Pentecost, 153

Persian religion, 65

perushim, 79

pesharim. See commentary

Peter, 101, 151; as first Christian, 23; 1 Peter, 23–34, 90–91

Pharisees, xiv, 13, 73–75; authority, 156; food, 105–7; interpretation of texts, 147–49; on location of God, 126; priesthood, 86–89; on purity, 95; tradition, 140

Philip (apostle), 13

Philo, 18, 51–52, 84, 95, 99, 104, 145

Pilate, Pontius, 70, 146–47

Pirke Abot (Sayings of the Fathers), 15, 155–57

Plato, 103

Pliny the Younger, 18, 23

Pollion, 154–55

Polycarp, 160

polytheism, 60

Pompeius Magnus, Gnaeus. *See* Pompey the Great

Pompey the Great, 56, 70

Potiphar, 27

practices, religious, 96. *See also* fasting; food; prayer; purity; Sabbath; sacrifice; table fellowship

prayer, 109–11; as communication, 112; formalization, 115–16; at set times, 111

priesthood, 40–41, 81; basic tenets, 80; as concept, 74, 91; interpretive function, 84–86; in Judah, 45–46; and lay authority, 81; pre-Exilic role, 82; roles, 95–96; as term of identity, 92; variations, 85–89

Priestly Source, 4, 82

property, 75

prophets, 143, 169–70

Prophets (book), xiii–xiv, 4, 143; in Septuagint, 7

prostitution, 55

Protestantism, xv, 115

Proverbs (book), 99, 131–32

Psalms (book), 17, 110, 120, 137

Pseudepigrapha, 7, 66; apocalypse in, 67; Dead Sea Scrolls, 9; grounding, 139; on the messiah, 42; temple, 125

Pseudo-Aristeas, 145

Ptolemaic dynasty, 46, 50

Ptolemy, 82

Ptolemy II, 7

purity, 79–80, 88, 107, 112–13, 126; defilement, 123

Q (source for Gospels), 12

Qumran, 53, 61, 63, 125; interpretation of texts, 142; prayer, 110; priesthood, 84–89, 95; reading of Torah, 97–98; temples, 123. *See also* Dead Sea Scrolls

rabbinic literature, 14–15, 78; and Hebrew Bible, 17; on Pharisees, 87

Raphael, 68

Rebecca's Children, xvi

religion: authority, 144–49, 154–55; commonalities, xvi; compartmentalization, 73–74; as concept, 60; interpretive strategies, xv–xvi; origins of, xi, xiii

Revelation, 14, 47, 63, 66, 90–91, 125, 133–34, 171; apocalypse in, 67; Michael, 68; prayer in, 111

Righteous Teacher, 123–24, 140, 143

Roman Empire, 50–51

Sabbath, 80, 88, 97, 126, 154

sacrifice, 39–40, 55, 82, 85, 95–96, 107–9, 112–13; Christians on, 108; after rebuilding of temple, 122; replaced by food, 114–15; replaced by prayer, 112

Sadducees, xiv, 73–75, 79

Samaias, 154–55

Samaritans, 76–79

Samuel (book), 4, 28

Samuel (prophet), 22, 42

Sarah, 34, 110, 150

Sariel, 68

Satan, 64–68

Saul (king), 22, 42

Sayings of the Fathers. See Pirke Abot

Schechter, Solomon, 10

Schiffman, Lawrence, 91–92

scholarship. *See* biblical studies

scripture. *See* texts

Second Temple period, 73, 84, 87, 141; Judaisms, 79, 81; sects, 73–74

sects, 74–78

seed of Israel. *See zera yisrael*

Segal, Alan, xvi

Seleucid dynasty, 46, 50, 56, 69–70, 82

Septuagint, translation of, 99

Servant Songs, 147

Shammai, 18, 78, 87, 155

Shavuot, 153

Shekinah, 129

Shiloh, 37

Simon, 152–54

Sirach, 5

Solomon (king), 22, 42, 120

sources (of sacred texts), 4

Stephen, 24

Suetonius, 18, 23

supersessionism, xvi

synagogues, 95, 98, 107–8, 126–27; design, 53

Synoptic Gospels, 12–13, 105, 132; food, 114–15

Synoptics, 59

tabernacle, 35–37, 82, 91, 122, 129–30, 134; diagram, 38; portability of, 109; vs. temple, 132–35

table fellowship, 104–9, 112–13; Christians on, 114; as sacrifice, 115–16. *See also* food

Tabor, James, 169–71

Tacitus, 18, 23

Taharot (Purity), 15

Talmud, 3–4, 16, 78; Babylonian vs. Jerusalem, 16; extra-biblical sources, 18

Tanakh: apocalypse in, 47; arrangement of, 4; prayer in, 110

Tannaim, 17

Targum Yerushalmi, 99

Targumim, 99

tefillin, 100

temple, 55, 76, 88, 91, 123–24, 156; basic tenets, 80; as concept, 74; destruction of, xii–xiii, 2–3, 119; Jesus as, 132; maintenance, 82; reading of Torah, 96; rebuilding of, 45–46, 121–22; as term of identity, 92; vs. tabernacle, 132–35

Temple Scroll, 142

tent. *See* temple

Tertullian, 106, 161

Testament of Abraham, 68

Testaments of the Twelve Patriarchs, 77, 168

texts: adaptive, 140; authority of tradition, 141; chart, 6; Dead Sea Scrolls, 9; interpretation, 149, 153–55, 161–62; Jewish, 15–16; names of, 5; translations, 5–6. *See also* canon

Thanksgiving Scroll, 148

theophany, 131
Therapeutae, 104
Thessalonians, 10
time line, 31–32
Timothy (book), 10
tithing, 88
Titus, 10
Torah: chart, 16; as concept, 74, 91; 1, dual, 157; given by Jesus, 152–53; in the home, 99–100; and Israel, 73–74; Jewish interpretation, xvi; meanings of term, 3–4, 16, 42; modern vs. ancient, 3; oral traditions, 14–15; portability of, 95–96; presence of God, 127–29; public reading, 96–99, 109, 115–16; in Septuagint, 7; study, 1, 128; as term of identity, 80, 92; text, 83; transmission, 157–58; unifying power, 79–80, 89, 92
traditions, 15
Trajan, 23–24, 160–61
translations, 5, 7
trinity, as pagan element, xiii
tzizit, 100

universalism, 51

Valentinus, 158
Veronica, 8
Vespasian, 18
vocabulary, 28

War Rule, 68
War Scroll, 7, 10, 169
The Way, 23–24, 63
white supremacy, 63
wine, 85, 103–4, 114, 155
Wisdom of Solomon, 5
wives, 75–76
Woman Wisdom, 131
works righteousness, xii
Writings, 4, 143; in Septuagint, 7
WWJD bracelets, 100

Yahwist, 4
Yuval, Israel, 109

Zadokites, 84–85; reading of Torah, 97
Zealots, 73–76
Zechariah, 65, 120, 167
zera yisrael, 61–62
Zeraim (Seeds), 15
Zoroaster, 64–65